Wisconsin's 37

WITHDRAWN

Wisconsin's 37

The Lives of Those Missing in Action in the Vietnam War

ERIN MILLER

with JOHN B. SHARPLESS

Foreword by
MAJOR GENERAL DON LOGEMAN,
U.S. AIR FORCE (RET.)

McFarland & Company, Inc., Publishers
Jefferson, North Carolina

LIBRARY OF CONGRESS CATALOGUING-IN-PUBLICATION DATA

Names: Miller, Erin, 1993– | Sharpless, John B., 1945– author.
Title: Wisconsin's 37 : the lives of those missing in action
in the Vietnam War / Erin Miller with John B. Sharpless ;
foreword by Major General Don Logeman, U.S. Air Force (Ret.).
Other titles: Wisconsin's thirty-seven,
the lives of those missing in action in the Vietnam War
Description: Jefferson, North Carolina : McFarland & Company, Inc.,
Publishers, 2018 | Includes bibliographical references and index.
Identifiers: LCCN 2018020752 | ISBN 9781476672007
(softcover : acid free paper) ∞
Subjects: LCSH: Vietnam War, 1961–1975—
Missing in action—United States. |
Vietnam War, 1961–1975—Missing in action—Wisconsin. |
Soldiers—Wisconsin—Biography. | United States—
Armed Forces—Wisconsin—Biography.
Classification: LCC DS559.8.M5 M55 2018 | DDC 959.704/38—dc23
LC record available at https://lccn.loc.gov/2018020752

BRITISH LIBRARY CATALOGUING DATA ARE AVAILABLE

ISBN (print) 978-1-4766-7200-7
ISBN (ebook) 978-1-4766-3161-5

Front cover photograph of helicopter in Vietnam jungle
© 2018 iStock; detail of POW/MIA flag

Printed in the United States of America

*McFarland & Company, Inc., Publishers
Box 611, Jefferson, North Carolina 28640
www.mcfarlandpub.com*

For Mike, Merl, Bill, Norm, Tom, Richard,
Robert, Paul, Don, Junior, William, Chuck, Jim,
Dick, Paul, Donnie, Paul, Dale, John, Rick, Ray,
Roy, Randy, Jim, Roy, James, David, Todd, Harold,
Biff, Dale, Pete, Wotsy, Al, Neil, Jim, and Bob,
and for those who remember them.

"But of others there is no memory; they have perished as though they had never existed, they and their children after them. But these also were good men, whose deeds have not been forgotten."
—Ecclesiasticus 44:9–10

"For you see we are all brothers, known to each other or not, and each, in turn, deserves an amen, or any word of recognition on his passing or in remembrance of that time. There is a special bond between us that time cannot break, it is the bond of war, of tears, of joy that holds each others names thru the years. I guess there is one thing I can say after all.... Our dear lord Jesus blesses us so that the load is not heavy, as we will carry each others names to our graves."
—Norm Pruett, SP. E5, Crew Chief, 1st plt.
"Widow Makers," 71st AHC, 16th CAG, Chu-Lai

Table of Contents

1965–1967

1968

1969–1973

Acknowledgments

I've said many times that I have been fortunate to have had the opportunity to write this book. It would not have been possible without the kindness and generosity of the many family members, servicemen, friends, and classmates involved. To avoid erroneously omitting any names, I will refrain from listing the nearly three hundred individuals who contributed, but will instead express my deepest gratitude for their time and help.

I do want to specifically thank the families who worked with me on *Wisconsin's 37* for sharing their memories, stories, pictures, and mementoes of their loved ones. It has truly been my privilege to know these men, and I am grateful for the opportunity. My thanks to Dave Allard, Denny Higgins, Cindy Hawkins, Sean Allen and the entire Allen family, Jane Kirkpatrick, Suzanne Redenius, Andy, Peter, and Jim Billipp, Nancy Konkol, Cindy Schmitz, Carol Grable, Greg Bush, Dorothy Fraczyk, Jerry Swanson, Darryl Downing, Nancy Greve, Beth Annen, Diana Imhoff, Sue and Tom Adler, Vivan Fellenz, Cheryl Clancy, Diane Zelzer, Dawn Cooper, Deborah Shoenick, Ann Fischer, Myron Frazier, Nancy Roehre, Lynn Schmitt, Jody Gee, Duane Gorsuch, Ron Hentz, Janice Kostello, Bob Brown, Karel Bretsch, Jeanne Wallrath, Don La Haye, Donna Leet, Mike Greenwood, Mary Black, Cynthia Manning and the Soulier family, Mike Schmidt, June Ellen Fettig, Mike Trudeau, Bobbie and Fran Connolly, Mike and Darlene VanBendegom, Mary Christie, Susan Ambrose, the Wilke family, the Kubley family, and Jerry Johnson.

Since I have no military experience, the last three years have been a hands-on approach to learning terminology, order of command, and weaponry and equipment. I thank especially the many service members who answered what must have seemed to them very basic questions regarding military life, reviewed chapters for inconsistencies, and mentally returned to Vietnam to share their memories of their fallen comrades. Special thanks to Ralph Dresser, Jim and Elaine McNeil, Ron Milam, Pat Forster, Mike St. Clair, Jim Herak, Terry Cox, Dave Wall, and Steve McComb, who took time to read through multiple chapters for accuracy.

Thanks also to Marg Sumner for her attention to detail and careful editing of this manuscript, and to Michael Seidel.

Thank you to Dave Mellon and Ken Davis for many things, but especially for their advice throughout this project.

I am extremely grateful to Don Logeman for kindly providing a foreword for this book.

I owe a debt of gratitude to John B. Sharpless, not only for his advice and his editing skills, but also for his willingness to encourage a 21-year-old student who wanted to write a book. Thank you for not turning me away.

Finally, thank you to my parents: To my father, David Miller, for reading and re-reading the pages in this book and for the many hours spent discussing what should go into those pages, and to my mother, Jody Miller, for masterfully editing every photograph. They were my sounding boards and biggest supporters.

Foreword

by Major General Don Logeman,
U.S. Air Force (Ret.)

Fifty years ago, my fighter squadron of twenty aircrews climbed into our brand new F-4 Phantom jets and flew from Eglin Air Force Base, Florida, to Ubon Royal Thai Air Force Base, Thailand. We were sent there to fly combat missions against North Vietnam. I was fortunate, indeed blessed, to be assigned to the 8th Tactical Fighter Wing at Ubon. The "Wolfpack," our Wing's nickname, was commanded by then-Colonel Robin Olds, a World War II fighter ace and one of America's premier fighter pilots. He commanded and led us—and he taught us to fly combat—with supreme confidence and extraordinary flying skills. Not surprising, a lot of wide-eyed anxieties and breathtaking memories from my 138 combat missions faded with the passage of many years. But those vivid memories came rushing back to me as I read the biographies in this book.

Erin Miller is a young historian from Madison, Wisconsin, not far from where I grew up in Fond du Lac. In 2015 Erin learned that a family friend had a brother who was missing in action from the Vietnam War. In the process of researching the specific circumstances of his loss, she discovered a list of 37 Wisconsin men also listed as missing in Southeast Asia. She was determined to document their tragic and heroic stories and share them with us all. Her biographical sketches reveal not only the courageous stories of their ultimate sacrifices, but also give us a glimpse into their personal lives growing up in the Midwest. We are witness to their youthful energy, their character, and the core family values that they brought with them from Wisconsin to their military service. Although each of these 37 warriors were different from one another, they all shared a common thread of devotion to country, family, and service to others above self.

One of these patriotic young men, Captain Roy Kubley, and I were friends and classmates at the University of Wisconsin. We were commissioned second lieutenants, entered active duty together in the Air Force, and learned to fly from the same instructor during pilot training in Oklahoma. Roy was a superb pilot—and he was an even better person. He is my oldest son's godfather. His brief but distinguished military career became the inspiration for my own flying career of nearly 34 years, and I think about him often.

As you read Erin Miller's biographies, you will undoubtedly be reminded of other lost warriors from past conflicts whom you have personally known or have read about in other publications. Erin has deftly painted each of these heart-rending stories into an individual portrait of selfless courage and tragic loss. Her collection of memories is yet another stark reminder of the priceless treasure of our youth and of the many freedoms we enjoy in America that should never be taken for granted. They have been handed down to us through generations, and they are being protected for us even today, at very great cost.

Major General Don Logeman entered the U.S. Air Force through the University of Wisconsin ROTC program. He flew jet fighters and reconnaissance aircraft on active duty for 33 years. He commanded the USAF Fighter Weapons School and the only tactical reconnaissance wing in the Air Force. General Logeman is a Command Pilot with 5,800 flying hours, including more than 300 combat hours. He is credited with one aeriel victory against a MIG-17 aircraft in Southeast Asia.

Preface
by Erin Miller

I've told the story of how this book came about many times over the last three years. I'm asked often, and I understand why. It's an unusual way for a college student to spend her free time.

It started with a Facebook post on November 12, 2014. On my news feed was a story about Staff Sergeant James VanBendegom, killed in Vietnam 47 years earlier and buried on Veterans Day 2014 in Kenosha, Wisconsin.

The post came from a long-time friend of the family, Cindy. In sharing it, she wrote that her brother, Richard, had been killed in Vietnam more than 40 earlier and was still missing in action.

I read her post several times. I noted her brother's name and the date she had written and I did an Internet search. I felt guilty for not knowing about him and assumed I could remedy that in a matter of seconds.

An hour later, I still didn't know what had happened to Richard. What I did know was that he was one of 37 names on a list of Wisconsin men who were "missing in action" during the Vietnam War, a war about which I knew little. I was frustrated. I felt I had done something wrong in not knowing that this list existed and that these men were missing. What's more, I was privately embarrassed at my own lack of knowledge about the war that had taken their lives.

But I was 21 years old, I was in school, and it was a list on my computer screen. I didn't know what to do with it, but I couldn't simply exit the page and forget the names were there. For Cindy and the VanBendegoms, they were very real. I saved the page.

Three months later, I was enrolled in a history seminar taught by Professor John B. Sharpless at the University of Wisconsin–Madison. He had assigned us a final paper with a simple guideline: Write something on Wisconsin's history. I instantly returned to that list. I decided that I would write about one of those servicemen, tell his story, and ensure that someone else knew his name.

The problem with this plan was the same problem I ran into when I attempted to learn about Richard, though: I didn't know where to find that information. I didn't know about the Library of Congress's POW/MIA database, which I would visit dozens of times over the next three years. Even if I had known, the stories the Library of Congress

3

contained were not the stories I wanted. I wanted to tell how these men had lived, not how they had died.

To do that, I had to talk to the people who knew them. A feat that might have been infeasible 20 years ago was made possible—even simple—by innumerable online memorials. The Virtual Vietnam Veterans Wall of Faces, like the physical Wall in Washington, D.C., exists as a cyber tribute to all those lost in the Vietnam War. On each page, family and friends leave remembrances and, often, email addresses.

I was nervous about sending those first emails. I never truly became comfortable with it. I never knew how people would react. I didn't want to hurt anyone or open old wounds. But I needed to try. I assumed most people would delete my message. I thought maybe, if I were lucky, someone might write me back.

What followed surpassed anything I could have imagined. I heard from a dozen people within 24 hours, and I realized that what I had started was possible, but it was bigger than a school assignment.

In the three years since, I've come to know these 37 men as so much more than names on a list. They were brothers. They were fathers. They were husbands. They played sports, they played music, they played tricks, and they played cards. They were from towns where I've been and towns I've never heard of. Some were career servicemen with years of experience; others were just beginning their careers. Some were draftees who had never factored the military into their plans until their country called them to service. Too many were younger than I.

During the Vietnam War, 58,220 American military personnel died. Of this number, 2,646 were listed as missing in action, their bodies left in Southeast Asia when all other Americans had gone home. This book tells of 37 of these missing servicemen. Their stories are as unique as they were.

I would never have known these men if not for the kindness and generosity of their families and friends. From sharing family stories and personal memories, to sending newspaper articles, letters, and pictures, hundreds of individuals have played a part in creating this book.

They have done more than that, though. I started this project to ensure that these men were remembered, but at some point I realized that I had become superfluous. They are remembered by so many without my help; I have simply written those memories down in these pages. I am grateful to have had that opportunity. I thank everyone who made it possible.

More than anyone, I thank Wisconsin's 37 men for their service and their sacrifice. It has been a privilege to come to know them from those who knew them best and to share a small part of their lives here. Their lives were cut short, but they were here, and they mattered. I will never again need a list to remember them. It is my hope that you won't either.

Note: Quoted material not cited in the notes comes from personal interviews (collected in the Bibliography).

Introduction
by John B. Sharpless

Wisconsin's MIAs and Erin Miller's Journey

When Erin Miller proposed the Wisconsin Vietnam War MIA project to me in early 2015, I was skeptical, but I kept that skepticism to myself. The obstacles to successful research on all 37 missing in action (MIA) servicemen seemed formidable. Let her give it a try, I thought. She had been a student in several of my classes, most notably my seminar in Wisconsin history. She had a love of history and a rare enthusiasm for historical detective work. I knew she had the skill and discipline to give it her best.

She also had a deeply sincere interest in the lives of the men and women who served in the Vietnam War. She had by that time already volunteered to serve as an interviewer for the Wisconsin Veterans Museum oral history project.

However, for this project, Erin was setting the bar at the highest level. She wanted it to be more than a perfunctory retelling of what appeared on the usual websites concerning MIAs. She definitely did not want a few limited paragraphs with the standard boot camp mug shot. She wanted the life stories of these young men told not only through the terse language of official reports from the war zone, but also from the remembrances of families, friends, and comrades. We also decided early on that we wanted photographs of these men at home with their families and with comrades at the front. We were committed to the idea that this book would be in part a collective biography, but it would also be like a family scrapbook.

It was a challenging task, and Erin has done well. She inspires trust. People responded to her sincerity. She has been invited into their homes, attended events recognizing the MIAs of Wisconsin, and developed a regular correspondence with veteran groups throughout the country.

Erin received no outside support or funding. She continued her research while pursuing a Master's degree and working part time. This project is truly a labor of love. All royalties from the sale of this volume will be donated to the Wisconsin Veterans Museum in Madison and the Highground Veterans Memorial.

My job was threefold. First, to serve as editor of the chapters as Erin wrote them. My goal here has been to encourage Erin to speak in her own voice and not to impose an overly academic style. Certainly, I have made suggestions on word choice, sentence structure, and citations, but I wanted each chapter to be accessible to the people of

Wisconsin and America. My second task was to press Erin on accuracy in the details of the Vietnam War and the combat operations she describes. We have tried to be as accurate as possible with the details of specific operations, equipment, and weaponry. Fortunately, we have had outside readers from each branch of the service who volunteered to read the manuscript.[1]

Finally, I've tried to serve as a counselor and mentor throughout the long and, at times, difficult project. It was not simply the frustrations when an avenue of inquiry came up short or when sources were unavailable. It was also the anxiety of connecting with people who still carried the heartache of losing a loved one, a close friend, or a combat companion. Not simply objects of research, the men whose lives are described in this book are now to her like close friends. Coming to know them has been for her an emotionally draining, but deeply rewarding experience.

Memories of the War and Its Legacy

The human costs of the Vietnam War are staggering. The total causality estimates (1954–1975) place the death toll between 1,353,000 and 3,207,000. Officially, 58,220[2] American service personnel died in the war zone during the war, including eight women.[2] Perhaps not surprising, proportionate to their numbers, enlisted men died with greater frequency than officers, and while the average age of a Vietnam war casualty was 23 years old, 11,465 of those killed were teenagers. The Army suffered the highest number killed of any branch of the service. The war's deadliest year was 1968.

The origins of American involvement in Southeast Asia date to the closing years of World War II, accelerating with our support of French efforts to recolonize French Indochina. Our involvement intensified with our pledge of support for the South Vietnamese regime following the Geneva Accords of 1954, understood to mark the end of the First Indochina War and, finally, the period of United States "direct involvement" from the early 1960s through 1975.

The war's beginnings are obscure. When the United States suffered its first casualty can be disputed. Lt. Col. Peter Dewey, often cited as the first American causality of the post–World War II Vietnam conflict, was shot and killed "mistakenly" by the Viet Minh on September 26, 1945. Air Force T-Sgt. Richard B. Fitzgibbon Jr., is listed by the U.S. Department of Defense as a casualty on June 8, 1956. Charles Ovnand and Dale R. Buis, two American military advisers to the South Vietnamese Army, died in July of 1959. The 3rd Radio Research Unit (RRU) of the Army Security Agency was the first to be deployed as a unit. Army Specialist James Davis was killed in December 1961 while serving with RRU.

Ending dates are more exact. Less than a month after the Fall of Saigon in April of 1975, the ill-fated Mayaguez rescue operation resulted in 15 servicemen killed in action, 3 missing in action and presumed dead, and 23 killed as the result of a helicopter failure. Three U.S. Marines (Marine Pvt. Danny Marshall, Marine Pvt. 1st Class Gary Hall, Marine Lance Cpl. Joseph Hargrove) were left behind on the Cambodian island of Koh Tang during the operation. They were presumably among the last fatalities and our last MIAs of the war.

The number of MIAs is usually placed at 2,646 servicemen. Early on there was some confusion over who among those "unaccounted for" were prisoners of war and who were among the dead. "Operation Homecoming," which followed the Paris Peace Accords of 1973, repatriated 591 American prisoners of war (POWs). The status of those who remained unaccounted for is controversial. During the ensuing decades the issue has been politicized and, at times, regarded with extreme bitterness. To a diminished extent, it remains so today.

According to Title 10, Chapter 76 of the Missing Persons Act, the definition of an MIA is:

> any member of the armed forces on active duty who becomes involuntarily absent as a result of a hostile action or under circumstances suggesting that the involuntary absence is a result of a hostile action; and whose status is undetermined or who is unaccounted for.

The Defense POW/MIA Accounting Agency (DPAA) is tasked with investigating, exhuming, identifying, and repatriating the remains of POW/MIAs for all past military operations, missions, wars, and conflicts.[3]

America's military involvement in Southeast Asia is a long, complicated, and highly controversial narrative. By the late 1960s, Americans were deeply divided over the war. At the time, some of the anger focused on the men who served. Perhaps at no time in our history have American servicemen been so vilified in a time of war. Over the centuries one common theme of warfare is that the persons sent into battle have little or no say about the policies and decisions that provoked the conflict or the strategy employed to carry the conflict forward. Whether conscripted or career soldiers, they served because it was their job to serve.

As the Vietnam War receded from our collective memory and formal diplomatic relations with the Republic of Vietnam were established, the vehemence of the debate over the war has thankfully ebbed. At the same time, the heated controversy surrounding the POW/MIA issue has to some extent declined as well.

Wisconsin's MIAs

On May 25, 1995, a group of Wisconsin bikers traveled to Washington, D.C., as part of a national trip for veterans and supporters of the military to honor and recognize all military MIAs. When they reached the Vietnam Memorial Wall, the bikers unloaded what became known as the Hero Bike—a custom-built motorcycle dedicated to the 37 men from Wisconsin still missing from the Vietnam War. Painted along the motorcycle are images from Vietnam, and dog tags from each of Wisconsin's 37 men are attached to the bike. They left the bike as a reminder of the men who had not yet come home. To date, it stands as the largest item ever left at The Wall.

In May 1995, 37 men were missing from the state of Wisconsin. In 2017, 25 remain missing; there are 12 whose remains—however minuscule—have been recovered. Four were found before 2000. Eight have been returned since the turn of the century, and three of those eight have been recovered in the last five years. Fortunately for our project, no mysteries or controversies surround Wisconsin's 37 MIAs. We know who was missing. The quest for their fate continues.

At one time, the DPAA classified five more Wisconsin servicemen as MIA/POW. Their names have appeared on occasional MIA lists in records over the last few decades. While we have decided not to include them in this book, they deserve mention:

- Eugene DeBruin was born in Kaukauna in 1933. He was a staff sergeant in the Air Force in the 1950s. In September 1963 while working for Air America, his plane was shot down over Laos. He was apparently a prisoner in several camps along the Laos/Vietnam border. The location and timing of his death, however, remain unknown. Controversy still surrounds his fate. At the time, he was a civilian prisoner and not technically a military MIA.
- Born in Fond Du Lac, Air Force Major Clyde Dawson was killed in action over North Vietnam on March 23, 1966. His body was recovered in 1977, and his name does not appear on most MIA lists.
- Army Specialist Fourth Class Valentine Vollmer was from Clintonville. He was killed in action in February 1968; his body was recovered in 1974 and identified in 1976, so he doesn't appear on most MIA lists.
- Air Force Captain Lance Sijan was born in Milwaukee. Captain Sijan, along with Lt. Col. John Armstrong,[4] ejected over Laos on November 9, 1967. Although seriously injured, Captain Sijan evaded capture for six weeks. He was ultimately captured and died in captivity. He was briefly categorized as MIA, but when his fate was known he was identified as a POW. He received posthumously the Medal of Honor.
- Air Force Captain Gary Edward Brunner was born at the Air Base in Pensacola, Florida, but graduated from Washington Park High School in Racine. He attended the Air Force Academy in Colorado. In June 1969 his C130 cargo plane was hit by enemy fire during a landing at Katum, the 5th Special Forces Group camp roughly 40 kilometers northeast of Tây Ninh, near the Cambodia border. He was among the four officers and two crewmen who died. They were designated as killed in action.

The sources for our research have been records of the United States government, newspaper reports, high school yearbooks, and most importantly, the information Erin received from family, friends, comrades-in-arms, and other servicemen in the theater of operation during the time of the MIA incidents. The latter have been in the form of face-to-face interviews, phone interviews, and email exchanges. We sincerely appreciate their cooperation. In all cases the people whose quotations are the result of Erin's interviews have had a chance to review the chapter. We have tried in every instance where the facts are vague or conflicting to obtain confirmation from multiple sources. Not surprisingly, some matters simply cannot be known with certainty. Indeed, in the final analysis, it is that lack of certainty that makes the loss of these men so difficult to comprehend.

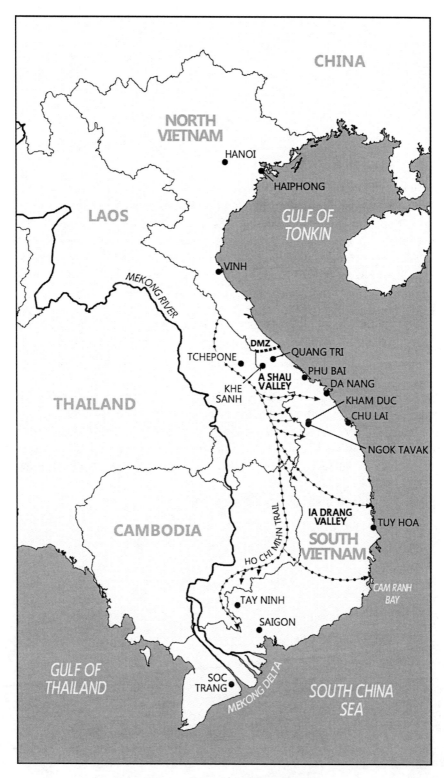

Southeast Asia during the Vietnam War.

A Note on Terms

During the Vietnam War, the term "missing in action" was used to describe combatants whose whereabouts were unknown. Given the lack of intelligence provided by the North Vietnamese during the course of the war, American officials never had solid information as to how many of the missing servicemen were being held as prisoners of war (POW) and how many were killed in the incidents that led to their disappearances. In some circumstances, it was heavily hypothesized that the servicemen had been killed, but without definitive proof, they were classified as "MIA."

In the 50 years since the end of the Vietnam War, information has revealed what happened to many of these men. The Defense POW/MIA Accounting Agency maintains a list of the men who were MIA at the end of the war. Today, the list makes a distinction between those who have been identified and accounted for since 1973 and those whose remains are still missing.

The 37 men in this book were classified as missing in 1995, the year that a bike was left at the Wall in Washington, D.C., in their honor. In the 20 years since, remains of some of the men have been recovered. The dates associated with their names in the chapters of this book are the dates of the incidents that led to their disappearance. In some cases, these have been revealed to also be the dates of their deaths. In others, that latter date is still unknown.

Searches for the unidentified continue today.

1965–1967

Captain Walter Frank Draeger, Jr.

United States Air Force, disappeared April 4, 1965

"He just was a really caring person.... Just a sweet person."—Beth Annen

"Mom would always say, 'He was so good.' She said he was such a good person."—Diana Imhoff

On August 4, 1964, President Lyndon B. Johnson informed the American people of an incident that had taken place in Vietnam's Gulf of Tonkin two days earlier during which the USS *Maddox* had exchanged fire with North Vietnamese torpedo boats. He announced that retaliatory air strikes were taking place as he spoke, and he informed the country that he had requested a Congressional resolution that authorized him to take any actions he deemed necessary to maintain peace in Southeast Asia. Unsaid by Johnson was that this could include military force. The resolution was not an official declaration of war by Congress, but with the resolution, the president no longer needed one.

The 1964 U.S. presidential election loomed large, and Johnson had set himself up as the candidate of peace, claiming his opponent, Senator Barry Goldwater, would lead the country into a nuclear war with the Soviet Union. At an Ohio campaign stop at the University of Akron, little more than a month after the Gulf of Tonkin Resolution was adopted, Johnson assured the public, "We are not about to send American boys nine or ten thousand miles away from home to do what Asian boys ought to be doing for themselves."

President Lyndon Johnson was elected on November 3, 1964. Captain Walter Draeger, Jr., arrived in South Vietnam the same day.

It was a long way from Deerfield, Wisconsin. Walter Frank Draeger, Jr., was born September 28, 1933. Named after his father, he was known in the family as Junior. Walter Sr. and Esther Draeger owned several acres of land and a dairy farm, and their three children, Beverly, Junior, and Bonnie, grew up knowing the value of hard work. In addition to the milking cows they raised, there were tobacco fields to be worked, crops to be picked, and endless other jobs that had to be done to keep the farm running. All three Draeger children had their chores, and Junior always seemed to finish his in a hurry. "[Mom] always said he'd rather be up in his room reading books," explains Beth

Young Walter Draeger, Jr., on his family's farm in Deerfield with his parents, Walter Sr. and Esther, and older sister, Beverly. Courtesy Beth Annen and Diana Imhoff.

Annen, Beverly's daughter and Junior's niece. "They'd buy book after book after book. He just liked to read."

Reading was one way to pass the time in a small town. Junior also played on the Deerfield High School basketball team and was a member of the school forensics team. "He would have been good at that," says Diana Imhoff, also Junior's niece. "He wasn't afraid to talk or give speeches."

Beth agrees. "He was pretty intelligent. Like Mom said, he was book-smart."

In addition to being a good student, he was a popular one. Junior was Deerfield's 1950 prom king and graduated in 1951.

Junior's post–high school plans did not include farming. "Farming wasn't his thing," says Diana. In the fall of 1951 Junior started college at the Virginia Military Institute. After one year, he transferred to the University of Wisconsin–Madison and enrolled in the Air Force ROTC.

He joined Delta Sigma Pi, the UW's professional business fraternity. "They're a business and social fraternity," says James Schaaf, one of Junior's fraternity brothers. "We did have parties. We had a party room, with beer on tap. We also had a lot of business speakers and field trips."

James was already an active member of the fraternity when Junior (called Wally by his fraternity brothers) pledged. During the first few weeks of initiation, the fraternity assigned senior members to the new pledges to guide them through the process, and Junior became one of James's "pledge sons." Initiation was an interesting experience, James remembers:

> Some of [the initiation activities] were kind of rinky-dink. We'd have a big fire in the fireplace and you'd take a mouthful of something very hot … and you'd have to run up a flight of stairs and down the other and spit it in the fire to put the fire out.

As for Junior, James knew him to be quiet guy and a "very, very nice person."

Junior was also a member of the Lutheran Student Association, the Finance Society, and the Marketing Club. Of course, much of his time was devoted to the Air Force ROTC. He spent part of the summer of 1955 training in Minneapolis and was commissioned as a second lieutenant in the Air Force Reserves on January 28, 1956, one month before graduating from the University of Wisconsin–Madison with a Bachelor of Business Administration degree in finance.

Immediately following graduation Junior took a job as a sales clerk with a Madison men's furnishing company called Olsen & Veerhusen. The job was temporary, and that spring Junior began active duty with the United States Air Force. He completed pilot training, and was awarded his Wings as a certified jet fighter pilot at Laredo Air Force Base in Texas on June 29, 1957. In July he began training at Moody Air Force Base, Valdosta, Georgia, with the 3550th Combat Crew Training (Interceptor) Wing. Junior flew the North American F-86D Sabre, the first swept-wing fighter aircraft in the United States military. During training Junior was awarded a certificate welcoming him to the "Mach Buster's Club," attesting that he had exceeded the speed of sound.[1]

Junior was promoted to first lieutenant on November 2, 1957. Three months later he departed for his first overseas assignment, with the 440th Fighter-Interceptor Squadron at Erding Air Base, a former Luftwaffe pilot training ground in West Germany, flying the F-86D Sabre as well as the Lockheed T-33 Shooting Star.[2]

In August 1958 Junior was released from active duty and returned briefly to Wisconsin. Diana and Beth, both growing up on the Draeger farm, remember his homecoming and the gifts he brought with him: a beret for Diana and their brother, Jimmy, and a doll for Beth.

A month after he returned to the United States Junior took a job in California buying raw materials for the Bomarc Missile program with the Boeing Airplane Company. He explained on his résumé that the job included "obtaining bids, writing purchase orders, and the associated follow-up work." He packed up his car, a Volkswagen Bug, and moved to the West coast.

Junior liked California. He liked it to so much that he purchased several acres of land near Salton Sea in Imperial County, property the family still owns today. "It's undeveloped," explains Beth. "I bet he would've gotten into real estate or something like that. Or something businesswise." In fact, during his time in California, Junior took several college courses in advanced accounting problems, cost accounting, auditing, and consolidations and mergers.

His next job, beginning in August 1960, was with the Dohrmann Commercial Company in San Francisco. He served as the assistant office manager in charge of billing operations until August 1961. Two months later he started with Belmont Reid & Company in San Jose, serving as a financial counselor working with stocks, bonds, mutual funds, and insurance.

Junior returned to active duty with the Air Force on July 28, 1962. Before leaving California he became engaged to a woman he met during his time there.[3]

Over the next two years Junior would go through several training programs. He began with the 559th Tactical Fighter Squadron at MacDill Air Force Base, Florida, where he transitioned from the F-86D to the Republic F-84 Thunderjet. On January 28, 1963, Junior received his commission as an Air Force captain and briefly departed

MacDill for survival training at Stead Air Force Base in Nevada. Because many ejections took place over water, Junior attended additional Tactical Air Command Sea Survival School at Langley Air Force Base, Virginia.

Junior spent ten months flying the Lockheed C-130B Hercules with the 4442nd Combat Crew Training Squadron at Sewart Air Force Base, Tennessee. In late 1964 he volunteered to fly a different type of aircraft: the Douglas A-1H Skyraider. "The A-1 has to be considered the most difficult aircraft of its era to fly," says Ray Jones, an A-1 pilot in Junior's squadron. While the Lockheed C-130B was a massive four-engine transport airplane, the A-IH Skyraider[4] was a single-engine, single-seat attack aircraft. The A-1 also differed greatly from the F-86D Junior had flown in Germany. Although both were single-seat fighters, the mission of all F-86D was aerial combat, while the A-1 was a designated ground-attack aircraft.

Walter Draeger, Jr., was commissioned as a 2nd Lieutenant in the Air Force on January 26, 1956. Courtesy Beth Annen and Diana Imhoff.

At the time, the Navy was the only U.S. military branch that regularly flew the Skyraider,[5] but the Pentagon had given more than three hundred planes to the South Vietnamese Air Force (VNAF) and needed American pilots to train them. The American pilots were called "advisors," a term used for the hundreds of American troops sent over in the early 1960s before any official U.S. involvement in Vietnam.

"Most people didn't even realize we had people there that early," explains Ray. "But [1964] was actually my second tour."

More than seventy Air Force fighter pilots volunteered for the advisory role in late 1964, but fewer than thirty were needed. The Air Force developed a competitive program to select the best pilots for the job, and both Junior and Ray were chosen.

The original training schedule called for two months of A-1H training at Naval Air Station Corpus Christi, Texas, followed by survival school and a two-week program specific to the job's advisory role. The overseas tour was intended to begin in January 1965. Shortly after Junior and Ray arrived at Corpus Christi, though, the plans were changed. There would be no survival school or preparation for the advisory role, and the two months of Skyraider training were reduced to roughly three weeks.

Their tour began November 3, 1964. The pilots arrived at Tan Son Nhut Air Base, in Saigon. Junior was part of the 1131st Air Force Special Activities Squadron, one of five pilots chosen to transfer to Da Nang Air Base.[6] Da Nang was the northernmost of the three operating bases at the time[7] and the closest base to the Demilitarized Zone and North Vietnam. There were several squadrons operating out of Da Nang, and Junior and Ray flew with the main force, the 516th VNAF A-1 Skyraider squadron.

"For all practical purposes we were part of the Vietnamese Air Force while we were there," Ray says. "We didn't need to teach [the Vietnamese pilots] anything. They just needed bodies to teach their new guys. They were flying combat and didn't want to train [the new pilots] so we trained and flew missions, too."

Although the Americans and South Vietnamese worked well together, there were some cultural differences. When the advisors arrived at Da Nang, the Vietnamese operations officer had set up an orientation program for them. He covered in detail the kinds of missions they would be flying and the procedures they should know. At the end of the meeting, he told them they would not cover any of that material again because it would be the same for each mission. Pre-mission briefings with the VNAF were short, maybe three minutes, compared to the usual hour-long briefings the men would have received in an American squadron.

Another difference for the Americans was the language used on the missions. Although their commanding officer had decreed that all missions be conducted in English, the Vietnamese pilots often communicated to the forward air control in Vietnamese. Some of the Americans learned basic words, like the numbers used to dictate coordinates in order to follow along.

The work was enjoyable, as was the location. They were in Danang[8] during the monsoon season, but that didn't bother Junior. "Today is Sunday, so I'm sitting by the waterfront, watching the fishing boats come in," he wrote his parents in February 1965.[9] "It's very pretty." He started the letter by thanking them "for the shirts and books" and mentioned having a good time on his trip to Bangkok the month before.

"Just found out for sure that we'll spend one year over here," he told them. "Three gone and nine months to go."

The next month was busy, according to another letter postmarked March 3, 1965:

> Guess you heard about the raids to North Viet Nam. They all left from Danang. Some of the Vietnamese pilots from our squadron went along with them. I've been getting quite a bit of flying time, taking the new pilots on instrument rides. It's pretty enjoyable work. Also have been managing to get some cross-country trips on the weekends.

He told his parents that when he wasn't flying he swam, played tennis, and watched a lot of movies, including a new one he recommended to his young nephew and nieces called *One Hundred and One Dalmatians.*

While Junior was enjoying his time in Vietnam, he was making plans for when he came home. Sam Warner, who knew Junior from the Tan Son Nhut Officers' Club, said that he talked of going back to school for his Master's degree, possibly in accounting. At the club Junior was usually with another American pilot who, Sam remembers, joked that Junior should become a milk farmer instead.

"They were always together until this guy came back and said his buddy had been lost," Sam says.

Operation Rolling Thunder, the lengthy bombing campaign carried out by the United States over North Vietnam, had commenced barely one month before Junior's mission on April 4, 1965.[10] It was a typical mission, an airstrike followed by armed reconnaissance, and Captain Walter Draeger, Jr., flew as the wingman to VNAF Lieutenant Dinh. Accompanying them on the mission were four North American F-100 Super Sabres. Lt. Dinh, flying low beneath Captain Draeger's aircraft, was hit by antiaircraft artillery offshore north of Quảng Khê. His aircraft immediately caught fire. Captain Draeger attempted to communicate with Lt. Dinh via radio, but received no response, and the plane crashed nose-first about one mile offshore.

The pilot of a Grumman HU-16 Albatross monitoring the radio communication contacted Junior, saying he was coming to help. In the meantime Junior remained, circling overhead. When the HU-16 arrived, Captain Draeger directed him to where Lt. Dinh had gone down. The pilot began search-and-rescue operations, while Captain Draeger provided cover above him. About half a mile from shore, the HU-16 radioed both Junior and the F-100s nearby. He said, "I see three boats lined up on the shore, could you make a high-speed pass and see if they're armed? I'd like to know before I search any closer to shore."

The F-100 flight leader declined. Over the radio Captain Draeger came through, saying, "Kayo Alpha, this is Fury Red Two.[11] I'll check it out for you."

Captain Draeger flew north to south along the shoreline, passing over the three boats. Then he pulled up. He began another communication. "Kayo Alpha, Fury Red Two. Don't go in any closer. The boats are armed and appear to be—"

The message broke off as all three gunboats opened fire. The pilots of the F-100s and the HU-16 watched as Captain Draeger's aircraft was hit and crashed into the water below.

The F-100s, low on fuel, returned to the base. The HU-16 pilot remained at the crash site to continue searching for both planes and their pilots. Eventually, he had to return to Da Nang AB as well, having found no sign of either Lieutenant Dinh or Captain Draeger. Walter Draeger, Jr., was 31 years old.

Three days later, Ray Jones flew as wingman to VNAF Captain De. They flew directly over the gunboats that had shot down Lieutenant Dinh and Captain Draeger, but were not fired on. As they were flying, Captain De tossed two cigarettes out his cockpit window, one for each downed pilot. For the Vietnamese, it was a sign of respect.

After collecting the testimonies from those who witnessed the mission, Ray felt sure that Junior qualified for at least a Silver Star. He submitted a recommendation. His commanding officers agreed, but upgraded the award to the Air Force Cross, the second-highest medal of valor in the United States Air Force.

Half a world away, in Deerfield, Wisconsin, the military arrived first at the home of Walter Sr. and Esther Draeger, then to the homes of Beverly and Bonnie. "I have some bad news," the officers said.[12]

On April 7, 1965, President Lyndon Johnson made another address, on another college campus. In stark contrast to his words before his election, Johnson now openly called the conflict with Vietnam "war." At Johns Hopkins University, President Johnson said:

Vietnam is far away from this quiet campus. We have no territory there, nor do we seek any. The war is dirty and brutal and difficult. And some 400 young men, born into an America that is bursting with opportunity and promise, have ended their lives on Vietnam's steaming soil.

Why must we take this painful road?

Why must this nation hazard its ease, and its interest, and its power for the sake of a people so far away?

    We fight because we must fight if we are to live in a world where every country can shape its own
    destiny. And only in such a world will our own freedom be finally secure.

Junior's plane was lost three days before President Johnson's address. Junior was the
first serviceman from Wisconsin classified as missing in action during the Vietnam
War.

    He would not be the last.

Commander James David La Haye

United States Navy,
disappeared May 8, 1965

"A true gentleman, an accomplished fighter pilot and courageous combat leader, a commanding officer personified. Rest in peace, valiant leader."
—George Schulstad

"CDR La Haye was a truly courageous fighter pilot and fine commanding officer whom I greatly respected."—Bob Pearl

The Battle of Midway in June 1942 is considered by many the turning point in the Pacific Theatre during World War II. It is appropriate, then, that the first large operational aircraft carrier named after a World War II battle would be the USS *Midway*. Commissioned in September 1945, the *Midway* participated in every major U.S. conflict from Korea to Desert Storm before she was permanently decommissioned in 1992, making her the country's longest-serving aircraft carrier of the twentieth century. Stationed at Navy Pier, in San Diego, the USS *Midway* is now home to a maritime museum. During her years of service, an estimated 225,000 men served aboard the *Midway*, and the museum now serves to tell their stories.

The massive carrier houses twenty-nine restored aircraft. There is only one Vought F-8 Crusader on board. And it has three names written on its side: CDR Doyle W. Lynn, CDR James D. La Haye, and LT (jg) Gene R. Gollahon. Theirs are only three of the many stories told on the USS *Midway*. They are stories that Commander La Haye's son, Donald, wants to be told.

James La Haye's story began in Stevens Point, Wisconsin, on July 21, 1923. One of five children—four boys and one girl—Jim was raised in Green Bay and graduated from high school in 1939 at age 16. Jim was smart, and an early high school graduation was only the start of how far his intelligence would take him.

The fall after graduation Jim and his older brother, Bob, enlisted in the National Guard. Bob was 18; Jim was not. His age was not a concern until 1940, when President Franklin Roosevelt called the National Guard into active service in preparation for a war in Europe. When the Army learned that Jim was underage, it released him, but not before he had reached the rank of E6, or staff sergeant, in only about a year of service.

While he was too young for the Army, the Navy had no such qualms, and Jim quickly enlisted with the Navy. It sent him to the Naval Academy Prep School in 1942 and then on to the Naval Academy in 1943. Jim joined the class of 1947, studying typical academic courses such as a foreign language—Jim studied Portuguese—English, history, and math, as well as subjects to prepare midshipmen for a career in the Navy or the Marine Corps. These included seamanship and navigation, ordnance and gunnery, electrical engineering, and marine engineering. The Academy's annual register for 1945–46 states, "A midshipman is an officer in a qualified sense. He is appointed a midshipman in the Navy, not merely at the Naval Academy." Jim also found time to compete on the fencing team while in school.[1]

Among his other high scores, Jim ranked 28 out of 823 in electrical engineering. It came as no surprise when he graduated early[2] with one of the most accomplished classes in the Academy's history in 1946, alongside the likes of future President Jimmy Carter. James La Haye was commissioned an ensign in the U.S. Navy. He married his wife, Gloria, in 1947, spent time on a surface ship, and then he entered flight school. When he graduated from flight school in 1951, his next destination was Korea with Attack Squadron 75 aboard the USS *Bonhomme Richard*.

This ship's name had a distinguished history. The original USS *Bonhomme Richard* existed before the formation of the United States as a 900-ton French merchant ship called *Duc de Duras*, used by the East India Company for trade in 1765. In 1779, after the American Ambassador to France had secured an alliance with the French King Louis XVI, the French demonstrated their friendship with America by giving it the ship *Duc de Duras*. The Continental Congress put the vessel under the leadership of Captain John Paul Jones, who renamed it in honor of the ambassador who had helped them acquire it, Benjamin Franklin, author of *Poor Richard's Almanack*. The *Duc de Duras* became USS *Bonhomme Richard*, or "Good-Natured" Richard.

This first *Bonhomme Richard* did not last long. On September 24, 1779, Captain Jones engaged in battle with the HMS *Serapis*. As the American ship burned the British yelled, "Have you struck your colors?"[3] Captain Jones replied, "Struck, Sir? I have not yet begun to fight!" It was the *Serapis* that struck her colors late that night, giving the United States Navy its first ever victory over an English ship in English waters. The *Bonhomme Richard* sank on its way to Holland for repairs.

It was not until 1944 that another ship paid homage to this significant naval victory. The second *Bonhomme Richard* saw action in World War II, but was placed on reserve in 1947. It was re-commissioned for service in the Korean War, and departed with Jim La Haye and Attack Squadron 75 (VA-75) on board.

Stationed in the Pacific, with ports of call in Sasebo and Yokosuka, Japan, as well as Pearl Harbor, the squadron performed dive-bombing missions, specifically targeting hydroelectric and industrial complexes in North Korea.[4]

While he was on the Japanese mainland, Jim picked up a movie camera. He began filming missions while in formation. Years later his son, Don, found some footage of a live bombing mission, with missiles and rockets shooting and machine guns blaring in the background.

Don and his sister were born before Jim left for Korea, and their brother would be born after Jim's return in 1952. He came home after completing more than fifty combat missions in Korea.

Home for the La Haye family could mean anywhere; they moved about every two years. After Korea, the family's next stop was Monterey, California, where Jim attended the Naval postgraduate school, earning a degree in aeronautical engineering. The family enjoyed their two years in California, which made the move to Troy, New York, where Jim studied at Rensselaer Polytechnic Institute for his Master's in Engineering Management, bittersweet. They only spent one year in Troy, though, and in 1956 Jim started with the VX-3 Experimental Squadron in Atlantic City, New Jersey, test piloting the Navy's first supersonic fighter, the Vought F-8 Crusader.

The Navy operated six experimental squadrons at the time, each responsible for evaluating a different type of aircraft, and in 1956 the VX-3 unit was charged with testing one of the fastest and most versatile aircrafts the world had seen until that point. Development on the F-8 Crusader began in 1952, when the Navy issued an order for a supersonic carrier-based fighter. Four years later Commander Robert Windsor set a record by flying more than one thousand miles per hour. The aircraft was designed for air-to-air fighting, bombing, and photoreconnaissance missions. The last American fighter aircraft built with guns as its primary weapon instead of missiles, the Crusader is often referred to as "the last of the gunfighters."

On July 25, 1957, a test flight turned into a real flying emergency for then– Lieutenant James La Haye when the F-8 he was flying at fifty-two thousand feet experienced a flameout. Lt. La Haye descended to thirty thousand feet, and the engine came back to life.

After Jim finished his work with the experimental squadron, the family moved to Jacksonville, Florida, when Jim was given the chance to fly the F-8 Crusaders as part of Fighter Squadron 32 off the USS *Saratoga*. He experienced another flameout on the *Saratoga*, except this time, he was forced to eject over shark-infested water, where he waited eight hours for a search-and-rescue team.

In 1960 he returned to the United States and resumed test flying, now for the Naval Air Test Center. Assignments at the test center varied, and many of the men alongside Jim were selected to be astronauts. More than once Jim brought home autographs for his kids from men whose names they would later hear on the news.

Jim did not become an astronaut. He spent several years testing the weapons systems of various naval aircraft, including the McDonnell Douglas F-4 Phantom,

Commander James La Haye, wearing one of the red berets he purchased for his squadron. A Vought F-8 Crusader is in the background. Courtesy Don La Haye.

Douglas A-4 Skyhawk, Vought F-8 Crusader, and Northrop Grumman E-2 Hawkeye. During this assignment, Commander La Haye flew the F-4 Phantom to Europe to demonstrate its capabilities to American allies.

In 1963 Jim was assigned to the Army War College in Carlisle, Pennsylvania, an assignment indicating that his higher-ups were considering him for his own command. After one year at the college, James La Haye became the commanding officer of VF-111, deployed on the USS *Midway* and headed to Vietnam.

The average age of the men aboard the USS *Midway* was 19. Commander La Haye was 41 years old. For those he commanded, James La Haye's experience was a source of reassurance and morale. Many of the men were heading to war for the first time, and knowing that their leaders were combat veterans helped them stay focused. Bob Pearl, one unit member, recalled years later, "His quiet, measured leadership style was just what we needed."

Commander La Haye's leadership extended beyond the ship. While in the United States, he entertained his squadron by inviting them to his home to watch college football games, and overseas, he bought red berets for the squadron to boost esprit de corps.

The USS *Midway* deployed in December of 1964, but Jim flew home to spend Christmas with his family in San Diego. Combat missions began April 10, 1965. The primary mission of VF-111 was combat air patrol, providing air defense opposition aircraft over the ship targets and during bombing missions. Additionally, the VF-111 F-8 Crusaders were used to attack ground targets with guns and Zuni rockets, while providing flak suppression for A-1 and A-4 bombers.

For all its versatility, though, the F-8s were designed for air-to-air combat, not for shooting at ground targets. They did not handle combat damage well. "We later learned that the horizontal stabilizer, upon full hydraulic failure, violently moves to the full up or down position," recounts Bob Pearl, an F-8 pilot. "One can't recover in either situation."

Commander James La Haye was the flight leader of two four-ship flak suppression missions on May 8, 1965, in Vinh, North Vietnam.[5] The mission targeted the Vinh Airfield and the Vinh railroad yard.[6] Vinh was known to be heavily defended, but everyone in the air that day was surprised by just how much flak they were getting; one claimed to have never seen so much before or after that mission. As flight leader, Commander La Haye rolled in to attack the antiaircraft sites first, approaching west to east so that he could easily head back out to sea.

Because so much was happening at once, some of the men couldn't see Commander La Haye begin his maneuver. Most, though, received his final transmission: "I'm hit."

His wingman, Lt. (jg) Tom Howard, had a visual on the plane and saw their flight leader level off and head for the water. While completing his weapons delivery, Howard lost track of Commander La Haye's plane momentarily; when Howard found him again, Commander La Haye's plane was considerably lower.

Over the radio another mission member heard Lt. (jg) Howard tell their flight leader, "Get out of it," and then yell, "Eject!"

As Howard prepared to descend with Commander La Haye, to his "shock and disbelief," the aircraft crashed into the water. There had been no ejection.

No one was entirely sure how it had happened. "Your Dad was a very calm and cool pilot and leader," Tom Howard wrote to Donald La Haye many years later:

> So the question comes up ... when he said "I'm hit!," what did he really mean? Was the aircraft disabled and damaged or was he also "hit" and wounded and disabled? Was his ejection system damaged? Or was he too low and couldn't control the UHT (elevator) and lost control into the water?

They knew exactly where the plane was. Commander La Haye crashed into relatively shallow water and his plane was visible beneath the water; however, it was too close to shore to be safely recovered. As a result, James was considered missing in action.

VF-111 lost three pilots during the 1965 cruise. All three took part in the May 8 mission. Commander James La Haye died that day. The second flight leader, Commander Doyle "Bud" Lynn, took command of the squadron upon Commander La Haye's death, but was killed in action 19 days later, also over Vinh. Lieutenant Gene Gollahon, Commander Lynn's section leader on May 8, was shot down on August 13.

The La Haye family settled in Virginia Beach after Jim's plane went down. Don joined the Navy and, in 1972, served in the Vietnam War as a submarine officer.

During America's Bicentennial celebrations in 1976 the decommissioned USS *Intrepid* was moored at the Philadelphia Naval Shipyard. On board the *Intrepid* was an F-8, and on the side of the F-8, painted in VF-111's squadron colors, were two names: Cdr. Jim La Haye and Cdr. Bud Lynn.

When the celebrations concluded the F-8 found its way to an air museum at Bradley

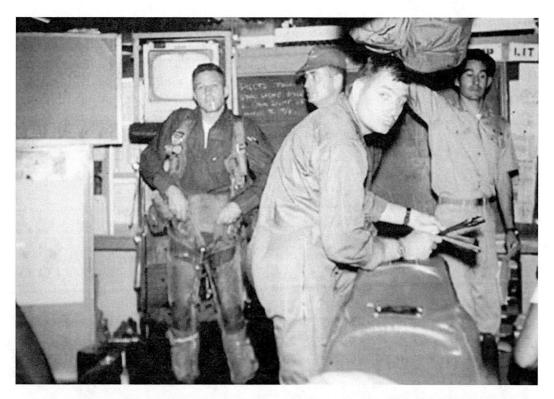

Left to right: Doyle "Bud" Lynn, James La Haye, and George Schulstad aboard the USS *Midway*. Bud was killed over Vinh nineteen days after James. Courtesy Don La Haye.

The F-8 Crusader aboard the USS *Midway* Museum serves as a memorial to the three men lost from VF-111's 1965 cruise, thanks in large part to the efforts of Jim's son, Don. Courtesy George Schulstad.

Field, Connecticut, where a member of the La Haye family spotted the family name. He informed Don, and Don began a project to have the plane refurbished. At the same time, San Diego was bringing the newly decommissioned USS *Midway*, his father's ship, to port. The Navy planned to turn it into a museum and it wanted an F-8 there.

The situation could hardly have been more perfect: Commander James La Haye's name on the same type of aircraft he had tested and flown, on the ship of the squadron he had commanded. Don contacted the museum, and it bought the plane. And then it scrubbed the names off.

Don argued that the names should remain on the aircraft. The museum explained that it did, indeed, plan to have names on the aircraft, but that the spots would be sold for $10,000. Don continued to argue that the plane should serve as a memorial to the fallen men who flew it. Eventually, with the help of the Crusader Association, he won that argument.[7]

Since the USS Midway Museum opened its doors in June 2004, more than 5 million people have visited the ship. More than 5 million people have seen the Vought F-8 Crusader on board, and more than 5 million people have read the names:

CDR Doyle W. Lynn
CDR James D. La Haye
LT (jg) Gene R. Gollahon

Captain Robert Ira Bush

United States Air Force,
disappeared June 9, 1966

"Bob was a happy-go-lucky guy. Good, solid fighter pilot. You could depend on him." —Elmer Nelson

"He was a very nice person and a hell of a pilot."—Frank Urbanic

In 1938 Franklin Delano Roosevelt was serving his second term as President of the United States. The country faced the ninth year of the Great Depression and followed the news across the oceans as Germany occupied and annexed Austria. Los Angeles dealt with heavy flooding and landslides, while a meteorite hit an empty field outside Chicora, Pennsylvania. Seeing-eye dogs were used for the first time, and the March of Dimes Polio Foundation was created. France won the World Cup, and the New York Giants defeated the Green Bay Packers to win the sixth NFL championship game. And on June 8, 1938, Robert Ira Bush was born.

Robert grew up in Racine, Wisconsin, the only child of George and Elizabeth Bush. Although he lived near the Lake Michigan shore, Robert was focused on the sky and his passion for flying. To pursue that passion, he enlisted in the Air Force soon after graduating from Washington Park High School, with a long-term plan to one day fly commercially.

On Monday, July 9, 1956, Robert departed for basic training at Parks Air Force Base, in Dublin, California, as a member of the largest single "buddy group" to enlist in the Air Force from Racine to that point. Buddy group enlistments ensured that the boys would go through basic training together, although there were no such guarantees for the remainder of their four-year commitments. After completing the six-week program, many of the boys pursued further training in administrative or technical fields.

Robert followed the latter path, taking radar training at Lowry Air Force Base in Denver. In addition to being one of the Air Force's seven technical schools in the country at that time, Lowry AFB was also a part of Strategic Air Command, a joint Department of Defense–Air Force command responsible for two of the three major nuclear programs at the time. Robert spent much of his time at the nearby Genesee Mountain Park Training Annex, where most radar training took place. In the decades following World

War II, radar (an acronym for radio detection and ranging) became an integral part of the military's strategic defense in many ways. Radar works by emitting electromagnetic waves. When an object moves into the radar's path, the energy from that object is reflected to a receiving antenna. From that energy, key information such as location and speed can be obtained. In Colorado Robert focused on radar-guided fire control systems, which provided data for accurate firing data for a target.

By June 1957 Robert had completed radar training. After a short leave, he arrived for his first assignment at Suffolk County Air Base, Long Island, New York. This was followed by an assignment at McGuire AFB in Trenton, New Jersey. For someone who longed to be in the air, though, Robert could be satisfied for only so long as a radar technician. He soon applied for and was accepted into the aviation cadet training program.

The program, which trained pilots, navigators, and bombardiers, consisted of three phases: pre-flight, primary, and basic.[1] The pre-flight stage provided an introduction to the military, which Robert hardly needed by then, as well as an academic introduction to flying. The cadets experienced their first flights during the primary phase. The basic phase introduced advanced flying techniques. The three training phases took place at different bases. Robert trained at Lackland AFB in San Antonio, Graham AFB in Marianna, Florida, and Reese AFB Lubbock, Texas. He received his Wings and his commission as a 2nd lieutenant in the U.S. Air Force Reserves at Reese AFB on April 29, 1960.

Robert's initial four-year enlistment was over, but his career was only beginning. Within a year he was flying jets with the 437th Fighter-Interceptor Squadron out of Oxnard AFB Base, Camarillo, California. An Air Defense Command (ADC)[2] base, Oxnard was one of five fighter-interceptor squadrons located within the Los Angeles Air Defense Sector (LAADS), an air defense organization responsible for the protection of much of southern California. Other such sectors guarded regions throughout the United States, using radar sites, both in the air and on the ground as well as fighter-interceptor squadrons like Robert's in the event of a nuclear attack. LAADS, its bases, and all other ACD bases throughout the country could identify and give advanced warning if a long-range missile attack were launched. For Robert, flying the McDonnell F-101 Voodoo supersonic jet fighter, Oxnard would be home for half a decade.

It was more than simply *his* home, though, because on October 21, 1961, Robert Bush married Carol Bird at the Chapel of the Flowers in Las Vegas. Eight days later, Robert was promoted to 1st Lieutenant.

Robert Bush's graduation photo from Washington Park High School, circa 1956. Courtesy the Vietnam Veterans Memorial Fund.

While Carol hailed from Oxnard, the couple occasionally drove back to Racine to visit Robert's parents. At the same time, Oxnard AFB had a thriving community of its own. There were steak dinners and small get-togethers and luncheons with crazy hat contests (for which Carol Bush once received an "honorable mention"). One weekend, after dinner and cocktails, the military wives put on a humorous show called "Weekend at OAFB—Show Place of ADC," which involved several dancing skits as the women depicted what their husbands did at work. On one of the smallest ADC bases in the country, the military families formed a tight-knit group.

This support network was important on September 6, 1963. While his home base was still Oxnard, Robert was performing test flights for the F-101 Voodoo out of Holloman Air Force Base in Otero County, New Mexico. The Voodoo, which broke world speed records in 1957 by reaching 1,207 miles an hour, was still a relatively new aircraft when Robert flew it with the 437th Fighter-Interceptor Squadron. The two-seat aircraft served as both a reconnaissance and fighter plane and it was armed with several air-to-air missiles. It was while testing these missiles that September that Robert's plane caught fire. Rather than abandon the burning aircraft over a civilian population, Robert piloted his plane safely away, while ordering his radar observer to eject. Once he was sure that his crewman and the civilians on the ground were safe, Robert also abandoned the plane. By then, he had received third-degree burns on 12 percent of his body.

Robert was hospitalized, first at Holloman Air Force Hospital, then transferred to Port Hueneme Naval Hospital, closer to home. By February 1963 he was back at work at Oxnard AFB. Not much could keep Robert down.

On October 29, 1964, Robert received the Distinguished Flying Cross for his heroism over the New Mexico town. He also received a promotion to captain. There were a lot of new events taking place in Robert's life at that time: He was with a new squadron (the 57th Fighter Interceptor Squadron) in a new aircraft (the Covair F-102 Delta Dagger), and in a new country (Iceland) at the Keflavik International Airport.

A year later, he would be in a similar situation. First, however, he returned to the United States. Robert spent the summer of 1965 at Hurlburt Airfield near the town of Mary Esther, Florida, learning to fly the Douglas A1-E Skyraider. Hurlburt had served as a training field during World War II and still had several older buildings and airplanes from that time. "It kind of took you back to that era," says Frank Urbanic, a member of Robert's training class, called Express 18. Frank jokes that their class name—Express—was a reference to how quickly the program turned out pilots.[3]

Their training period lasted only four months, during which time the men transitioned to a new aircraft. Unlike the newer jets Robert was accustomed to flying, the A1-E Skyraider was developed shortly after World War II and had already proven its worth during the Korean War. The low-flying Skyraider was perfectly suited for Vietnam's jungle environment as well. Learning to fly such an aircraft could be difficult, Frank explains, but Express 18 turned out to be a class of "outstanding pilots."

Six pilots from that class went on to serve in the 602nd Fighter Squadron, assigned to Udorn Royal Thai Air Force Base in Thailand. Robert's tour commenced on November 20, 1965. With him from Express 18 was Elmer Nelson. "The people that Bob and I trained with in that class ... had a rather difficulty history," Elmer remembers. "Of the

Robert liked to go fast, whether that was in one of his own cars or in a Voodoo 101. Courtesy the Vietnam Veterans Memorial Fund.

six, there were six guys shot down." Two from that group were never hit, but two went down once, and another two, twice.

Robert was among the latter. On May 26, 1966, Robert was forced to bail out of his aircraft, landing in a rice paddy. It was no easy feat, Elmer explains:

> The A1 did not have an ejection seat in the airplane. The way we got out was we rolled the canopy back and basically jumped out of the cockpit and pulled the ripcord on our parachute. We had to have a controllable situation and plenty of altitude to get out. So we lost a lot of pilots in those first six months.

The 602nd had very high losses, the highest of any fighter squadron in Southeast Asia at that time, they were told. The squadron began with thirty-two airplanes in January 1966, and only fifteen remained by July. Robert survived that May jump with little more than a cut on his chin from his parachute strap. He spent one hour and fifty-five minutes on the ground awaiting rescue, while seven Skyraiders provided cover overhead. He was posthumously awarded the Air Force Commendation Medal for his actions on this mission.[4] Afterward, he took an eight-day leave in Hong Kong.

The Skyraider was a designated fighter plane, but in addition to combat missions, the 602nd trained Vietnamese pilots and conducted search-and-rescue operations. Late in the evening of June 8, 1966, Captain Robert Bush and Major Theodore Shorack, Jr., another Express 18 classmate, prepared for a search and rescue of a downed F-105 pilot. Accompanying them were two HH-3C Jolly Green helicopters and two additional

Skyraiders. Major Shorack's plane took off at 11:57 p.m. on June 8, with Captain Bush following at 12:01 a.m. June 9.

The downed pilot was located and picked up less than two hours later, and the formation began its return to base. During the maneuver, a midair collision occurred between Major Shorack's aircraft and Captain Bush's. Robert's plane burst into flames. Major Shorack did not appear to have had time to escape his aircraft. Robert bailed out immediately, but he did not have the necessary altitude to deploy his parachute. It tangled and failed to properly open. A search was later conducted for both men, but neither were found. Both were listed as missing in action.

On Wednesday, June 9, 1966, in Quảng Bình Province, North Vietnam, Robert Ira Bush died. Due to the time difference, the date in America was still June 8, making Robert exactly 28 years old. In those 28 years, he married a woman named Carol Bird. He served more than eight years in the Air Force, and flew in a world-record-setting jet. He saw Iceland, Thailand, and Vietnam. He piloted three types of aircraft, operated a radar system, and won an award for heroism. He jumped from three burning planes. Twice he survived.

It was a life cut short, but it was one hell of a life nonetheless.

Commander William Tamm Arnold

United States Navy,
disappeared November 18, 1966

"He was a hell of a nice guy."—Norm Wold

"He was a super young man and aviator.... And a great loss to his fellow squadron mates!"—Mickey Miefert

"Bill was the one who came in after me and I lived to tell the tale, and appreciate him for the qualities that made him a good friend and aviator.... I won't ever forget him."—Tom Saucier

The University of Wisconsin–Madison's Naval ROTC unit maintains a Wall of Honor. It draws the eye immediately on entering the innocuous brick building on University Avenue. Red velvet roping draped across large shell cases forms a walkway to the right wall, where thirteen plaques, black with wood frames, are arranged in rows. Each plaque displays a picture of a graduate who lost his life in service of his country.[1] Commander William T. Arnold, USN, UW NROTC Class of 1963 does not smile in his portrait. In his dress uniform, he appears the consummate professional. Near the bottom of the frame, inscribed in silver, a quotation reads, "To honor is to remember."

Born June 25, 1940, William "Bill" Arnold grew up in West Allis, Wisconsin, the second of William and Lois Arnold's three children. Billy, as he was called growing up, played the trumpet at West Allis Central High School, ran track, and played on the junior varsity basketball team.

Bill was born to fly. He sketched planes as a boy, built model planes that he tacked to his bedroom ceiling, and flew with his dad, a pilot himself. At the local airport Bill worked as a line boy, washing, fueling, and assisting in airplane repairs. Eventually he soloed himself.[2] When the University of Wisconsin–Madison NROTC offered him a scholarship, he accepted.

The NROTC building, a former garage purchased by the University in 1942, served as an enlisted radio operator school from August of that year until the end of World War II. It was also one of the first training locations for the United States Naval Reserve (Women's Reserve), better known by its acronym, WAVES.[3] It became home to the UW Naval ROTC on November 1, 1945, and is still used as such today.

About 200 midshipmen were enrolled in the NROTC in the early 1960s. The men were led by Commanding Officer Reginald Rutherford as well as several Naval instructors and a Marine major. Bill's first-year curriculum consisted of one semester of orientation and a second of naval history. During the summer, midshipmen embarked on a 3rd Class Midshipmen Cruise, a six-week opportunity at sea to experience Naval and Marine life firsthand, while also training in antisubmarine warfare. Bill spent his summer cruise aboard a destroyer, departing from Boston and twice making port, once in Quebec and once in New York City.

After their sophomore year, which was dedicated to learning navigation and naval weapons, recruits declared for either the Navy or the Marines; Bill chose the Navy. Bill's junior year in NROTC focused on engineering, also Bill's UW major, and his senior year focused on administration, while it also prepared all the midshipmen for life as an ensign.

Bill was an active member of the NROTC program, eventually becoming a battalion commander for the unit. Because of his leadership abilities and academic success, he was also selected as a member of the honorary military society, Scabbard and Blade. He earned a Bachelor of Science degree in mechanical engineering. Bill's sisters, Suzanne and Jane, had joined him in Madison after his freshman year, and all three graduated the same day in June 1963. He was commissioned an ensign in the U.S. Navy that afternoon.

Following graduation, Bill was stationed aboard the USS *Shangri-La* (CVA-38) while it conducted operations in the Caribbean. After the aircraft carrier returned in October, Bill attended flight training at Naval Air Station Pensacola and Naval Auxiliary Air Station in Kingsville, Texas. He was then assigned to Attack Squadron 22 (VA-22). The "Fighting Redcocks" flew Douglas A-4C Skyhawk aircraft, the Navy's main light attack aircraft in the opening years of the Vietnam War. The single-engine aircraft's primary job was to attack and destroy surface targets. Bill's first deployment was aboard the USS *Midway* (CV-41); his second, aboard the USS *Coral Sea* (CV-43).

Between deployments VA-22 was stationed at Naval Air Station Lemoore near the California city of the same name. Although they had some time to enjoy California when not deployed, VA-22 trained constantly. They performed practice missions and rehearsed descending on a set target. During these trials, they flew either high level (through the mountains) or low level (reaching as low as fifty feet above the ground).[4] They also spent several weeks at Naval Air Station Fallon for weapons training. "When you were out on cruise, you were 100 percent qualified to be there," says Mickey Miefert, a member of VA-22. Because the A-4s were equipped with nuclear capabilities, the squadron was also prepared to carry out strikes against the Soviet Union or China at a moment's notice if called on to do so. They never were.

The *Coral Sea* departed California for Southeast Asia in July 1966, stopping in Hawaii, Japan, and the Philippine Islands along the way. Shore time was appreciated. "When we went to sea, we went to operate," remembers Mickey. "When we came to port, we partied." It was a well-run ship with plenty to do. Everyone had daily jobs and chores, but life aboard the carrier was reasonably comfortable compared to that of troops on the ground.

When the *Coral Sea* reached North Vietnam, it usually kept about 50 to 100 miles

The UW NROTC Wall of Honor recognizes alumni who were killed while serving official duties with the military or civilian service, were Prisoners of War, or were distinguished for exceptional acts of heroism. NROTC alumni William Arnold and Norman Billipp have plaques on the wall. Photograph by the author.

from the coast, and rarely stayed in the same place for long. For the pilots, life was hectic. Most flew at least one sortie a day, sometimes two. Occasionally, they were ordered to stand down for several days while another ship became the primary attack carrier. After the brief respite, missions would begin again. Typical missions were either bombing or reconnaissance, and all operated under the rules of engagement.

The rules of engagement (ROE) were the guidelines that dictated operations of the U.S. military in Southeast Asia. They began under President Kennedy to keep the United States in an advisory, rather than military role in South Vietnam. The ROE eventually evolved into rules of war that were to be obeyed by commanders and combat troops during missions. The rules initially served to prevent friendly fire mishaps and civilian casualties and damage, but over time took on an increasingly political role as well. They often put the U.S. in a defensive rather than offensive position, requiring them to first be attacked before attacking and obliging officers to request permission before conducting certain assaults against suspected enemy troops. The need to consult the Secretary of Defense or other high civilian authorities before an attack complicated missions.

One of the more frustrating rules for pilots prohibited strikes against third-country shipping. From 1969 to 1972 this prevented bombing missions against Haiphong Harbor, the major shipping port and third-largest city of North Vietnam, where it was known that the Soviets and Chinese were supplying material to the North Vietnamese.[5] Instead of attacking the harbor directly, pilots were forced to track the transported material through the jungles along the Ho Chi Minh Trail, a series of roads running from North Vietnam through Laos and Cambodia into South Vietnam, and used by the North Vietnamese to transport people and equipment.

Although they could not bomb the shipping harbor itself, the U.S. could monitor what was being transported and regularly did so. Bill's first mission as flight leader was one such assignment in early November 1966. Tom Saucier piloted the second aircraft involved in the mission and remembers that night clearly:

> It was usually rainy and overcast. The plan was to refuel inflight from a tanker and proceed north over water until abeam Haiphong at about ten thousand feet. Bill was then to move ahead of me and descend to four to five thousand feet so he could drop a series of parachute flares, and I would then be a little above him and in a position to take pictures of the British, French, Russian, etc. ships at the dock in Haiphong or at anchor alongside one of the many islets just off the harbor. We did not usually take pic-

William Arnold was passionate about flying and dedicated to the Navy. The top photo is displayed at the University of Wisconsin–Madison NROTC Wall of Fame. Courtesy Jane Kirkpatrick.

> tures, as there were special aircraft on board the Coral Sea equipped to take very high-quality pictures. Maybe it was an experiment, of which there were many during those early days of the air war.

Amid the heavy antiaircraft fire the pair were receiving, along with the constant warnings of SAMs[6] ringing throughout the plane, Tom found himself flying behind and below Bill's aircraft as two flares went off, each flashing with 1 million candlepower. Tom was momentarily blinded and ending up directly above Haiphong.

Something disrupted Tom's radio, and he was suddenly cut off from all communication. His directional instruments were not functioning properly and with no further guidance from his plane or his commanding officers, Tom leveled out his aircraft's wings and tried to establish his position so he could navigate back to the ship.

At that moment, Bill flew up beside Tom and flashed his lights. With Bill's guidance, both men made their way to safety.

"What made this such an unforgettable flight for me ... was the professionalism Bill demonstrated on his very first flight as a flight leader," Tom says. He continues,

> He could have simply orbited over water and safety while I flailed around in a very dangerous place and then rejoined me when I eventually headed east [toward] safety. He didn't wait, but flew into danger, turned his *lights on* so I could see him, and led me back to safety. After we were back on board,

> I tried to express my gratitude and he just waved it off. Wouldn't hear of it. Said anyone would have done the same.

Anyone might have. Bill did.

A few missions later, on November 18, 1966, Bill was the wingman on an armed reconnaissance mission off the coast of North Vietnam, south of Cape Mui Ron. The weather that day was cloudy and rainy, but approximately seven miles out the flight leader determined that the mission should be carried out and initiated his bombing maneuver. Lieutenant (Junior Grade) William Arnold completed his maneuver as well and radioed the flight leader, saying "I'm in the clouds, coming down." The flight leader could not see Bill's aircraft and received no further communication. He did not see an ejection, nor any sign of debris in the water. Search-and-rescue operations were launched from the *Coral Sea*, but nothing was found.

It wasn't clear what happened in the skies that day. Discussing the incident years later, Bill's friend Stuart Brandes, himself a Navy veteran, knows one thing: "A bombing maneuver in a high-speed aircraft in rain and clouds takes bravery. Some don't come back."

Bill was 26 years old when he was officially listed as missing in action. He was twice promoted while missing and received a final posthumous promotion to commander when he was declared dead on May 18, 1978. He was awarded the Purple Heart and the Air Medal.

Every year Wisconsin's Naval ROTC program offers The Commander William Arnold Scholarship to a midshipman "who embodies the spirit and devotion to country demonstrated by CDR Arnold." Bill Arnold flew more than 165 missions in Vietnam, and while no one knows what happened on the last one, they know what happened in the ones that came before. Throughout his life and his career, Bill displayed high levels of professionalism, dedication, and courage. He is still remembered for those qualities today.

Captain Roy Robert Kubley

United States Air Force,
disappeared January 31, 1967

"Roy was an outstanding young man with unlimited potential."—Ralph Dresser

"He was a patriot, a bona fide hero, and a lifelong inspiration to me and others like me."—Don Logeman

"He was one of the good guys."—Dick Peshkin

More than 9 million Americans served in the military during the years of the Vietnam War. Approximately 3.4 million served in Southeast Asia and more than 2 million in Vietnam. Between 1 and 1.6 million engaged in combat or were exposed to enemy contact. Over 200,000 servicemen came from the United States Air Force.[1] Of these, 1,269 men were selected and assigned to Operation Ranch Hand. Among them was Captain Roy Kubley.

To those who knew Roy, it came as little surprise that he should be selected for such an elite assignment. "If I were to characterize Roy, he was quietly gung-ho," says Don Logeman, a friend from college and pilot training. He continues,

> He was very motivated towards the military. I don't know that either of us talked about making a career out of it, but he probably would have if he had lived. He was that kind of guy, serving his country.

Roy was born in Glidden, Wisconsin, on July 8, 1939. He graduated from Glidden High School in 1957 and enrolled at the University of Wisconsin–Madison, where he joined the Air Force ROTC. It was a popular decision at the time: Roy's class had somewhere around five hundred cadets. "All dedicated, patriotic young men," remembers Don. "Roy was certainly at the head of that list."

Roy was at the head of the list academically, too. AFROTC training began by providing an overview of the military and the Air Force, then moving on to aspects such as leadership, management, and organization. One day a week the cadets participated in basic military training at the Wisconsin Field House, marching, shoe shining, and undergoing uniform inspections.

Roy enjoyed it and excelled at it. By the end of his four years, he had reached the rank of cadet colonel, the highest rank one could achieve in ROTC. He served as the corps commander the first semester his senior year, with Don taking over for second semester. Roy had been awarded *The Chicago Tribune* ROTC Gold Medal in 1960, and in 1961 both he and Don were the recipients of the Professor of Air Science (Commander's) Plaque. Roy also received the Air Force Association Silver Medal Award. In his free time at the UW, Roy served as a member of the Arnold Air Society, did volunteer work and spoke at high schools about the ROTC program.

Recognizing Roy's potential, his officers offered him private piloting lessons while still in school. Don Logeman, afforded the same opportunity, explains:

> Pilot training is a costly project. If any of us selected for pilot training didn't have the skills, it would be to the Air Force's advantage to find out sooner rather than later. So they offered us lessons at the airport.

Both young men were worth the investment. Roy graduated in 1961 with a degree in civil engineering, a pilot's license, and an assignment at Vance Air Force Base in Enid, Oklahoma, for USAF undergraduate pilot training. The program began on November 20, 1961, with forty-eight recently commissioned 2nd lieutenants, Roy and Don among them. Thirty-four men would graduate with their wings thirteen months later.

Cadet Colonels Don Logeman (center) and Roy Kubley (right) receiving the Professor of Air Science (Commander's) Plaque from an unidentified Air Force Colonel at the UW AFROTC in 1961. Courtesy Don Logeman.

Training at Vance AFB consisted of flight training with one of two airplanes: the Cessna T-37 Tweet, a small, easily maneuverable plane, or the Lockheed T-33 Shooting Star, a more advanced, single-engine, two-seat jet. In addition to flying, there was also coursework and regular military training. At the end of the course, they would be graded on all these areas and given their pick of aircrafts and assignments, depending on their placement in the final class rankings.

The men worked tirelessly during the week, and although they had weekends and holidays off, there was little to do in Enid. "We didn't care," says Don. "Twenty-two years old, sent off to fly jet airplanes. It doesn't get any better than that." Don was married and lived in town, while Roy, a bachelor, lived in a private room in the bachelor officer quarters on base. He was a frequent dinner guest at the Logeman house, and when Don's son was born in October 1962, Roy was asked to be his godfather.

When training neared its end, all the available assignments were posted. The class gathered and, in order of rank, stood and selected which assignment they wanted. Roy chose an assignment in France, flying a Lockheed C-130 Hercules military transport aircraft. A position overseas, a big airplane, and lots of flying—Roy got exactly what he wanted.

The C-130, a four-engine cargo plane, used a yoke projecting from the floor rather than a stick for controlling. It was far different from the small jets Roy had flown in Enid. There was so much room inside the cabin that a pilot, copilot, navigator, crew chief, a bunk, and a coffee machine fit in the space. Before leaving for Paris, Roy attended additional training at Sewart Air Force Base, outside Nashville, to become acquainted with the aircraft.

Training lasted roughly two months, during which the airmen learned to start the engines, taxi, steer, and take off as well as to maneuver a multitude of approaches and landings. Flights consisted of a flight instructor on the right and a trainee on the left. In the classroom they learned what could go wrong during a flight and how to handle it. In the air, they put that knowledge into practice when their flight instructor killed one engine on each side of the plane and waited for the novice pilot to respond. Again and again they simulated crisis conditions until the quick response of experience was automatic.

There was more to do after hours in Nashville than there had been in Enid, and Roy quickly became friends with another C-130 pilot-in-training, J.P. Morgan. J.P. says, "Roy was a big, raw-boned farm kid, and fun to be with."[2] The two spent much of their free time in Nashville's Printers Alley, famous for bars and blues. They also took off a weekend and drove to Fort Knox, where they met an older couple who dubbed them "Honorary Kentucky Colonels."

Roy's overseas assignment began May 4, 1963. He was part of the 35th Tactical Squadron, one of three squadrons in the 322nd Airlift Division at Évreux-Fauville Air Base in Évreux, France, east of Paris. As at Enid, bachelors like Roy had quarters on base, while married men like J.P. lived nearby. J.P. and his wife had a small, completely unfurnished apartment, so Roy "borrowed" some items from the bachelor's quarters for them to use. One item was an ironing board, which served as the couple's dinner table.

From his base in France, Roy flew all over the world. There were missions to India

Godparents Roy Kubley (center) and Linda Alsip at the baptism of Don Logeman's son, Brian, in the chapel at Vance AFB, October 1962. Courtesy Don Logeman.

and the Middle East and night flights over Libya. Most of the division's tasks involved hauling cargo and ammunition, although amid the Cold War there were some instances where they carried nuclear material across Europe. They also monitored several Soviet-controlled areas. J.P. explains:

> Before East and West Germany were reunited, Berlin was located in the middle of Eastern Germany, and there were corridors you flew in and out of just to get to Berlin. One of our missions was to activate those corridors—to actually show we could do it because Berlin was controlled by the four powers. The Russians controlled the air space and they would harass us quite often when we flew.

American units in France began to return to the United States in the early 1960s.[3] Roy departed Évreux-Fauville AB in May 1964 for Lockbourne Air Force Base[4] in Columbus, Ohio. He left again shortly thereafter for a training assignment at Hurlburt Air Force Base, just west of Fort Walton Beach, Florida. There, Roy continued flying cargo planes, but began piloting an older model used in World War II called the Fairchild C-123 Provider. Hurlburt AFB had housed the Doolittle Raiders in 1942 as they prepared for the firebombing of Tokyo during World War II. In the 1960s, it once again served as a training ground for men undertaking a unique mission. Nine in Roy's training class were selected for a defoliation assignment in Vietnam called Operation Ranch Hand. Roy was one of them.

Operation Ranch Hand began in 1962 at the request of South Vietnam's President Ngo Dinh Diem after much discussion with the White House. Ranch Hand's primary mission was the defoliation of the dense jungles in North Vietnam and Laos, which the

Vietcong and North Vietnamese Army used for protective covering. The ultimate out-come of this mission was to protect American lives from ambush, although it served the dual purpose of eliminating the enemy's food sources in the jungles.[5] By the time Roy joined in November 1965, the unit had turned its attention to Laos and the Ho Chi Minh Trail, aiming to remove the foliage covering the long road the Vietcong and North Vietnamese used to transport supplies. Several varieties of herbicides were used in the operation, but the best known was Agent Orange.[6]

Following training at Hurlburt, those selected for Operation Ranch Hand were sent to Langley Air Force Base, Hampton, Virginia, for an additional three weeks of spray training. Afterward, they returned to Hurlburt to pick up three C-123s, each modified to carry 1,000-gallon herbicide tanks, spray booms beneath each wing, and a spray boom at the tail, and to ferry them to Vietnam.[7] The trip took 11 days, with stops along the way in California, Hawaii, Midway Island, Wake, Guam, and the Philippines before reaching the destination of Tan Son Nhut Air Base in Saigon. Roy's second tour overseas, his first in Vietnam, began November 1, 1965.

At the time, Ranch Hand kept around seven planes on base. As only three or four men per aircraft were needed for missions, the Ranch Hand unit in 1966 rarely exceeded more than twenty-four or twenty-five people.[8] Many lived together; officers typically rented "villas" just off base and lived three or four to a house. Dick Peshkin, who served with Roy in Vietnam, recalls, "Roy could fill a door, but only from bottom to top. He was slender and athletic. He was a good guy.... His nature, it was wonderful and care-free."

Roy was also, Dick notes, an excellent aviator, necessary for Ranch Hand missions. Their large planes, combined with the low altitude and slow speed they flew at, made them easy targets. Their unit was known to be one of the most, if not *the* most, shot-at unit in Vietnam. Unit members flew almost daily, a deliberate choice by the men to avoid sitting and worrying about what could happen during the next mission. Missions required a pilot, seated on the left, who controlled the airplane; a copilot, seated right, who controlled the speed; and a crew chief, seated in an armored box behind the 1,000-gallon defoliant tank, who operated a small gasoline-powered pump to propel liquid to the spray bars.[9] Sometimes there was also a navigator. Missions started early in the day to allow the aircraft to take off in the dark. They were flown east to west as the sun rose to reduce visibility. The men often put in a day's work before noon. When they weren't in the air, members of Ranch Hand were often planning the next mission or doing routine maintenance on their airplanes.

There was some time to relax. Just prior to Roy's arrival the base had installed new handball courts, an ice cream store, and a movie house. Nearby Saigon had an athletic club and good food, including a popular Chinese restaurant, "Cheap Charlie's" (which served excellent corn chowder with shrimp). Even on the job, they usually had a good time. On one mission, Roy's crew took chicken wire and threaded a cloth through it, on which they wrote, "F*** Communism." They let loose the sign after their mission, but the bridle broke and the sign flew off. They came out of their plane laughing at the idea of their message lost somewhere in the Laotian treetops. Overall, despite the dangers, the men were in good spirits and devoted to their work.

In May 1966 Roy was promoted to captain. On July 29 his aircraft was severely damaged during a mission he piloted, but he remained in control and successfully completed the assignment. The action earned him his first Silver Star; his second would come for a similar incident in November. Around this time Roy's aircraft was shot down, forcing an emergency landing in a rice paddy. After the helicopters pulled the crew out, the crew threw a "glad to be alive" party at a club in Saigon. J.P. Morgan, Roy's friend from France, was assigned nearby and attended the celebration. "Roy was just ecstatic to be alive," he says.

With the end of his tour nearing in October 1966, Roy approached Ralph Dresser, the commander of Ranch Hand, who had arrived with Roy from Hurlburt. He wanted Ralph's opinion on extending his tour. Roy had flown more than three hundred spray missions at this point and loved his job. "Guys wanting to extend was not unusual," Ralph writes, "and because Roy was not married I encouraged him to consider it. His only regret was he would not be able to get back to the States to his beloved Porsche sports car." So Roy extended, embarking on his third overseas tour. In December Ranch Hand, now an independent unit officially designated as the 12th Air Commando Squadron, relocated to Bien Hoa Air Base.

In December 1966 a newspaper article on Operation Ranch Hand, originally printed by a paper in Saigon, was reprinted in multiple newspapers across the United States.[10] It explained how, between January and September 1966, the squadron had defoliated one thousand square miles of Vietnam and seventy thousand acres of crops. It explained how the herbicides began to affect foliage within two to three days and how only dead trees remained four to six weeks later. The article reported that the squadron had won 4 Silver Stars as well as 430 Air Medals, 61 Distinguished Flying Crosses, and 15 Bronze Stars. It quoted Captain Roy Kubley, age 28, as saying that defoliating pilots were the only real fliers in jet-age war and that, after one mission, "a board of review would have taken my wings away" if he were flying in the United States. Though probably joking, he emphasized the difficulty of the flying skills required of the men in Ranch Hand.

Roy's mission on the morning of January 31, 1967, was near the town of Tchepone. It was a focal point in the Ho Chi Minh Trail in central Laos and had been targeted by Ranch Hand before. Dick Peshkin explains:

> To get to Laos from North Vietnam were mountain passes. You had to go up a fairly steep road and at the border you turn southwest, and there was a fairly high plateau with not many trees. Mostly savannah. Then it started to decrease in ground altitude and then, perhaps one hundred kilometers to the west, was the Mekong River.... There was a little town nearby and it was known as a nasty place to be flying because they had heavy machine guns.... So coming from the plateaus—one hundred feet higher than the river—there was a break in the hill as you went down to the river and it was fairly narrow. Two, three airplanes could get in, so about five hundred feet wide. One of the most important things, when flying conventionally powered rotary engine airplanes, was you never fly uphill.

Roy's was the lead plane in a three-plane formation that day. He was flying as an instructor pilot, occupying the copilot's chair. Dick continues:

> They were on the plateau just to the southeast of the river going through the notch where there was a road, and they got hit going down that road and it disabled an engine. You have very little time to shut off the engine because you have to do that to reduce the drag that may be coming from a bad propeller. You gotta work fast. Also, you gotta be careful about controlling the elevators because if you pull back on the stick, you lose airspeed very quickly and if you lose too quickly, you do a snap-roll. It was observed that the plane went nose up, snap-rolled, and dove into the ground upside down.

Rescue crews arrived at the scene soon after the crash, but were unable to reach the aircraft due to the heavy antiaircraft fire in the area. No one, however, believed that they had survived. Unable to be retrieved, the entire crew was listed as missing in action.[11] By the end of February, their status had been changed to killed in action.

Before he left for Vietnam, while he was training for Ranch Hand, Roy crossed paths with Don Logeman again. The men talked, but not about Roy's mission. "Typical of his discretion and quiet attitude, he never said much about his combat," remembers Don. "Later I learned how significant and highly dedicated a warrior he was.... I never realized he was that much of a hero until later on."

Captain Kubley was awarded ten medals after his death, presented to his parents at a ceremony at Duluth Air Force Base in Minnesota. Among the awards were his third Silver Star and the Gallantry Cross, given by the Republic of Vietnam. Along with the latter decoration came a message from Major General Hoàng Xuân Lãm, commander of I Corps in Vietnam: "Despite intense ground fire, Captain Kubley was courageous, and set a brilliant example of sacrifice and gallantry in fulfilling his mission under hazardous conditions.

"Captain Kubley died for the cause of freedom."

Private First Class
Duwayne Marshall Soulier

United States Marine Corps,
disappeared May 1, 1967

"He wasn't the kind of guy who got mad. I used to say he was a lover, not a fighter.... I don't think he had a mean bone in his body."—Cynthia (Soulier) Manning

Roughly one of every 12 eligible Americans served in the military during the Vietnam War. Roughly 25 percent of those who served were drafted. Compare these statistics of the general population to those of the forty-two thousand Native Americans who fought in Vietnam, where one of every four served, and more than 90 percent volunteered. While Native Americans constituted approximately 0.6 percent of the American population, they represented 1.4 percent of the wartime military.[1] One such volunteer was Private Duwayne Soulier, a member of the Red Cliff Band of Lake Superior Chippewas.

Duwayne Soulier was more often known by his middle name, Marshall, or his nickname, Wotsy. He was born on December 31, 1946, and grew up on the Red Cliff Indian Reservation in northern Wisconsin. The reservation was small, with a population of only about five hundred, and nearby Bayfield was not much bigger. Kids spent most of their time outdoors. Few people owned cars. When the children from Red Cliff wanted to see a movie after church on Sundays, they trekked the three miles to the Bayfield theatre without complaint. "It was just a good life," Marshall's younger sister, Cynthia Manning, remembers.

The Soulier family was large and close knit. "We had family, and that's basically who we did things with," Cynthia says. Every year, almost immediately after school let out, their father, John, packed up Marshall and Cynthia, their older brother, Lawrence, and younger brother, John, and took them to Sturgeon Bay for the summer. From June through August the Souliers harvested crops in a farmer's field. Of everything they picked, cherries were the kids' favorite.

Not only were they paid 20 cents for every pail they filled, but the cherries were delicious. Cynthia says:

> We were told that we could not eat the good sweet cherries. They had trees of red cherries, and we could not touch them because people would come in and pick their own. So when it got dark at night we'd climb the trees and eat until we were sick. I'm sure they knew.

After working, they would walk a few miles and cool off in a lake. The evenings were filled with night games or movies or board games inside. Summers were fun, and the money they earned helped pay for school clothes. They returned to the reservation only a day or two before school started in the fall.

Marshall attended a one-room Catholic elementary school, then Bayfield High School. The high school was also small, totaling roughly two hundred students during Marshall's four years.

Most of the kids had gone to school together since kindergarten, either in the public or the Catholic school, and many were from Red Cliff. "There wouldn't have been a high school without the reservation," says John Norwell, a student one year ahead of Marshall at Bayfield.

At school, Marshall was typically laid back. "We used to say he went to school just to eat the meals because he was very carefree," Cynthia remembers. Marshall rode the bus to school alongside his good friend, Merlin Allen.[2] He didn't play sports, but a classmate, Rod Hiekel, thinks he probably could have if he'd chosen to. "He was good enough," he says. "He was a good ball player—baseball and basketball."

The class of 1965 had roughly fifty-five students, about half of them boys, and most of those boys joined the military after graduation.[3] "It was their ticket out of there," John explains. Rod, also a Marine, agrees: "I would say that well over half the class ended up in the military." Marshall's oldest brother and two of his older sisters were living in Milwaukee when he graduated, and he moved in with them. From there he enlisted in the U.S. Marine Corps.

Marshall completed boot camp and advanced infantry training, arriving in South Vietnam in the summer of 1966. Marshall had an MOS of 0351,[4] an antitank assaultman, and was attached to 1st Battalion, 5th Marines. In the fall of 1966, the unit carried out several operations in the vicinity of Tam Kỳ, capital of the Quảng Nam province, as well as operations in the province of Quảng Tín.[5] In December 1966 Marshall was transferred to Mike Company, 3rd Battalion, 5th Marines (3/5), where he served as an assistant gunner.

Wotsy (middle row, left) smiling during a typical Wisconsin winter. His younger sister, Cynthia, is wrapped in a scarf on the sled. Courtesy Cynthia Manning.

It was while assigned to 3/5 that Marshall showed interest in serving with a Marine combined action program (CAP) squad. The CAP was established in 1965 with the goal of pacifying rural Vietnam. CAP squads were assigned to hamlets and villages where they worked with local Vietnamese militia to protect the inhabitants from attacks by the Vietcong. They conducted military operations and trained Vietnamese forces, called Popular Forces (PF), while gathering intelligence at a local level. Marshall's squad was called CAP India and operated just west of Tam Kỳ.[6]

Marshall was well liked within CAP India. He was a notorious prankster, and his sense of humor and fun-loving nature were infectious within the unit. Marshall had grown up fishing, and he and several other members frequented a nearby river. Sometimes they swam; other times, they fished with hand grenades. Rather than eat what they caught, they often traded for bread with the PF to make sandwiches. The unit members called Marshall "Chief," and someone drew a caricature of him on the back of one of his sweatshirts, a sign of their respect and camaraderie.[7]

Cynthia sent care packages and wrote her brother often while he was in Vietnam. She and her best friend took pictures of home to include in the letters. Other members in his platoon noticed the letters Marshall was writing and receiving, and they began writing Cynthia and her friends themselves. Soon, the girls were writing letters to most of the squad.

In one letter Marshall told Cynthia that after completing his tour of duty, he would enjoy his leave, then return to Vietnam. "He felt that ... he needed to be there," Cynthia explains. "We were in this, and he felt that he needed to go back and continue what he started. Very strong, being the Marine way."

Marshall's enlistment would end midsummer 1967. On May 1, 1967, Private Duwayne Marshall Soulier was medically evacuated from the 1st Hospital Company in Chu Lai, for a fever of unknown origin. In recent years, however, the Soulier family has been contacted by Marshall's team leader, Stanley Pace. Stan told the family that Marshall was accompanying another Marine on a mail run when their jeep ran over a mine. The explosion killed the other Marine and wounded Marshall, who was evacuated for his wounds.

On the evening of May 1, two Boeing Vertol CH-46 Sea Knight transport helicopters departed Chu Lai for the USS *Sanctuary*, a hospital ship operating in the waters off the coast. One of the helicopters was transporting men on stretchers; the other carried those who could walk on. Marshall was on the latter.

Kevin Kelly was carried via stretcher onto the other helicopter. He remembers that evening clearly:

> It was still daylight but it was getting dark when they came in with two very large helicopters.... We went out and we took off together in those helicopters. We were going to the *Sanctuary*. We were over land—not for very long—and there was some shooting and I could see tracers going up. That lasted five seconds, maybe. We continued out and we got to the *Sanctuary*. My helicopter landed on the *Sanctuary*. While it was on this little landing pad, the other helicopter was circling and then crashed into the sea.

It is believed that the second CH-46 lost power while waiting to unload onto the *Sanctuary*.[8] When the helicopter crashed in the South China Sea, the crew immediately began evacuating the patients. Strong swells suddenly flipped the helicopter, however, and within ninety seconds the CH-46 was completely underwater. Of the four crewmen and thirteen patients aboard, three crewmen and six patients escaped the sinking helicopter. Eight people did not.[9] On May 13 and May 17 search-and-rescue operations recovered the bodies of Lance Corporal Early Dillworth and Lance Corporal Joseph Lipton. Six Marines were listed as killed in action/body not recovered. Duwayne Soulier was one of them.

Several months earlier Marshall's siblings in Milwaukee had bought a recorder and sent him a tape from home. They sent Marshall the recorder as well so he could mail them back a message. He had recorded a tape, but had not yet sent it to his family. The Souliers found it in his duffel bag after the military returned his personal belongings.

"He died when he was 20 years old," Cynthia says. "He didn't have a lot of time to do anything."

Marshall's loss was felt throughout Red Cliff, and it resonated for decades. In 2006 local veterans ensured that he would never be forgotten.

Private Duwayne Marshall Soulier, circa 1966. Courtesy Cynthia Manning.

Three years earlier Bayfield's VFW Post was informed that, due to its low activity and membership, it was going to be closed. Rather than accept this, the remaining members began a fundraising effort. They raised enough funds to demolish the old post, and volunteers built a new one. The post hosted youth groups and organized community activities. Its membership grew. With a new building, a new purpose, and new members, a new name was needed. The post was renamed The Duwayne Soulier Memorial VFW Post 8239.

Inside, it is unlike any other. Lining the walls are portraits of every citizen of Red Cliff to have ever worn a uniform, from the Civil War, to Iraq and Afghanistan. "You feel such a sense of pride when you go in there to see that," Cynthia reflects. Her stepfather, an Army veteran, has a spot on the wall. So does her oldest brother, Eddie, who fought with the Navy during the Korean War.

The place of honor is reserved for Marshall. His photo is larger than the others, framed by his service medals. A rubbing of his name from the Memorial Wall in Washington, D.C., is placed beneath it. Above the photograph is an oil painting done by fellow Vietnam veteran, Larry Bychowski. The painting shows Marshall crouched in the fields of Vietnam, an eagle and an American Flag behind him, a feather in his helmet.

"It just gives you such a feeling, it's hard to explain," Cynthia says. "You can almost see him."

Sergeant James Neil Tycz
United States Marine Corps, disappeared May 10, 1967

"When he was in the field, he was serious. When he was not in the field, he clowned around a lot.... He was just a kid."—Roger Wines

"He was right by the book, but also had that good ol' Recon wild streak."
—Ted Biszko

"Swift, Silent, Deadly" is the motto of the United States Marine Corps reconnaissance battalions. Vietnam War Marines often included another word: Surrounded. Dropped behind enemy lines, members of these elite teams gathered critical information directly by observing and often engaging with the enemy. Each Marine division had one operating recon battalion. From the time 3rd Recon Battalion landed in Vietnam in May 1965 until they were decommissioned in November 1969, roughly twenty-eight hundred Marines served within its ranks. Approximately 40 percent of these Marines were killed or wounded.[1] Four were awarded the Medal of Honor, and thirteen received the second-highest medal of valor, the Navy Cross. For his actions on May 9 and 10, 1967, Sergeant James Neil Tycz was among those thirteen.

With his high-pitched voice and 5'9" frame, it was hard for the Tycz[2] family in Milwaukee to imagine Neil as a platoon sergeant. "In movies these are big guys," says his older brother Phillip. "He wasn't a take-charge-type kid. He was very humble."[3]

Theirs was a large family. James Neil Tycz was born April 10, 1945, and like most of his seven siblings, he was known by his middle name.

Neil began high school in 1958 at St. Francis de Sales Seminary, intending to become a priest. After a short time he decided on a different path and transferred to South Division High School, where he ran cross country and lettered on the tennis team.

The camaraderie and hard work that came along with sports were only part of the reason Neil competed. "He was in it for laughs, too," wrote his cross country teammate, Warren Gerds, in 2005.[4] "He was always a gas to be around." Neil found humor in almost everything he did. Warren recalls a time when Neil greeted him with a playful call of "Whitey, you scrounge!" Warren's brother, also present, found it so funny that he repeated the line for years.

Neil's was the life of a typical Wisconsin teenager. There was little to suggest the makings of a hero. Outside of school, Neil was among those from South Division High School who frequently hung around Milwaukee's popular pizza parlor, Pepe's. He and his older brother dug up night crawlers and sold them to a bait shop in town for a penny per worm. Neil totaled that same brother's 1958 Pontiac Bonneville the very day he got his driver's license.

Growing up during the Cold War, Neil acquired a strong anticommunist sentiment as a teenager. He graduated from high school in 1963 and enlisted in the United States Marine Corps. He was 19 years old, aiming to do something meaningful with his life.

Neil completed the Marine Corps's basic training program. After that, he began Marine reconnaissance training. "A lot of physical training, a lot of mental," explains Ted Biszko, who trained alongside Neil for roughly a year before they deployed to Vietnam together. He remembers:

> Once we got our squads together, we started training in the mountain trails and the watercrafts. Like in the Navy. We started doing that all the time after the mountains and the bush work in California.... Then we were sent down to San Diego with the Seals. We'd be in the water for days with some food. Insertions, extractions.... We trained all the way until the day we went to Vietnam. We never really knew where we were at. We slept on decks of boats. We never were very organized about where we were assigned to. They kept rotating the old guys back to train the new guys, too.[5]

Training was intense, but so were the Marines. They had to have a certain "edge" to volunteer to conduct the dangerous, covert missions recon Marines conducted, and Neil definitely had that edge. While training with Navy Seals onboard a submarine, someone told Neil he had no guts. Neil told him to stick out his hand—and promptly shot the outstretched hand with a spear gun. The incident was brushed aside. The Marines on board roughhoused on a regular basis, and no one questioned Neil's guts again.

Neil had the confidence and the dose of craziness it took to be a recon Marine, but he also had the brains and the dedication. "He was a happy-go-lucky guy, but boy, when it came to the book, the Marine Corps book, he was right on it," Ted says. "He probably would have been a hell of an officer if he got out of Vietnam."

Many members of the training unit were assigned to various battalions after completing recon training. Neil and Ted were not. Both were sent to teams in 3rd Platoon, Alpha Company, 3rd Recon Battalion in the 3rd Marine Division. The role of recon Marines was long-range reconnaissance; that is, to gather intelligence behind enemy lines. To do this, seven-man recon teams were dropped, usually by helicopter, miles into remote sites to observe and report enemy activity. Usually, the teams were within reach of supporting artillery, which could be called on in the event they identified a large enemy target or were themselves discovered.

While observation was their job, many patrols involved direct confrontations with the Vietcong or NVA. There was no official front line in the Vietnam War; enemy forces could be in any village or along any path that the Marines traveled. Recon Marines were alone in dangerous territory. There was a reason their units were composed of volunteers. There was also a reason their casualty rate was so high.

Recon Marines were isolated on their patrols. Their success depended on their training and each other. Ted recalls one mission he had with Neil. Their team had finished their patrol, but no helicopters were available to retrieve them. They had to walk back to their base, a five-day journey in near-constant pouring rain. During the trek they found themselves in the middle of an abandoned village, which, they discovered after some investigation, was being used as a Vietcong training camp. They conducted their reconnaissance, left some booby traps, and quickly moved on.

It was not the last close call they had on that mission. After they made their way out of the mountains, the group reached flatter terrain and started across a highway when everyone suddenly dropped to the ground. Ted assumed they were taking a break and sat down behind a blueberry bush. He coughed, the bush moved, and the team realized the Vietcong were hidden among the flora. The highway erupted in a firefight.

Amid the attack, a medevac helicopter arrived to retrieve the lieutenant, who had been wounded. Their platoon leader was pulled on board, and as quickly as it had arrived, the medevac took off again, leaving the rest of the team in the same position as before, but without their platoon leader.

"So what now?" Ted remembers thinking. Without the team leader, the men felt Neil was the most qualified and urged him to take charge. Neil wanted to continue moving forward. Another Marine, senior to Neil in rank, wanted to go back the way they'd came. The team overruled the senior Marine, and Neil led them safely back to base.

"When we got back, somebody asked us, 'Where'd you come from?'" Ted remembers. "We said, 'See those mountains? Somewhere up there.'"

It was one hell of a mission, but most missions were hell. "Nobody ever thought we'd come back from patrols," Ted says. "We were away from the troops, starving half the time.... They gave us a map. Our orders were: search, destroy, and capture. How can you do that with six guys?"

The men did not wear helmets or flak jackets when on patrol. They coated their faces in grease paint and hygiene was understandably forgotten while scouring the jungle. Despite this, Neil always carried a toothbrush with him, even while out in the bush. Before patrols, Neil often led his team in prayer. He felt strongly that the Marines were doing important work in Vietnam, but he didn't revel in the violence that came with the job.

Throughout early 1967, Alpha Company frequently engaged with the NVA regulars and Vietcong in the vicinities of Phu Bai and Khe Sanh. Enemy activity had increased, especially in Khe Sanh. As April waned, multiple battalions from the Marines 3rd Division fought the NVA for control of Hills 861, 881 South, and 881 North to eliminate the enemy, which was threatening the nearby Khe Sanh Combat Base. This series of battles became known as "The Hill Fights," or "The First Battle of Khe Sanh."[6]

The Hill Fights were coming to a close by the time Alpha Company's Team Breaker[7] began its patrol on May 9, 1967.[8] Seven men made up Team Breaker. Sergeant James Neil Tycz had recently been promoted to platoon sergeant. He was 22 years old, and had been in the Marines more than three years. He was also nearing the end of his tour and although several friends discouraged him from taking the patrol, he felt a responsibility to lead it. Second Lieutenant Heinz Ahlmeyer, Jr., was new in country and assigned to the patrol to learn on the job from a more experienced recon Marine: Neil. Also on the team were Private First Class Steven Lopez, Private First Class Carl Friery,

Members of Alpha Company, 3rd Recon Battalion, 3rd Marine Division, in Khe Sanh, March 1967. Always looking for a laugh, Neil is lying down in front of the unit insignia. Courtesy Roger Wines.

Lance Corporal Clarence Carlson, Lance Corporal Samuel Sharp, Jr., and Navy Petty Officer 3rd Class Malcolm "Doc" Miller.

The team departed Khe Sanh Combat Base late in the afternoon of May 9, just as the helicopter carrying Corporal Ted Biszko returned to the base from his team's mission. Ted took a moment to ask Neil about his new team, and where they were headed.[9] Neil told him they were headed north of where Ted had just been. Ted told him they wouldn't come back. It was how they always spoke, always expecting trouble and preparing for the worst. Neil jumped in the air and kicked his legs like the Roadrunner from the cartoon *Looney Tunes*, shouting "Beep, beep!" Ted did the same. It meant that "Charlie" Coyote couldn't catch them.

A helicopter dropped the team 9.3 miles from the base. They were inserted on a treeless landing zone, with Hill 665 to the south and a shallow stream to the north. For recon Marines, such open spaces were disconcerting, and they quickly began their work: uncovering recently filled holes and bunkers where the Vietcong had been living and checking on the damage done by the recent bomb strike. After several hours Neil radioed headquarters for an extraction. He was told that a helicopter would pick them up in the morning.

Neil wanted to leave the area. They were near the landing zone (LZ), and it was possible the helicopter that had inserted them had been spotted. Neil and 2nd Lt. Ahl-meyer discussed the situation, and Team Breaker remained near the LZ for the night.

The attack began shortly after midnight on May 10, 1967. A company of more than one hundred NVA soldiers surrounded Team Breaker, so close that the Marines could hear them talking to one another. The NVA opened fire, and the Marines returned it. During the chaos Neil radioed the combat operations center at Khe Sanh, requesting extraction helicopters—and help.

Ted Biszko was ready to provide it. At base, he was awakened and told that Neil's patrol had run into trouble. Someone asked if Ted would gather his team and go in for an extraction. Ted didn't hesitate. He told his men it was a suicide mission, but they were going in.

Twice, Ted's team boarded helicopters to pull out Team Breaker. Twice, the CH-46s were viciously repelled.

On the ground, the Marines' situation was dire. Both 2nd Lt. Ahlmeyer and Sgt. Tycz had been hit in the opening minutes of the attack, and Heinz Ahlmeyer was seri-ously wounded. Neil, while hurt, could still fight. Corporal Carlson was nearby and described what happened next in Lawrence Vetter's book, *Never without Heroes:*

> A grenade came in, and, by God, [Tycz] went for that grenade. He grabbed it and threw it back at the enemy. It went off.... I can't remember exactly, but it was like Tycz was trying to protect a Marine who had gone down. It might have been Lieutenant Ahlmeyer. Then another grenade came in, and he went for that one, too. That one went off in his hand.

Three hours into the battle, Sergeant Tycz, 2nd Lieutenant Ahlmeyer, Lance Corporal Sharp, and Navy Petty Officer Third Class Miller, their corpsman, were dead. The pilot of the second helicopter that had been turned away, Captain Paul Looney, was also killed during the rescue effort. Despite the odds, a third helicopter managed to land, and Private Friery, Private Lopez, and Corporal Carlson escaped, wounded, but alive. Due to continued heavy fire, they were forced to leave behind the four fallen members of Team Breaker.

Sergeant James Neil Tycz was awarded the Navy Cross for his "extraordinary hero-ism" and "unselfish act of courage" in those early morning hours beneath Hill 665.

All the Marines were listed as killed in action, body not recovered. They would remain so for more than three decades.

Efforts to bring them home began in 1991, when a Vietnamese woman claimed to have found the dog tags of both Heinz Ahlmeyer and Neil Tycz. Shortly thereafter two Vietnamese sources arrived at the U.S. Office for POW/MIA Affairs in Hanoi with the names of ten U.S. personnel, including Neil, and the locations of their remains, but no further proof. One month later, a Vietnamese man approached the office with three teeth, one bone, and several dog tags. This witness, too, mentioned Neil's name.

This was enough evidence for JPAC to begin investigating further. For 10 years teams traveled to Vietnam in hopes of finding the men. They were successful in 2003 and delivered to the identification lab in Hawaii 31 teeth and tooth fragments. Three belonged to Neil Tycz.

James Neil Tycz, Heinz Ahlmeyer, Samuel Sharp, and Malcolm Miller were buried in Arlington National Cemetery on May 10, 2005, exactly 38 years after their deaths in Khe Sanh.

The day their son left for his final patrol, Sigmund and Agnes Tycz received a letter from him. The letter speaks volumes about Neil, about his humor, his compassion, and his dedication to his men and his country[10]:

Dear Mom and Pop,

Hi! It's very close to "black out" (all lights off), but before that time, I just have to write an overdue letter to the best parents in the world, and anywhere else. After being with the 2nd platoon for very close to a year I have been transferred. I am now the platoon sergeant and second in command of an entire reconnaissance platoon.... The change is a little strange, of course, but I know once my men and myself get used to each other, everything will be just great. They're a platoon of good marines and I plan on keeping them that way, with my newly acquired "Sarge's growwwl!" (Would you believe—my squeak??!)

Since my last patrol, Khe Sanh has kept me pretty busy. About a week ago a couple infantry platoons discovered enemy fortified positions in our front yard.

From our different "recon" patrols, we have known that there were many numerous enemy troops in our area; the two infantry platoons have been hit extremely hard, which has set off a large operation to our west and surrounding terrain.

Although he didn't have the loud, booming voice of a typical Marine sergeant, Neil Tycz was one of the best and most experienced platoon sergeants in Alpha Company. He was awarded the Navy Cross for heroic actions on May 10, 1967. Courtesy the Vietnam Veterans Memorial Fund.

The battle has been going on for, it seems, eternity.

Most of the contact has been with North Vietnamese Communists, very well armed, well trained and in positions that make the defensive fortifications of World War II look like sand castles.

Due to all available helicopters being used for resupply and "med evacs" (flying out the killed and wounded in action), my patrol is on standby, waiting for choppers to insert us into our area to be patrolled.

We've been sand bagging our living quarters for quite some time and are not really minding this work. Our base is frequently hit by enemy mortars during the night.

The most unpleasant detail is acting as stretcher bearers at the airfield.

An afternoon participating in evacuating the dead and wounded has made me learn to hate: Demonstrators (gutless traitors is what they are); a minority who actually supply the enemy with blood and supplies, and those overprotecting parents who put boot camp drill instructors in jail because they try to turn their boys into men that can stand up to a hard core enemy.

Our company has been hit pretty hard, too, with casualties; 100% casualties in one of our eight man patrols hit by mortars while waiting for helicopters to pick them up....

Mom and Dad, I have had opportunities to write sooner than tonight but I hope you will understand that writing about an unpopular war like this one is not easy....

I want to say what I think and feel, but I do not want to cause worry at home.

None of us here like this war, especially after seeing a friend or a fellow Marine wounded or worse, but the majority (I hope for the sake of democracy) believe in fighting off Communist aggression in a weakened country.

I firmly believe in bombings in North Vietnam of supply plants and arsenals. Why fight a trooper as well supplied and armed as these North Vietnamese are?

Unless we prove to the Communists that we do mean business, I feel that this war can and will last a long time.

I had an interruption just now. Our lieutenant passed me the word that we go in at 7:30 a.m. tomorrow. None of us want to go, but that's our job and I pray I will never fail to do it....

Your Marine Son,
Neil

Beneath his signature, Neil had sketched an American flag, along with a brief note: "The U.S. is in. It is free!"

Lance Corporal Merlin Raye Allen

United States Marine Corps, disappeared June 30, 1967

"Merl was my mentor, he took me under his wing and he taught me about recon and he taught me about Vietnam. He was my friend when I needed one, that's how Merl was!"—Jeff Savelkoul

Jeff Savelkoul knew the four-hour route from Minneapolis, Minnesota, to Bayfield, Wisconsin, well. He'd made the trip four times over the course of sixteen years, with one goal in mind. Three times, he stopped shy of that goal, at the end of a driveway in the small town. The fourth time was different. On that trip, Jeff made it past the driveway and to the front door of the Allen family's house. Reaching that door, he says now, was "one of the greatest things I've ever done in my life."

The reason for Jeff's trips to Bayfield was his best friend, Merlin Raye Allen.

Merlin, more commonly known as Merl, grew up all around Wisconsin. He was born in Madison on October 22, 1946. As a child he lived in Winneconne and Omro before the family settled in Bayfield. The second oldest of six children, Merl was a prankster at heart. Many Sundays he would drive his younger siblings to church, convince them to give him their money for the mass offering, then use the money to buy everyone bakery rolls and donuts. He had a great sense of humor and was always playing tricks. If his pranks ever landed him in trouble, it was never for long. Vivacious and fun, Merl had a smile that could win over anyone.

Merl attended Bayfield High School and played on the school's basketball team, the Trollers. The town was on Lake Superior, and Merl spent much of his time outdoors, fishing, swimming, and hunting. His favorite place to spend his days was York Island, which his father owned until the early 1970s.[1]

His best friend growing up was his sister, Marilyn, older by only eleven months. When Merl first expressed a desire to join the Marines, their father asked Marilyn to speak with him. "I was going to college when Merl was thinking about enlisting," she explained in a 2013 interview.[2] "The war was escalating. Dad asked me to come home and try to talk Merl out of it. There was no talking him out of it."

After graduation in 1965 Merl spent a portion of his summer working at his uncle's machine shop and with the Interlake Steamship Company, aboard the *William G.*

Mather. Later in the summer Merl and his friend, John Powers, made a cross-country road trip. The two drove John's oil-guzzling sedan, loaded with 50 pounds of potatoes and a case of motor oil, to Alaska. The potatoes froze as they approached their destination. They made stops in Sacramento, California, and Reno, Nevada, as well, where they won enough money to buy gas for the ride home. Merl loved Alaska and told the rest of his family that they needed to see it, too.

Merl and John made the round trip in ten days because they needed to be back to report for basic training. The two had enlisted together through the buddy program, which guaranteed that they would go through basic training together. Merl followed basic with six months of communications training, where he learned to be a field radio operator. Upon arriving in Vietnam, he was deployed first with the 2nd Battalion, 4th Marines, the "Magnificent Bastards." He volunteered for a reconnaissance battalion soon after.

Marine recon battalions supported divisions by gathering intelligence. Individual teams of six to ten men conducted patrols before or after larger assaults. Only four Marine recon battalions were activated during the Vietnam War: the 1st, 2nd, 3rd, and 5th. Merl served with 3rd Division's 3rd Reconnaissance Battalion, Alpha Company, Team Striker.

With 3rd Recon Merl was stationed first in Danang, then in Khe Sanh. It was here where he greeted Jeff Savelkoul, new to the battalion, by saying "Says you here for recon? Name's Allen from Bayfield, Wisconsin. How long you been in country? Oh ... FNG, huh?[3] Recon's this way."

It was atypical, says Jeff, to accept new unit members so easily. "They usually screwed something up," he says. "Also, you just never made friends quickly because it was too hard seeing them hauled off in body bags." Yet Merl and Jeff hit it off immediately. They were both from the Midwest, both were radio operators, and both were excited to be in recon. More than that, though, they were both "big dreamers," says Jeff. They talked about the world they'd left behind and made plans for what they would do when they went home. They decided to become heavy equipment operators and return to Vietnam one day as civilian operators.

Within the unit the Marines joked that Merl either had to camo his teeth or stop smiling and keep his mouth shut. "Merl was always scheming up something," says Jeff. As bunkmates, Merl and Jeff made a table out of ammunition crates. He spent much of his time writing letters to his family and to others. He wrote Anne Randall, an American model and actress, and she replied by sending pin-ups for all the boys in the unit. He sent a letter to the Bicycle Playing Card Company, requesting multiple ace of spades playing cards. The North Vietnamese viewed the card as a "deadly omen," so the Marines began picking the ace of spades from their card decks and leaving them in the bush. After receiving Merl's letter, the company sent 3rd Recon fifty-two packs of cards made up entirely of the ace of spades. "Merl was our hero," Jeff remembers. While most unit members carried one or two cards with them on patrols, Merl carried his entire deck.

Merl played a large part in keeping up his unit's morale. Third Recon Battalion had a dangerous mission in a dangerous place, and the battalion suffered roughly 40 percent casualties from 1965 to 1970. Khe Sanh was a valley in the northwestern corner of South Vietnam near the Laotian border, south of the Demilitarized Zone. The Marines held a combat base there until it was evacuated during the Battle of Khe Sanh in 1968. It was a strategic location because many North Vietnamese troop-carrying trucks passed nearby, but it was also surrounded by hills from which North Vietnamese fighters conducted guerrilla warfare.

While 3rd Recon was stationed in Khe Sanh, the hills were estimated to be hiding two to three divisions of North Vietnamese, while Jeff estimates that fewer than three hundred Americans were on base at any given time. More often than not, the recon Marines were in the field.

Radio operators like Merl and Jeff were responsible for calling in and receiving information during missions. "We tried to stay as far away from the antennae as we could," Jeff explains. "They always shot the guy with the antennae because the guy next to him was usually the leader."

From April through June 1967 the North Vietnamese launched a series of coordinated attacks in the hills surrounding Khe Sanh. Third Marine Recon Battalion's Alpha Company sustained heavy casualties, including four members of Team Breaker and a helicopter pilot in May.[4] Alpha was replaced by Bravo in Khe Sanh, and sent to Phu Bai to rebuild the company.

Merl Allen at Marine Corps Recruit Depot, San Diego, sporting the infectious grin he was well known for. Courtesy Cindy Hawkins.

Operations from Phu Bai centered on the Co Bi-Thanh Tan Valley, the main route for enemy traffic traveling into the city from the northwest. Although the Marines had been launching missions at the valley since 1966, the summer of 1967 saw a rapid buildup of North Vietnamese troops as they prepared to pull off the infamous Tet Offensive in the early months of 1968. Co Bi-Thanh Tan was the staging area for two North Vietnamese battalions, or roughly eight hundred troops.

Only two recon teams were operating at full strength in June 1967: Team Striker and Team Nettlerash 1. On June 29, 1967, Team Nettlerash 1 had been out on a three-day patrol, and Team Striker was sent to replace them. Although Nettlerash 1 had faced little enemy fire during its time in the field, when the helicopter carrying Striker approached, it was suddenly fired on and forced to return to base. The next day, June 30, the landing zone was shifted slightly, and Team Striker set out again.

The team consisted of Lance Corporal Merlin Allen, Lance Corporal John Killen, Lance Corporal Glyn Runnels, Sergeant Eugene Castanada, Lance Corporal Dennis Perry, Lance Corporal Mariano "Junior" Acosta, Navy Hospital Corpsman 3rd Class Michael Judd, and Lance Corporal Jeff Savelkoul. Captain John House II was the helicopter pilot.

On base at Phu Bai were two intelligence organizations.[5] It's possible that the information regarding the eight hundred North Vietnamese troops at Co Bi-Thanh Tan was lost between them. It is also possible that each section thought the other had briefed Team Striker about the hidden fighters. In fact, no one warned Team Striker about the force awaiting them that day.

As the helicopter descended to the landing zone, it was suddenly hit with small arms and antiaircraft fire. Captain House was attempting to pull out of the ambush when they were hit by a rocket. "It blew a huge hole in the side of the chopper, severed the fuel line, sprayed jet fuel all over the chopper and us and ignited," explains Jeff, who, at that moment, was standing in the back of the helicopter. Jeff saw the rocket strike and then saw the flames. He writes:

> The inside of the chopper was like an 8-foot culvert with a pile of burning tires in it—that thick, black, oily, smoke-like acetylene w/o oxygen. You couldn't see and you couldn't breathe. EVERYTHING was on fire! I could see streaks of light coming in where bullets were coming thru, but I couldn't see anyone else. How I didn't get hit was a miracle!

Years later, Jeff Savelkoul and Mariano Acosta reconstructed the events of that day, and Jeff knew without a doubt how he had survived: "I was in the void behind Merl, and was shielded from the blast by him—my best friend!" Jeff and Mariano also concluded that many of the men in the aircraft died instantly, including 20-year-old Merlin Allen.[6]

Back in the United States, the Allen family wasn't in Bayfield when the officers came to deliver the news. They were on their way to Alaska. Merl's sister, Cindy, remembers:

Lance Corporal Merlin Allen in Vietnam, possibly Khe Sanh. Courtesy Cindy Hawkins.

> We had been expecting a letter from Merl before leaving. We delayed our trip by a few days hoping to get one. Finally, Mom and Dad had mail forwarded to Dawson City, hoping his letter would catch up. Actually, the letter arrived after we had left, but the postmaster chose not to send it along with the other mail after the Marine officers had come to Bayfield. The town knew of Merl's death before we did, and the local paper had published the story before our return. We were notified in Dawson City to contact the Mounties. The Mounties shared with us a contact name and number of a Marine officer in Minneapolis. When Dad called, he spoke with a family member and they confirmed that it was a fatality. We immediately turned around and drove nonstop to Wisconsin in silence.

Jeff spent 13 months in recovery, with burns over 65 percent of his body. When he was released from the hospital, he drove four hours from Minneapolis to Bayfield for the first time to meet the Allen family. But he turned around and drove home. He

Merl's family, along with Khe Sanh veterans Jeff and Junior, at Merl's memorial on York Island before his remains were recovered in 2013. Back row: Jeff, Sean, and Casey; middle row: Alden, Cindy, Eleanor, Marilyn, and Mariano. Sheila is kneeling. Courtesy Cindy Hawkins.

was afraid for them to see him, he said. "If I looked this bad, what would they think their son endured?"

What Jeff didn't know was that the Allen family had never been given accurate details about Merl's death. Upon returning to Bayfield, the Marine officers told them that there were no survivors.

Sixteen years after Merl's death, Jeff made it to the Allen's front door and was welcomed by the family. After years of wondering, they finally knew what happened to their son and brother. But all of them still hoped for the day when Merl would come home.

That day came in 2013, when, after multiple trips to the crash site, a Joint POW/ MIA Accounting Command recovery team recovered and positively identified the remains of Merlin Allen and Michael Judd.[7]

Also found at the crash site: a rosary belonging to Jeff Savelkoul and a full deck of fifty-two aces of spades, wrapped in plastic, belonging to Merl Allen.

On June 29, 2013, the eve of the 46th anniversary of his death, a ceremony was held for Merl at the Bayfield High School gymnasium, where he once played basketball. More than five hundred people attended, including his brothers and sisters, Jeff Savelkoul, and Mariano Acosta. They shared their memories of Merl as a slideshow of a young boy with a wide grin was presented. At the end of the ceremony, the family, Jeff, and Mariano boarded a landing craft tank from World War II while *Taps* played and a Marine honor guard performed a twenty-one-gun salute. They buried Merl on York Island, his favorite place, alongside his parents.

Staff Sergeant
James Lee VanBendegom
United States Army,
disappeared July 12, 1967

"He was a good guy to be around. You know, you would want him around. There would not be a dull moment."—Mike VanBendegom

"He loved life."—Darlene VanBendegom

"Jim's story is such a long and sad, difficult journey," Darlene VanBendegom says of her brother-in-law.

Jim's brother Mike agrees: "It's a very, very bizarre, long, drawn-out story."

It began November 28, 1948, when James Lee VanBendegom was born, the second of Bob and Virginia VanBendegom's four sons. Jim and his brothers, Mike, Bob, and Gary, were raised in their father's hometown of Kenosha, Wisconsin. Virginia came from the state of Oregon. The two met on a blind date when Corporal Robert VanBendegom was stationed at Pendleton Field, Oregon, in 1941. They married in 1945, after Bob completed a twenty-eight-month tour overseas in the Chinese Burma Indian Theater during World War II, where he served as a ground crew member with the legendary Flying Tigers. Bob's military service would have a lasting impact on young Jim.

While Bob was an only child, Virginia had ten brothers and sisters living on the West coast. For two weeks every summer, the VanBendegoms traveled cross-country to visit her family. The annual road trip was always memorable, Mike says:

> It was crazy. My dad worked for a factory. He'd come home Friday afternoon, we'd load up the family station wagon, and we'd start driving west.... By Tuesday we'd be in Washington, the state of Washington. We'd hang around with my cousins and my uncles and aunts for a few days, get in the car, and we'd drive all the way the hell back to Kenosha, and he'd be back to work, two weeks later, the following Monday.... We'd be four boys packed in—and my mom and dad—packed in the station wagon, driving west, no air conditioning.... I don't know how they put up with it.

When Jim was 15, Bob and Virginia decided to move to Portland, Oregon, to be nearer to her family. They sold their house and set the boys up in new schools. Bob took a job in Portland, and Jim and his older brother Mike reluctantly said goodbye to their girlfriends as the family headed west.

The move lasted three months. "They drove their mom and dad nuts," Darlene, Mike's girlfriend then and, later, his wife, remembers. Mike and Jim were determined to return to Kenosha. So their parents sold their Portland home and re-enrolled the boys back in their Kenosha school. Bob returned to his old job, and the boys were reunited with their respective girlfriends.

Only one school year apart, Mike and Jim were a force to be reckoned with while growing up. The brothers shared a room, they played baseball, double dated, and worked a paper route together. Jim also worked at the Sunnyside Grocery Store in Kenosha and saved his money from both jobs to buy a motor scooter.

Jim kept busy when not working. He was a popular student at Tremper High School, and often had dates on the weekends. "He was just a fun-loving, carefree guy," says Darlene. Charismatic and charming, he was also religious and hardworking. His family attended church every Sunday, and Jim was a member of the Trinity Church choir and Luther League.

Jim liked hands-on, outdoor work. He spent much of his free time hunting and fishing. Bob took all four boys fishing most Sunday mornings. "That was always a circus," Mike laughs. "Four boys in a boat and my dad trying to fish." Bob usually gave up trying to keep order and let them fight in a tangle of rods and fishing lines.

All the VanBendegom boys admired their father, but Jim perhaps most of all. "He saw my dad like a hero," Mike says. Jim's favorite class in school was shop. Their father was a machinist, and Mike feels that Jim would have followed a similar path had he not followed his dad's lead and enlisted in the military first.

Jim dropped out of high school in the fall of 1966 to volunteer for the draft. He spent January of 1967 receiving basic and advanced training at Fort Jackson, South Carolina, as an infantryman and recoilless rifle specialist.

He returned to Kenosha for a thirty-day leave in May, gung-ho and confident in his decision. Jim was proud to be in the military. He was proud to follow in his father's footsteps, and took a picture beside his father, dressed in the uniform of a United States soldier.

Jim spent his leave doing what he always had. He wanted to be one of the hometown guys for a month so he worked, he hung out with his friends, and he spent time with his family.

Mike and Jim still shared a bedroom. Reflecting on Jim's leave, Mike says, "I remember looking at him and thinking—he was sound asleep—and thinking, 'Wow. That's really something. What is gonna happen to him?'"

On June 18, 1967, the VanBendegoms drove Jim to Chicago's O'Hare International Airport. They said their goodbyes and waved him off. It was Father's Day. A week later, Jim left Oakland, California, for Vietnam.

Jim was assigned to B Company, 1st Battalion, 12th Regiment of the 4th Infantry Division. Known as the Red Warriors, the unit was sent to the Ia Drang Valley, a jungle area with scattered clearings just east of the Cambodian border. In early July 1967 U.S. troops stationed nearby noticed a lot of activity by several NVA Regiments.[1] The unit called in a series of airstrikes to the area to clear it out. After the strikes it was standard operating procedure to send American troops to the targeted area to conduct a bomb damage assessment.

At this stage in the war, though, the routine had been employed regularly enough that the North Vietnamese knew what to expect once the bombing began and they planned accordingly. When the airstrikes started in early July, the NVA pulled out and crossed over into the relative safety of Cambodia to wait out the assault. When it was over they returned to the strike zone and waited for the units they knew would come to inspect the damage. It was a set-up.

The morning of July 12, 1967, 1/12 Regiment's B and C Companies were assigned to assess the area. Both units were vastly undermanned. Jim's B Company had only 69 of what should have been 120 men, while C Company had 75.

C Company engaged the enemy first at approximately 7:49 a.m., but the heaviest part of the fighting began roughly three hours later. B Company's 3rd Platoon was attacked from the west and southwest. The platoon's lieutenant requested immediate assistance. When 1st and 2nd Platoons arrived thirty minutes later, they walked directly into the trap the NVA had laid for them. By 1:00 p.m., the battle was over.[2]

Jim and his father, Bob, before Jim left for Vietnam. Bob's service during World War II was part of Jim's motivation to enlist in the U.S. Army. Courtesy Mike VanBendegom.

B Company was all but wiped out. Twenty-nine men died on the field, and sixty-nine men were wounded. Seven were taken prisoner, including Jim.[3]

Jim was severely wounded. "He had been shot in the neck, the shoulder, and the buttocks," Sgt. Cordine McMurray recalled in June of 1973. It's unclear why the North Vietnamese didn't kill Jim when they found him wounded on the battlefield or why they took him to an underground hospital, where Sergeant McMurray met him. McMurray stayed with Jim for two and a half days until Jim died. Jim's last words to the sergeant were, "All I want to do is go home."

Jim was 18 years old. He had been in Vietnam for three weeks.

For the family in Kenosha, the hardest part of the story was just beginning. Mike wasn't home when the news arrived. He was in Milwaukee with Darlene, picking out bridesmaid's dresses for her brother's upcoming wedding. His father and brothers were also out. Virginia met the Army officer at the door, where she was told that Jim was officially missing in action.

"We were shocked," Mike said. "My mom says that was probably one of the only times she ever saw my dad cry."

There was little they could do but wait. The officer who came to their door became their caseworker, and it was left to him to inform the family if any news arrived of Jim.

The officer came back, in 1969, and he brought a photograph with him. "This is your son in there," he told them, pointing at the image of a group of Americans POWs being led to a notorious North Vietnamese prison, which the Americans called the Hanoi Hilton. But the family disagreed; it wasn't Jim. The government insisted, and Jim's status changed from missing in action to prisoner of war. As was the custom with prisoners, bracelets were made and sold with his name on it, and people across the country waited for him to come home, along with hundreds of other Americans being held by the North Vietnamese.

In 1973 the Paris Peace Accords put an end to the war, with the assurance that, as U.S. troops withdrew, American prisoners would be released from the North, and the dead repatriated. American POWs began returning home on February 14, 1973. Their homecoming was broadcast live. The VanBendegoms watched as, one by one, the prisoners disembarked from the plane. Jim was not among them. From February to April 1973, 591 prisoners were released to the U.S. Although the family had known it was not Jim in that picture, they had clung to the hope that they were wrong. That they were right was a crushing blow.

"We did the funeral with no body, and it was horrible," Darlene remembers.

Jim's story was still not over. On March 14, 1986, a Vietnamese woman approached U.S. officials at a refugee camp in Thailand with human remains she had smuggled across the border. She hoped to sell the remains for money to join her family in the United States. The woman herself had not dug up the bones, but had paid a prospector to look for remains for her to sell. The remains consisted of some larger bones, bone fragments, and a lone dog tag that did not match anyone listed as missing from the Vietnam War. The bones were brought back to the United States and put on a shelf.

Those bones were taken out again in 2000. Recent advances in technology led the Joint POW/MIA Accounting Command (JPAC) to believe it would be possible to identify some of those remains. Working in conjunction with the Armed Forces DNA Identification Laboratory in 2009, members of JPAC used two forms of DNA analysis, mitochondrial DNA and Y-chromosome short tandem report DNA, to find one match among the bones and bone fragments with DNA samples in their system. The samples had been provided by the VanBendegom brothers years earlier. The identified bone was a single left radius (an arm bone) that belonged to Jim.

This time the news reached Virginia VanBendegom by phone, on October 17, 2014. "We've found the remains of your son," the military told her. They were sending him home.

The family initially intended to hold a small ceremony, but the Kenosha VFW Riders Group, headed by family friend Rob Roberts, wanted to recognize Jim's sacrifice.

The result, says Darlene, was unbelievable.

It began when the family departed Kenosha to retrieve his remains in Milwaukee, escorted by the Riders Group along Highway 94. The highway was shut down for miles.

At Mitchell Airport, the captain of the Delta commercial jet carrying Jim's remains

Kenosha residents came out to honor Jim when his remains were returned on November 11, 2014. He is buried beside his father. Courtesy Cindy Fredericksen.

disembarked before the casket was unloaded and stood at full salute. "He saluted the entire time we were there," Mike says.

Then, finally, Jim's body touched down in Wisconsin.

The city of Kenosha embraced Jim VanBendegom's return. As the family drove home, they found overpasses flooded with people, saluting and waving flags. The Riders Group led the escort. The owner of a local Culver's closed the restaurant to come outside with the customers and acknowledge Jim and the family. Classmates who had also served in Vietnam carried Jim's flag-draped coffin. Two active duty military officers from B Company, 1st Battalion, 12th Regiment of the 4th Infantry Division came for the service, and a bugler played *Taps* as Staff Sergeant James VanBendegom was laid to rest with full military honors. His funeral was held on Veterans Day 2014. He was buried in Kenosha next to his father.

Jim's last wish was to go home. It took forty-seven years, but he made it.

Lieutenant Michael John Allard

United State Navy,
disappeared August 30, 1967

"I remember Mike the way younger people remember someone older—I really looked up to him. He was ... a good athlete, smart, and a tremendously nice guy."—Mancer Cyr

"He was a good officer and gentleman and treated us 'line boys' with respect, appreciative of our efforts to keep his aircraft ready for flight."
—Frank Wilson

"I was incredibly blessed to have had Mike in my life ... if even for a brief time. I couldn't have asked for a more loving or caring husband and father for our children."—Denny Murphy Allard

When asked about fellow Wausau High School graduate Michael Allard, Mary Lou McCarten quotes her mother: "When you speak of someone, they are not gone. Their memory is still with us."

The quotation is appropriate because Lieutenant Michael John Allard has never been forgotten. Born September 12, 1940, Mike was the youngest of five Allard children growing up in Wausau, Wisconsin. It was the kind of town where everyone knew everyone. More than fifty years later, many of its residents remember Mike.[1]

Michael Brockmeyer remembers biking to and from John Marshall Elementary School with Mike a couple times a day. With only a few blocks between the school and their houses, the boys often rode home for lunch on their Schwinns, cutting each other off and bending "the fender struts into the spokes," Michael says. After supper, they played in the streets until the lights went out.

Most people remember Mike's love for football. "[He] wanted to play football all year," Michael explains, "in the spring and summer during baseball season and even in the winter on those icy Wausau streets." At Wausau High School Mike started as a tight end on the varsity team, coached by Win Brockmeyer.[2] The former University of Minnesota All–American remains the winningest high school coach in Wisconsin, but he taught his players more than football. One of Mike's teammates, Barry Libman, recounts a lesson Brockmeyer taught them at Mike's expense:

> During a practice scrimmage [Mike] missed a block and as his man went around him he threw out his leg to trip him. Mike's leg was at an awkward angle so when his man ran into it, he tore up Mike's knee. As Mike lay on the ground writhing in pain, Brock stood over him. He gathered all the players around and chastised Mike for the stupid move of trying to trip his man. Brock wanted everyone to learn from Mike's misfortune. Brock never missed a teaching opportunity, even in a bad situation.

Mike missed the rest of his senior season, a year when the Lumberjacks finished 7–1 and became the first Wausau team to win an uncontested Big Rivers Conference championship.

Mike was involved with other extracurricular activities beside football during the school year. He played volleyball, participated in the ski club, and did curling. He performed in the senior class play, served on the student council, enrolled in the Latin Club, took engineering courses, and participated in Rotary Club. During the summer Mike was a camp counselor at Tesomas Scout Camp in Rhinelander, Wisconsin. He worked alongside his friends, Dick Christensen and Donnie Watson, teaching the scouts first aid and archery and taking them hiking, swimming, and camping. All three counselors were in military service during the Vietnam War, Dick as a stateside Army medic, and Donnie and Mike as pilots.[3]

Mike's friends remember the respect he had for his older brother, Dave, who received an appointment to the United States Naval Academy in Annapolis after high school. "He … wanted in the worst way to follow him to Annapolis," writes Michael Brockmeyer. "When he couldn't do that, he found another way to fly." After graduating from Wausau in 1958 Mike enrolled in the ROTC at Marquette University, a Jesuit school in Milwaukee.

At Marquette Mike joined Sigma Phi Delta, the engineering fraternity. One of his fraternity brothers, John Tumpak, describes Mike as "a very, very nice, outgoing person" who "lived and breathed for the Green Bay Packers." Most of their conversations revolved around either Wisconsin's professional football team and its coach, Vince Lombardi, or Mike's high school football coach, Win Brockmeyer, for whom Mike continued to show extraordinary respect.

Mike remained a tremendous football fan and played when the opportunity arose, which it did at the annual Marquette Army and Navy ROTC units' football game. In 1961, Mike scored the Navy team's winning touchdown.

Mike graduated from Marquette with an engineering degree in 1962. That summer, he proposed to his girl-

Mike with his three sons, May 1967: Paul (left), Mark (right), and Bart (center). Courtesy Denny Higgins.

friend, Denise, in a grotto to the Virgin Mary near Blue Mound Round in Milwaukee. They married shortly after she graduated. Their three sons were born within three years.

By then, Mike's military career had begun. He spent one year aboard a landing ship in California before being accepted into flight school. In the interim period, Mike returned to Marquette's campus to speak with the current NROTC class. John Healy, present that day, remembers how highly Mike spoke of shipboard life. "I was ... impressed with his presence and the fact that he would take time to stop by campus (in uniform and while on leave) to speak with us," John recalls.

Soon after, Mike began his career in Naval Aviation. Instructed by, among others, a young John McCain (later Senator John McCain), Mike learned to fly the Douglas A-4 Skyhawk. In the early years of the Vietnam War, this single-seat aircraft was the Navy's main fighting aircraft; in 1964 the first Skyhawk lost contained the first and longest-held prisoner of war, Lieutenant (Junior Grade) Everett Alvarez.

Mike was still in the United States in 1964. After completing his Naval aviator training, he was assigned to Attack Squadron 153 (VA-153). Because he'd spent some time as a "black shoe,"[4] he was a few years older than most of the other squadron members. The unit, composed of roughly twenty men, trained together for over a year at Naval Air Station (NAS) Lemoore, in California, and NAS Fallon, Nevada, before departing for their tour aboard the USS *Coral Sea* in mid–1967. Their destination was Yankee Station in the Gulf of Tonkin.

The squadron's first day of operations was August 30, 1967. The first mission of the day, a bombing run over North Vietnam, was to be flown by Lieutenant Commander Gary Starbird. Lieutenant Michael Allard flew as his wingman. When the two pilots reached their target, the flight leader's bombs failed to release. L. Cdr. Starbird assumed the wingman position and instructed Lt. Allard to take command as they redirected toward an alternate target. As Mike began his run, the plane went into a nosedive and was unable to pull out. L. Cdr. Starbird called repeatedly for Lt. Allard to eject, but received no response nor did he witness any parachute ejection before the plane crashed into the ground. Although he was classified as missing in action, there was little doubt that Mike was gone. He was 26 years old.

Lieutenant Michael Allard in pilot's in front of a Douglas A-4 Skyhawk. Courtesy Denny Higgins.

Onboard the *Coral Sea*, VA-153 pilot Gene Corsini sat down to receive his mission briefing when a friend from another squadron asked where Mike's aircraft had gone down. It was the first Gene had heard of the crash. "I thought, 'What? We just got here. How can this be?'" He continues, "How can we have lost one of our own on the very first day?"

"We were very saddened by his loss," says Frank Wilson, also of VA-153. "It was a heavy blow to us when he failed to return from his last mission."

The Navy held a small memorial service for Mike in California, without a body. Meanwhile, his wife had thirty days to pack and leave the military base with her three sons, the eldest of whom turned three just two days after his father's death.

For Mike's family and friends, life went on, but they remembered. Mike left a legacy of three successful sons: Mark, an orthopedic surgeon; Paul, a mechanical engineer and financial planner; and Bart, a CPA with his own business. As a teacher, Michael Brockmeyer ensured that future generations knew of his friend. Each time he took his class on a school trip to Washington, D.C., one of their stops was Michael Allard's name on the Vietnam Wall. He explains:

> I told them of Mike Allard's beaming and devilish smile and the jokester he was. He was just a regular kid, just like me and just like every one of them. I told them that he was reckless with his body, that he always threw himself into the middle of things and you always wanted him on your side in a fight or on Thom Field. I told them that he was smart, he was happy, he was loved, and he enjoyed life … just like they did.

Many others have visited the Wall to see and touch Mike's name. "Every time we have a class reunion or a few of us get together, someone brings up Mike," says Mary Lou McCarten. "Everyone liked Mike; he was that kind of guy."

For decades, it seemed that the memories were all that Mike's family and friends had left of him. That changed on May 8, 1992, when representatives from a Senate select committee and the Defense Intelligence Agency met with a Vietnamese representative at the U.S. embassy in Moscow. The Vietnamese representative told the Americans that he had "friends" who possessed the remains of three servicemen, including Michael Allard, and that the "friends" believed they would be paid if they handed the remains over to the U.S. government. The American representatives explained that the United States does not make such exchanges, but they recorded the information regarding Michal Allard.

In September that year three more witnesses claimed to have seen the aircraft crash in the same area, around the same time Mike's plane went down. One of them also revealed that an illegal excavation of the crash site had been conducted several years earlier. An American-led site excavation was undertaken in July 1993.

Several years later, the Central Identification Lab in Hawaii called Mike's brother and sister, asking for blood samples for a DNA comparison. For the first time, the family was told of the possibility that Mike's remains had been recovered.

In the early 1990s the technology was not yet capable of extracting DNA from the remains stored at the lab. Four years passed, during which time the Allard family was contacted intermittently and given little information, before the lab was finally able to conclude that the DNA was a match. Thirty-four years after his death, Michael Allard had been found.

Mike's family is presented with an American flag during his burial at Arlington National Cemetery, 2001. Courtesy Denny Higgins.

On March 19, 2001, Lieutenant Allard was buried at Arlington National Cemetery. A fifteen-piece military band, twenty-four sailors, and six white horses led an American flag–draped casket to Section 66, where Mike was laid to rest. Mike's three sons and his brother had the honor of walking behind the horse-drawn caisson from the church to the burial site at Arlington Cemetery.

Nearly 100 friends and family members gathered to remember Michael Allard, and to say goodbye.

Lieutenant Colonel
Donald William Downing

United States Air Force,
disappeared September 5, 1967

"Don was a really good brother, and a good guy, and we still think about it after all these years.... We were all extremely proud of him."—Darryl Downing

"He was an easygoing, wonderful person. He never got mad. He was a good kid."—Nancy (Downing) Greve

Pictures, found in old newspaper articles and online memorials, offer only brief glimpses of a young pilot's life. In one, he wears a suit and tie. In another, an Air Force dress uniform. Others are more casual shots of a young man in a pilot's jacket or flight suit. There's an endearing quality to the photos that allows Donald Downing's natural personality to shine through. Those who knew Don remember him as the kind of person they wanted to be, and the kind they wanted to be around. He was studious, he was fun, he was calm, he was considerate. As a career Air Force man, Don didn't have to go to Vietnam. He volunteered because, in addition to all else, he was brave and he loved to fly.

Donald William Downing was born March 17, 1934. He grew up in Columbus, Wisconsin, the eldest brother of Shirley, Nancy, Chuck, and Darryl. The family moved to Janesville when their father, William, took a job with Wisconsin Power & Light in 1948, where Don attended Janesville Senior High. There, he kept active playing several sports. "He was pretty athletically inclined," says Darryl. Don golfed. He boxed. He had a fondness for baseball, which his dad had played in his youth. He sprained his sister Nancy's thumb more times than she can remember when she acted as his catcher while he practiced. Don was one of eighteen students to letter on the school's new wrestling team in 1952.

Don had one hobby, though, that had nothing to do with sports. "He had a love for flying from early days," says Darryl. Within the Downing family, it was something of a joke to say that Donald Downing got his pilot's license before his driver's license. It was an exaggeration, but not by much. Don not only had a pilot's license when he was 16 years old—he had a plane. Don and a friend split the $500 cost of the plane and flew it out of a corn-lined airstrip in a farmer's field.

During high school, flying was an exciting pastime, but not a priority. After graduating from Janesville High School in 1952, Don took a job at Gibbs Manufacturing & Research Corporation as well as pursuing a career in baseball. He tried out for the Fond du Lac minor league team as a pitcher, but an arm injury that summer put an end to his baseball aspirations. He switched gears and pursued a different passion. With a plane and license already in hand, Don headed to a recruiting station. He enlisted in the Air Force on November 4, 1953.

In 1953 the United States Air Force, as an independent and separate branch of the military, was still new, having been established only six years earlier through the National Security Act of 1947. The military had used aircraft long before then, of course, purchasing its first aircraft in 1909, but through World War II, the Air Force remained an extension of the Army.[1] Because of its newness, the Air Force did not yet have its own service academy such as the Army's West Point or the Navy's Annapolis. Officer candidate school and Air Force ROTC programs were still being established so the primary route for enlisted men like Don in the Air Force was through the aviation cadet training program.

When the military began to train aviators in 1912, graduation requirements differed from what they would one day become. Among other conditions, the pilot had to conduct a flight of at least five minutes in winds of at least fifteen miles per hour, reaching a height of at least twenty-five hundred feet at some point during the flight. In April 1917, at the onset of World War I, America had only ninety-six qualified officers. The number of graduates from the cadet program—pilots, navigators, and specialists— would rise to over eleven thousand by the end of the war, drop again during the interwar years, and increase to more than two hundred fifty thousand during World War II. After 1945 the military had more aviation officers than it needed and temporarily shut down nearly all the cadet training programs across the country.

In the early 1950s, though, as the Cold War heated up in Korea, developing Air Force officers once again became a priority. When the programs began to accept applicants again, the candidates faced a rigorous admission process, involving twelve "paper-and-pencil" tests and six psychomotor tests. If they passed, they met with an equally intense four-phase training program, a place where, Don told his family, "you had to salute the bubbler and ask if you could have a drink." It began with twelve weeks of pre-flight training at Lackland Air Force Base in Texas. It was followed by eighteen weeks of primary flight, sixteen weeks of basic flight, and twelve weeks of advanced flight training. When Don graduated in May 1955 as a 2nd lieutenant in the United States Air Force, his parents and Nancy traveled to Texas to watch him get his Wings.

Don attended pilot training at Vance Air Force Base in Enid, Oklahoma, then received an out-of-country assignment in Newfoundland, Canada, flying Boeing KC-97 refueling tankers for Strategic Air Command (SAC). Both a Major Command of the Air Force and a Specified Command of the Department of Defense,[2] SAC controlled two of the three components of the United States military's "nuclear triad" during the Cold War: land-based strategic bombers and intercontinental ballistic missiles.[3] The approximately quarter-million members of SAC operated under the motto "Peace Is

Our Profession." They were responsible for the most powerful weapons on the planet, prepared for an atomic war with the Soviet Union.

Don returned to Janesville at least once during the Newfoundland assignment. It

was an occasion that everyone enjoyed because, among other reasons, Don always brought gifts when he visited. For her high school graduation, Don sent Nancy a throw pillow with her picture on it—drawn by him. He gave Darryl a baseball glove during one trip home and $20 worth of change in another. When Don visited, Darryl never failed to ask him to go flying, and Don never failed to take him. "He was a good brother," says Darryl. "I kind of idolized him and obviously wanted to be like him—that's why I took up flying, too."

After several years in Newfoundland, Don was assigned to Hanscom Air Base, twenty miles outside Boston. It was one of many bases assigned to Air Force Systems Command (AFSC).

Following World War II the Air Force created the Air Research and Development Command, devoted to research and engineering to aid aircraft and intercontinental ballistic missile development. In 1961 it was re-designated the Air Force Systems Command. It had four major divisions: Ballistic (San Bernardino, California), Space (El Segundo, California), and Aeronautical Systems (Dayton,

Captain Donald Downing began flying when he was 16 years old. He served 12 years in the Air Force before his aircraft went missing in 1967. Courtesy Nancy Greve.

Ohio), with Electronic Systems research at Hanscom Field.

AFSC operated Boeing KC-97 Stratofreighters, capable of carrying special electronic test equipment. In 1960 Captain Donald Downing was the copilot of a KC-97 on its last trip before its retirement. Over seven years the aircraft had logged more than four hundred thousand miles and had ventured to the North Pole eight times. The KC-97 was being replaced with a faster, more efficient version of itself called the KC-135 Stratotanker. Don trained in California to pilot this sister ship.

He didn't remain in California long, though, before returning to Massachusetts and his fiancée, Marion. The two met on a blind date on New Year's Eve, 1959, were married September 10, 1960, and had four children in four years: Dawn, Linda, David, and Brian.

The family remained in Massachusetts for several years, with Don flying the KC-135 Stratotanker. In 1963 he was a member of the first crew to test a KC-135 Skyscraper, a modified version of Don's aircraft, used for missile radiation measurement experiments at Kwajalein in the Marshall Islands.

In 1963, Don and his family relocated to Hawaii, hardly a difficult move, Darryl recalls. They liked the island, and the rest of the family enjoyed visiting them. They didn't know much of what Don did on the island. "He had been flying big four-engine jets, doing some secret work," Darryl explains. "He couldn't talk about it."

Both the KC-97 and the KC-135 were transport aircraft, but Don flew jets as well. Those, recalls Nancy, were what he most enjoyed. When the opportunity arose, he volunteered to fly jets in Vietnam. Sixteen years in the Air Force and involved with SAC/AFSC, Don certainly did not have to go overseas. He had just begun to look for piloting jobs in civilian life. United Airlines offered him a position, but with the stipulation that he begin working inside the airport rather than inside a plane. It was not a move he wanted to make, and with the war raging on across the ocean, he saw an opportunity to keep flying and serve his country in Vietnam.

"He didn't mind flying fighter planes by himself," says Darryl. "So he decided to try and get into the fight and go to Vietnam. He thought he would spend six months or something and then come back."

Not everyone agreed with him. He was 33 years old, a married father of four, and unlike many of the men fighting overseas, he clearly had a choice. In mid–1966 the family returned to Massachusetts and in July 1967 Don chose a tour of duty in Vietnam.

Don joined the 557th Tactical Fighter Squadron at Cam Ranh Bay Air Base in South Vietnam. The 557th, a part of the 12th Tactical Fighter Wing, flew the McDonnell Douglas F-4 Phantom, possibly the most versatile jet aircraft in Vietnam. Capable of flying at more than twice the speed of sound, the Phantom was operated by the Air Force, Navy, and Marines to provide air defense, close air support, and bombing missions throughout Southeast Asia.

Don kept in touch with his family while he was overseas, writing often and receiving many letters in return, thanks in part to Darryl and Nancy, who wrote him daily. His

The Downings' last family photo before Don deployed to Vietnam. Left to right: Marion, Brian, Dawn, Linda, David, Don. Courtesy Nancy Greve.

work was different than anything he had done before, largely because he was flying at night, with the lights off. Although everyone tried to keep in contact with each other during missions, he wrote home, "surprises do happen."[4] But while the work was new, the scenery was surprisingly familiar. In the same letter, Don wrote that Vietnam was so beautiful it could be another Hawaii. He told his mother that in his three months overseas, he had completed 45 missions and expected to reach 100 before the end of the month.

That letter reached his mother September 6, 1967. Don went missing September 5.

It was a night mission, the third that Don had flown. Captain Donald Downing was the aircraft commander of a Phantom identified only as 63–7547, the second of a two-plane flight on a mission over Quàng Bình Province, North Vietnam. Also in the aircraft was 1st Lieutenant Paul Raymond. The lead plane selected a target and alerted the second aircraft that it would begin the assault. Don replied that he would do the same. As the lead aircraft began its assault, they saw a large "fireball" descending through the air. They immediately tried to contact Captain Downing and 1st Lieutenant Raymond by radio, but were met with silence. The lead jet remained in the hostile area for roughly twenty-five minutes, attempting to reach the downed aircraft before returning to base. In the darkness, they had not seen any ejections.[5]

Both families were told that the men were missing in action. Without a definitive answer, the Downings held out hope that Don might return. Marion continued to write him letters for a while, but it became increasingly difficult, she said, to maintain a one-way correspondence. She sent him a Christmas package in 1968 and cried when she found it sitting on the doorstep four days before the holiday. She told her eldest daughter that her father was missing, but to the younger three, she simply said he was in Vietnam and would come home.

The family hoped and prayed, but twelve years after he was declared missing, the government declared Don killed in action, his plane likely having been blown up that night in September 1967.

"The Air Force handled it well," Darryl says. "Each of the kids were given the chance that, if they wanted to go to school, the government would pay their tuition. The Air Force really tried to take care of them." With Don's change in status, Marion could remarry, but she never did.

For his time in Vietnam, Don was awarded a Bronze Star, a Purple Heart, a Distinguished Flying Cross, and two Air Medals. The family has his awards. They have his dog tags, found and returned to them decades later. They have his letters. They have a brick with his name at the local VFW. And they have their memories of the calm, kind man they knew, who loved his family and who loved to fly.

Captain Harold John Moe
United States Marine Corps, disappeared September 26, 1967

"He was a very unassuming, family-oriented guy."—George Rodosky

"He was very dedicated and loved the Marines."—Mary Miller

"Harold was just a delight."—Mary (Moe) Black

Professional. Dedicated. Dependable. Certain words come to mind when one thinks of the United States Marines. "Gentle" and "kind" are not typically among them. But then again, Harold Moe was not a typical Marine. He didn't drink, he didn't swear, and when others partied he went home, bringing with him every dollar he earned. Married with six children, Harold was both a Marine and a family man, and love of family and love of country went hand in hand. Others took note and respected him for it. Harold, his sister says, was the kind of person who made an impression on people. Forty-five years after his death, his family learned just how true that was.

Harold was born July 11, 1938, the second child and eldest son of Bernard and Cleo Moe. "As a kid, I looked up to him," says his sister, Mary Black, ten years younger than Harold. Blond hair, blue eyes, and a bright smile, Harold John Moe was a good role model because he was a good person. "He never gave my parents grief.... He was kind. A hard worker." Cleo Moe called her son "Sunny," and she never meant it to be spelled with an *O*.

As a teenager, Harold worked as a farmhand on a farm outside Eau Claire, Wisconsin, driving tractors, feeding cattle, and baling hay. Whatever needed to be done, Harold did it.

Off the farm, Harold spent a lot of time running around town—literally. He was fast, and went most places on foot until he earned his driver's license. As soon as he could drive, though, that became his preferred mode of transportation. Harold loved cars. He put this passion to good use by driving a student restricted to a wheelchair to nearby Altoona High School, despite the fact that Harold attended Memorial High School[1] in Eau Claire. Harold transferred to Altoona his final year of high school to help the boy get around better inside the building.

Although only a few miles apart, Altoona was a much smaller town than Eau Claire.

Founded in the 1880s, the town got its start as a railroad town. In the 1950s, most men still worked at the railroad-switching yard. Likewise, Altoona High School was decidedly smaller than Memorial High School. Harold graduated in a class of sixteen. He didn't mind the transfer, though, especially because his girlfriend, Nancy, attended Altoona as well.

As in so many of Wisconsin's small towns in the postwar period, life in Altoona was simple. Kids made their own fun. Playing backyard football and attending high school basketball games were common pastimes. Basketball was the school's strongest sport, and the team was routinely good. Harold tried out the one year he attended and made the team. His girlfriend was a cheerleader and a drum majorette. Together, they made for a traditionally "cool" couple.

They married on July 26, 1958, one month after Nancy graduated from high school. By then, Harold was already in the United States Marine Corps, having enlisted the previous March and completed basic and infantry training in California. Harold served with the Marines as a motor vehicle operator in the 3rd Marine Division, first with Service Company, Headquarter Battalion, then with Company B of the 3rd Maintenance Battalion.

Before pursuing the military, Harold had studied at the University of Wisconsin–Eau Claire for one semester. Later, while in the service, he would finish his college education at Santa Anna College in California. Harold also continued his Marine education over the years. In 1961 he trained at Naval Air Technical Training Command (NATTC) in Memphis, then Naval Air Technical Training Unit at NAS Jacksonville. When he returned to El Toro in 1962, he joined Marine Fighter Attack Squadron (VMFA) 312, the "Checkerboards," as an aviation electric technician.

The Moe family grew over the years: Kim, Mike, Kevin, Greg, and twins Jimmy and Jackie. The twins were born in 1966 when Harold and VMFA 312 were stationed at MCAS Beaufort, South Carolina. By then, Harold had received further training at Quantico's Officer Candidate School and NATTC Glynco. He now qualified as a radar intercept officer (RIO).

Since February 1966 VMFA 312 had been permanently stationed in Beaufort to provide much-needed training to aircrews using the new McDonnell Douglas F-4 Phantom II. The supersonic jet played a critical role in the Vietnam War, carrying up to sixteen thousand pounds of armaments and serving as the primary air superiority fighter aircraft for the Navy, Air Force, and Marine Corps.

By 1966 Harold had eight years of service in the Marines, more than many of the men in the squadron. The Marine Corps was short of experienced enlisted officers at the time. Some enlisted Marines were specifically chosen for promotion to help eliminate the shortage. Harold was promoted to sergeant and then selected for the Warrant Officer Program. When he was selected for flight training, he was promoted to 2nd lieutenant.[2]

While devoted to his country and his squadron, Harold's main concern was always for his family. "He was not a drinker, not a partier," remembers George Rodosky, who met Harold at Beaufort and served with him overseas. "Every nickel that he had went home." When he did go out with the squadron, remembers another squadron mate, Richard Alvarez,[3] all he drank was a Pepsi.

Harold Moe in uniform. He served nine years in the Marine Corps after enlisting in March 1958. Courtesy the Vietnam Veterans Memorial Fund.

After initial F-4 flight training in Beaufort, the squadron deployed to Yuma, Arizona, for training on live bombing ranges. After Arizona came Vietnam.

Harold arrived at Chu Lai Air Base in South Vietnam in March 1967, where he joined Marine Air Group (MAG) 13.[4] The air group was composed of four squadrons, three flying the F-4B Phantom, and one support squadron, Headquarters and Maintenance Squadron (H&MS). Records show that Harold was assigned to the latter.[5] The mission of MAG 13 was to provide fighter cover and close air support for infantry Marines. "You were always busy," remembers George. "The average soldier in World War II was there for years and got like fifty to sixty days' combat, whereas in Vietnam, you were only there for thirty months and you had maybe ten or eleven months of combat. It was just constant."

"You'd fly typically early in the morning," explains George:

> They'd get all the airplanes up, and as soon as you came back from a mission you'd go into the debriefing area and guys would fix the airplanes to go back out again.
They'd fill them up with fuel and new bombs and ordnance on them and make sure everything was good to go. Turnaround time was maybe an hour or an hour and a half. You'd get a lunch break ... and then get ready to do it again.

Marine pilots and RIOs assigned to MAG 13 typically flew close to three hundred missions during their time in Vietnam. While they usually flew multiple missions a day, there was an occasional day off, especially during the monsoon season. "Some days you couldn't find your way to the runway. You'd get 10 inches of rain in an afternoon," George says. "You couldn't keep anything dry." The Marines lived on platforms called hardback tents, or "hooches." Raised about two feet off the sand and framed by an outer canvas siding, the buildings housed six to eight men of the same squadron.

Squadron members grew close, but it was more than simply sharing quarters. Knowing and believing in your comrades was essential. They needed to know that they could trust the man flying with them in high-pressure situations.

Harold, called both Hal and H.J. by others in his unit, was a trusted member of MAG 13. He was quiet and serious and he stood out because of his overall demeanor and dedication to his family.

"He was a very gentle, kind man," says Richard Alvarez. Richard was new to the Marine Corps. On September 26, 1967, it was Richard that Harold spoke to in the early hours before his final mission. Richard says:

He stopped for a moment and looked intently at me and said with wet, glistening eyes, "God, I love my wife and children. I have to see them again and tell them how much." He said a little more, but these words are burned into my heart.[6]

Richard, young and unsure of how to handle such an emotional moment, simply nodded. More important, though, he remembered.

That morning, six months into his tour, 29-year-old 1st Lieutenant Harold Moe served as the RIO on an F-4 bombing mission over an antiaircraft site in North Vietnam that had repeatedly harassed American aircraft. His plane, piloted by Major P. M. Cole, was one of two taking part in the morning mission. Witness statements from the two men in the other aircraft, Captain M. M. Simpson and Captain E. F. Miglarese, detail what occurred after they took off.

On reaching the heavily defended site, the two planes discovered that they would not have a forward controller; rather, the flight would be "self-controlled." Shortly after arriving at the target, they encountered a combination of small arms, automatic weapons, and antiaircraft fire. Despite this 1st Lt. Moe and Major Cole completed their bomb run with "pinpoint precision."[7] As they pulled out, Harold realized their aircraft had been hit and the right engine was on fire.

Major Cole radioed the other plane, first informing them of the damage and then adding that their situation "didn't look good at all."[8] Harold, meanwhile, read his pilot the emergency procedures and directed the plane out over the sea. By this time, the tail of the aircraft was aflame, and they were losing control of the plane.

The men had to eject, but Harold recognized they were flying directly above friendly ships. Were they to abandon the plane then and there, they would put everyone beneath them at risk. As the cockpit filled with smoke and control of the plane grew more difficult, Harold elected not to eject. He remained in the aircraft and directed his pilot to a clear area farther out to sea. As the plane began simultaneously rolling and rapidly descending in a nosedive toward the open water, Harold and Major Cole ejected. Major Cole's parachute opened; 1st Lieutenant Harold Moe's did not.[9]

"It's hard to think about that tragic incident," George Rodosky reflects.

For the Moe family in Wisconsin, it was hard to forget the warm September evening when a taxi driver delivered a telegram informing them that Harold was missing in action. For Nancy Moe, still on base in Beaufort, South Carolina, the loss was devastating.

Unknown to the Moe family, Richard Alvarez never forgot that day, that mission, or the conversation that preceded it. He made a career out of the Marines and, always, Harold Moe's last words to him remained with him. Whenever he knew someone traveling to the Vietnam Veterans Memorial Wall in Washington, D.C., he urged them to look up Harold's name. Then, in 2012 Richard decided to look up Harold's name, too, not in the Capital, but on the Internet, searching for an Eau Claire newspaper that might lead him to the Moe family.

He contacted a reporter at the Eau Claire *Leader-Telegram*, who, in turn, located and reached out to the Moe family. Through a series of emails and telephone calls, after four and a half decades, Harold's children received his final, heartfelt message. Harold was, after all, a dedicated family man.

Harold was also a Marine. In combat, men need to be able to trust the men with whom they serve. They need to believe that, if the worst should happen, the men standing beside them will do all they can to keep them alive, for they hold each other's lives in their hands. On September 26, 1967, Harold's final actions very likely saved the lives of countless crewmen on board ships in the South China Sea. Harold was posthumously promoted to captain and awarded a single mission Air Medal with five gold stars for his decision to remain in the aircraft and direct it safely to open water. "In giving his own life to avoid jeopardizing the lives and safety of others," the award certificate states, "Lieutenant Moe upheld the highest traditions of the United States Naval Service."

1968

Gunnery Sergeant
Richard William Fischer

*United States Marine Corps,
disappeared January 8, 1968*

"He was an honorable man."—Ann Fischer

In the Madison East High School yearbook, class of 1965, Richard Fischer listed "missionary" as his career plan. "Yeah, right," laughs his sister, Ann, who, ironically, is a pastor. It seemed an odd choice, then and now, for Dick knew before graduating from high school that he would one day join the Marines. "He was very adamant about going to Vietnam," Ann says. He felt called to it, even if no one quite understood why.

Richard was born June 15, 1947, in Rockville Centre, Long Island, New York. He was raised in Levittown, with his older brother, Jay, and younger siblings, Carl and Ann. Until Ann was born, the boys shared one of the two bedrooms in their house. Once Ann arrived, their father, John, raised the house's roof and built the boys' beds in the attic.

Life changed drastically on July 27, 1958. While driving through Ohio on the way to a vacation in Wisconsin, the entire Fischer family was involved in a serious car crash. Rear-ended in the age before seatbelts, only Ann was left unscathed. Dick was thrown from the car, fracturing his leg; their mother, Eleanor, was also injured; and John, Jay, and Carl were killed. Jay was 13 years old; Carl, 9.

Eleanor took Dick and Ann, ages 11 and 7, and returned to her hometown of Madison, Wisconsin. She got a job and moved in with her parents, who served as surrogate parents to the children as well. "They kept us from getting at each other," Ann says. They were typical siblings. Each night it was their responsibility to wash the dishes, a chore that entailed more than just washing. There was drying to be done, the counter and stove to be wiped clean, and the floor to be swept. Somehow, Ann remembers, she always ended up doing the washing, and the wiping, and the sweeping, while Dick took his time, carefully drying and putting away the dishes.

They had fun, too. "He was a typical boy," Ann says. One winter, Dick and his friends built an igloo in the backyard. Ann was charged with hauling buckets of water from the basement for the boys to freeze into blocks. When the igloo was finished, the interior was tall enough for the kids to stand up, and Ann was welcome to join the boys inside.

Their father had been something of an inventor. He loved to take old things and refashion them into something new. Dick had inherited this passion. Except instead of *old* things, his projects were usually made from *Ann's* things. He borrowed her hula hoop to make a snorkel (which didn't work) and took the wheels off her roller skates for a skateboard (which snapped in half the first time he stepped on it).

He put this creativity to good use in the Junior Achievement program, a national after-school program that teaches finance and entrepreneurship to kids of all ages. In 1964 Dick was named the JA vice-president of manufacturing and received a plaque designating him as the highest officer of manufacturing in the program.

At Madison East High School, Dick played on the basketball team as a sophomore and junior, and lettered on the school's first swim team. He loved the water and dreamed of working as a lifeguard in Madison, a goal he achieved during high school. After several summers of training, he was assigned to Esther Beach. The job was all he hoped it would be, except for one minor, unexpected

Born in New York, Dick Fischer was raised alongside his sister, Ann, in Madison, Wisconsin, where he spent much of his time on the lakes. Courtesy the Wisconsin Veterans Museum (Madison, WI).

detail: no bathrooms. As a result, Dick became quite friendly with the local homeowners. The arrangement worked fine because the people appreciated their lifeguard. The kids, especially, loved him and made him a T-shirt with "Super Lifeguard" written across the front. He wore it proudly.

When he wasn't working, Dick spent his summers outdoors. He and a group of friends were part of the Four Lakes Yacht Club. They also filled in for local sailing teams when additional crew members were needed for practice or competitions. Dick was an avid bike rider, taking advantage of Madison's multiple bike paths.

Before graduating from high school in 1965, Dick told a fellow lifeguard that he desperately wanted to join the Marines and serve in Vietnam, where the war was still in its early stages. The lifeguard convinced Dick to wait a year. He was smart. He should give college a try, and then see what he wanted.

So Dick tried. He spent one year at the University of Wisconsin–Madison. And then he enlisted in the United States Marine Corps.

He wasn't alone. Three of his cousins enlisted at roughly the same time, one to the Army, two to the Marines. Their father, Dick's uncle, was also a Marine. His uncle's service played a role in Dick's choice of the Marine Corps but his desire to serve was his own, and it was strong. "He was adamant," Ann remembers, even though he didn't need to be. He wasn't concerned about receiving a draft notice, a factor that motivated many young men during the Vietnam War to enlist so they could select their own service branch. The military wasn't pressuring Dick to enlist. They were actually *dissuading* him. Department of Defense Directive 1315.15, "Special Separation Policies for Survivorship," protected family members from the draft if they had lost another family while serving in the military so it did not technically apply to Dick. However, because his family had already lost two sons in the automobile accident, his recruiters urged him to reconsider, but he wouldn't. He enlisted and in September 1966 he left for San Diego.

Basic training at Marine Corps Recruit Depot, San Diego included eight weeks of hand-to-hand combat, bayonet training, and swimming, along with some personal maintenance skills the men might not have otherwise learned, like sewing buttons on a uniform. Training began with a head shaving and a photograph. Dick, whose brown hair had always been unruly, returned home and told his family he would show them his military ID only if they promised not to laugh. They promised, but the change was so striking that they laughed anyway. Dick had also lost weight during training and had to buy a new belt while home to keep his jeans up.

After basic training Dick received advanced weapons training and basic maneuver tactics at Camp Pendleton, California. He also attended the administration school. Following this, he reported to Camp Lejeune, North Carolina, where he received several weeks of weapons specialist training as a machine gunner. From there, he would depart for South Vietnam.

Before leaving, Dick returned for a final visit home. The family gathered for an early Thanksgiving meal, but the mood was hardly celebratory. The adults were reminding Dick, again, that he didn't have to go. They said he had a choice, but he felt differently. "He said he needed to do this," Ann remembers. "He had a really strong calling and he couldn't make everyone understand." Frustrated, he left.

Dick shipped out soon afterward. While still in the United States, he stopped at the PX store on base and bought Christmas gifts for his family. His mother and Ann each received pearl earrings and a necklace.

Dick was assigned to Mike Company, 3rd Battalion, 5th Regiment, 1st Marine Division. So, too, was one of his Marine cousins. Their paths crossed once overseas, marking the last time anyone in the family saw Dick alive.

In late 1967 Mike Company was operating in the Điện Biên District of Quảng Nam Province in south-central Vietnam. Typical missions involved small daytime patrols and night ambushes outside nearby hamlets or villages, searching for local Vietcong. "We were always on patrol," says Jim Blankenheim, who joined Mike Company in February 1968.

> Battalion HQ wasn't too far, but we were always on patrol. Companies didn't spend too much time in the rear. It was like there was no rear. Any place you were, you were in contact with the enemy. Ambushed, mined, shelled—you name it, they could do it.

Dick spent more time at HQ than he might have liked. Due to his typing abilities, he often worked in administrative management, another effort to enforce the unofficial

Dick Fischer outside the Mike Company bunker in Quảng Nam province, South Vietnam, circa 1967. Courtesy Ann Fischer.

"sole surviving son" policy. Still, he was there to serve and he did his job well. In a letter sent to Eleanor after her son's death, Dick's commanding officer described him[1]:

> Lance Corporal Fischer was alert and intelligent on the job. He was possessed of a cheerful, outgoing personality, which was distinctively marked by many as the traits so often thought of as Marine—self-assuredness, aggressiveness, independence, and a pride in personal physical prowess or endurance.

At the same time, Dick wanted desperately to be in the field as a machine gunner. He did his work at headquarters, but continually requested to be sent out. In the end his persistence won. The date was January 8, 1968, when Lance Corporal Richard Fischer went on his first patrol.

The night's mission was about twenty miles southwest of Danang, less than a mile south of Mike Company's command post, outside the village of Duc Ky.[2] The Marines established an ambush site at the edge of the jungle, roughly seventy-five yards from the village. Separating the Marines and the village were rice paddies. The area was flat and open, offering little concealment, and the ten men on patrol were alert and aware that they could be ambushed just as easily as they could do the ambushing. After the Marines had spent several hours in this position Vietnamese civilians awoke and became aware of the Marines at the ambush site. Several more hours passed, and Dick separated from the squad and was reported missing.

Marines protect their own, and within two hours, additional elements of Mike Company had surrounded the village. They were immediately hit with heavy small arms fire, but proceeded to question the villagers about Dick's whereabouts. The villagers claimed to know nothing of the missing Marine. More Marine units aided the company in their search but after two days, they had found no sign of 20-year-old Richard Fischer.

The news reached the family back home in Wisconsin. Amid the shock and grief, though, there was always hope; missing was not dead.

Ann and her mother held onto that thought for many years after the war had ended and after the Department of Defense officially changed Dick's status in 1978 from missing in action to killed in action, body not recovered.[3] They joined the National League of Families, an alliance of MIA/POW family members advocating for the return of their servicemen. Over the years they received many government reports and few answers. Eleanor eventually transferred the "next-of-kin" position to Ann, tired of false hope. Ann would later transfer the role to her daughter, Jamie.

Unknown to them, they weren't the only ones hoping to find Dick. Information regarding Dick's disappearance first turned up in 1970. A Vietnamese witness came forward, stating that he knew a member of the local Vietcong cadre who had witnessed the burial of a U.S. Marine in Dien Ban District in early January 1968. Despite the flaws in his story, the report notes, "Fischer is the best candidate among those Americans who are unaccounted for in the area."

The Joint POW/MIA Accounting Command (JPAC) received bits and pieces of information throughout the next two decades regarding a possible burial site. In 1992 and 1993 a team traveled to the area and interviewed witnesses, including one woman who verified that Dick had been shot and killed the day he disappeared. She had helped bury him.

In August 1994 the JPAC team excavated the site. It had been more than twenty-five years since Dick's death. Vietnamese soil is highly acidic, making it difficult to preserve much of anything, and the main excavation site was now a farmer's field near the La Tho River. Despite these odds, the dig uncovered several small bones and two buttons.

The team felt confident that the remains belonged to Dick Fischer, but the imprecision of DNA testing at the time prevented them from saying so conclusively. Should they attempt any sort of identification, they feared they would destroy the bones without proving anything.

DNA testing grew in sophistication over the next decade. Smaller DNA samples were needed to run a test, and the amount of information that could be gleaned from those samples improved. Given these advances, the interviews, and the location, the JPAC team needed only to find someone from Dick's family with which to match his DNA to say with certainty that his remains had been located.

In April 2007 they hired a genealogist to find Ann and Jamie, who quickly provided the necessary samples. Then they waited. Ann had waited decades to know what happened to her brother, but to have the truth so close was almost unbearable. "It was the longest summer of my life," she says. She called the agency multiple times, only to be informed that the tests hadn't been performed yet, or the results weren't back yet, or they were still gathering information.

In September the JPAC team called her. The DNA was a match.[4]

It had been forty years since the family had gathered for their early Thanksgiving, an evening that had ended so unpleasantly in an argument and Dick's leaving the house. On Monday, November 19, 2007, they gathered once again—to bring him home.

The funeral was held at Christ Presbyterian Church in Madison. Dick had had a headstone in nearby Forest Hill Cemetery since 1978. In 2007, he was finally buried there with full honors. His mother, Eleanor, was buried nearby. Numerous East High School classmates and coworkers from the lakes attended the service. Former Mike Company members were present as were Vietnam veterans who had never met Dick, but came to honor him as their fallen brother.

The recovery and the service provided closure for the Fischer family. The empty diamond beside his name on the Wall in Washington, D.C., was filled in, a cross placed beside it to signify that he'd once been lost, but now was found.

Looking back at Dick's high school yearbook, Ann thinks maybe his career plans weren't that far off. Determined as he was, maybe he knew his course better than anyone could have imagined. "We both chose a path of peacekeeping, in our own way," she reflects. "I chose that of a pastor."

"He chose that of a warrior."

Captain Paul Stuart Gee

United States Marine Corps, disappeared January 16, 1968

"He was a very interesting person. He was quiet. He was multitalented. He was a fine musician.... A good phrase to describe him would be 'quietly competent.'"—Art Lohuis

"Paul was a quiet gentleman."—Chuck Kohls

"The very first name I looked up on the Wall at the Vietnam Memorial in Washington, D.C. was Paul's. I think I just needed to confirm he was gone."—Terry Cox

The Forest Park Presbyterian Church began in 1928 without a denomination, without a minister, and without a church. The building came first. Situated in Milwaukee on 124th Street, the "Little White Church" would be renovated and relocated more than once before settling on three acres of land in New Berlin. An affiliation with the Milwaukee Presbytery came in 1929. Ministers, though, would come and go. It was not until 1953 that the church appointed a full-time pastor. Joining the Forest Park family was the Rev. Garth Gee, who brought with him a large family.[1]

The Reverend Gee and his wife, Rosabelle, were accustomed to moving. The youngest of their five sons, Paul, was born in Shawano, Wisconsin, on August 21, 1943. In addition to Shawano and New Berlin, Paul also lived in Crandon and Waukesha, where he attended Waukesha South High School. Paul was well liked and well known at Waukesha South. This was due in part to his enthusiastic involvement in the school community, particularly the fine arts. Throughout his four years Paul was a member of junior choir, ensemble, quartets, acapella, and Scitamard.[2] He also worked on the Central Star student newspaper, was selected for the school's premium singing group, the Madrigals, and participated in several school plays, including a starring role in his senior year production of *Brigadoon*. After graduating in 1961 he remained in Waukesha and attended Carroll College.[3]

Carroll is considered Wisconsin's pioneer college. It was established by settlers in 1841 and given a charter in 1846, two years before Wisconsin was granted statehood. When Paul attended 120 years after its founding, Carroll was a small, private, liberal arts institution affiliated with the Presbyterian Church. The college held mandatory chapel every Thursday at 10:45 a.m. They held an annual Religion in Life Week during second semester as well as Fund Week, where organizations on campus raised donations for charities.

About 50 percent of the student body was involved in Greek life. Paul was a member of Delta Rho Upsilon and served as an officer his senior year. Paul lived in the fraternity house as an upper-classman and was infamous for driving his car the three blocks to campus.

Just as in high school, the fine arts were a large part of Paul's collegiate life. He sang in the choir as a freshman and took part in dramatics as well as the Carroll Players theater program during his sophomore and senior years. More informally, Paul played folk music with his fraternity brother and roommate, Art Lohuis. With Art on the banjo

Paul Gee's senior photo from Waukesha South High School, circa 1961. Paul was a prominent member of several choirs and fine arts organizations. Courtesy Waukesha South High School.

and Paul on the twelve-string guitar, they performed covers of Peter, Paul, and Mary as well as the Smothers Brothers and Bob Dylan for "pizza and beer money."

Paul graduated in May of 1965 with a B.S. in geography. He'd been a member of Gamma Theta Upsilon, the International Geographical Honor Society, all four years of college. Upon graduation he immediately found a job as a cartographer with the Southeastern Wisconsin Regional Planning staff. He held the job throughout the remainder of 1965 and early 1966 before handing in his resignation. Aware that he would soon receive a draft notice,[4] he enlisted in the Marine Corps Officer Candidate School in Quantico, Virginia, hoping to become a pilot.

More than 700 college graduates arrived on March 21, 1966, for the fortieth Officer Candidate Course. The program was designed to challenge candidates both physically and mentally. Operating on little sleep, the men performed daily calisthenics, runs, and marches, completed obstacle courses, hiked hills carrying pounds of weaponry, engaged in hand-to-hand combat, and conducted target practice, all while under the nearly constant harassment of the infamous Marine drill sergeants. By graduation on May 27 the 585 men who had completed the course had been reshaped into Marine officers.

Paul returned to Wisconsin in June and visited another fraternity brother, guitar player, and former roommate, Chuck Heidner. The two had worked together at Camp Minikani for two summers in college, taking older campers on canoe trips around Manitowish Waters, and Chuck now worked as an assistant camp director in Merton. During his visit Paul asked Chuck if they could go for a run around the camp, a distance of about four miles. This request, coming from the man who once drove three blocks to class, surprised Chuck, himself a four-year letter winner in track. What surprised him more was that Paul ran circles around him. Marine training had paid off.

There was more training ahead. Paul next traveled to Florida to Naval Air Station Pensacola for flight school. He would not be learning how to pilot the plane. He had been selected for MOS 7584—naval flight officer (NFO)—for advanced training.[5] The NFO controlled the weapons systems aboard the aircraft during missions. NFOs also qualified for copiloting duties in certain types of aircraft. At Pensacola, NFOs attended the same classroom lectures as the aviators: aerodynamics, aircraft engines and systems, meteorology, navigation, and flight rules and regulations. They underwent intense physical training, with an emphasis on swimming, as many ejections in Vietnam took place over water. For that reason part of training also included simulated ejections as well as practice escaping from a submerged aircraft.

The last step in Paul's training was to learn to operate weapon and radar equipment. This took place at NAS Glynco, Georgia. The training involved classroom work, with an emphasis on math, as well as real experience operating the systems in the aircraft. For Paul, Glynco also included music. He'd brought his guitar along and, as at Carroll, he'd found someone to perform with. Terry Cox, who knew Paul during training, remembers:

> My time with Paul was mainly centered around our music. We would sit for hours in our room and play guitar together ... mainly old folk tunes. We used to draw a pretty good crowd. Paul was the only guy I knew who could play a twelve-string guitar, and I was in awe of that.

Paul was awarded the Naval Flight Officer insignia upon completing his training at Glynco in 1967. He was then given an assignment with Marine Composite Reconnaissance Squadron 1 (VMCJ-1), departing shortly thereafter on an overseas cruise to Danang, South Vietnam.

VMCJ-1 first arrived in Vietnam in April 1964, flying the Vought RF-8A Crusader[6] and the Douglas EF-10B Skyknight for photoreconnaissance missions. One year later the Skyknight performed a historic feat when it became the first Marine aircraft to use jamming equipment against enemy radars in support of an Air Force strike. For several years it remained the sole aircraft capable of performing this task.

The Skyknight (nicknamed Willie the Whale because of its rotund shape) was a two-seat Korean War–era fighter aircraft that the Marine Corps had modified to carry electronic jamming equipment. Six jammers were stored in its fuselage. An antenna in both the nose and the tail gave off jamming signals, and the nose also contained receivers to pick up signals from the enemy.

VMCJ-1 flew missions out of Danang in support of nearby Air Force units. Tom Driscoll of VMCJ-1 explains:

> All the aircraft flying up to Vietnam took the same highway, so to say. It was all NATO and UN rules, and rules from our government. So they had SAM[7] sites set up all along there so they knew the routes the American aircraft were going to fly. North Vietnam was the most heavily defended by SAMs in the history so far of warfare. It was like suicide.

The Air Force lacked jamming aircraft of its own so it relied on the VMCJ-1 pilots and navigators to take out the SAM sites before they could carry out their own missions along the heavily defended path. Tom continues:

> When they would get up to a certain place, I believe if a SAM site was close or active, they would get a red light ... so they would turn on their jammers, which would scramble their radar and blind the North Vietnamese to their sighting ability. Which is why it was so critical that this old piece of junk flew up before the Air Force bombers. There would be a couple hundred aircraft that would go up at a time on these major massive strikes and little old Willie the Whale and Captain Gee would jam all the enemy weapons.

VMCJ-1's base in Danang was a hectic work environment. Pilots were always coming and going, and there never seemed to be enough crew chiefs to launch the number of aircrafts that needed to be sent out in a day. If the stress got to Paul, he didn't show it. "He was just always really nice," says Tom. "He was just a calm, always-in-control guy."

On January 16, 1968, 1st Lieutenant Paul Gee departed Da Nang Air Base at 3:45 p.m. His aircraft, piloted by Captain William "Dave" Moreland, was intended as the second of a two-plane flight in support of U.S. Navy operations in the Gulf of Tonkin, but the lead aircraft was unable to take off. Captain Moreland and 1st Lt. Gee successfully conducted the mission alone. Ten minutes prior to their scheduled landing time at 5:55 p.m., Captain Moreland radioed to say they were approximately fifteen miles from Da Nang Air Base, in sight of the airfield, and were switching from radar control to tower control.

This was the last communication with the aircraft. It did not return to the base, and both 24-year-old Paul Gee and 26-year-old Dave Moreland were listed as missing in action.[8]

In July and August 1973, the Joint Casualty Resolution Center conducted search-and-recovery operations off the Danang coastline. Divers discovered the wreckage of an EF-10B aircraft. Among the few items recoverable was a helmet bag with the name "Gee" stenciled on the side. This was considered evidence for a presumptive finding of death, and Paul's status was changed from missing in action to killed in action, body not recovered.

"Paul's family loved him deeply and were heartbroken when he was reported missing in Vietnam," writes his sister-in-law, Jody Gee.

> Once his status changed, they mourned his loss deeply and often wondered what he'd be like "now" as they all got older. His extended family … still share stories about him. We're sure he would have made an even greater difference in this world had he lived to fulfill his full potential.

During VMCJ-1's yearlong tour in Danang, the unit undertook several charity projects. The largest was rebuilding an orphanage. In the years to come VMCJ-1's presence, and Paul's, continued to make a difference in the city. The Forest Park Presbyterian Church in New Berlin established the Paul Gee Memorial Fund after his death. The Gee family requested that all money raised through the fund be donated to various charities throughout Southeast Asia. It is still used to that purpose today.

Colonel Robert Frederick Wilke
United States Air Force,
disappeared January 17, 1968

"He was very charming, good looking, fun, and funny, as I recall, and was great to us.... He was really special."—Susie Wilke

"He was a truly wonderful man. Kind, fun, sensitive, smart and good looking."—Susan Ambrose

"I will never forget his sacrifice and courage under heavy antiaircraft fire."—Thomas Moe

On March 23, 1961, an American C-47 Skytrain was hit by antiaircraft artillery by the Pathet Lao, a Laotian Communist organization. The hit tore off a wing and sent the plane crashing into the jungle below. Only one man aboard escaped the aircraft. On reaching ground Major Lawrence Bailey was quickly captured by the Pathet Lao. He spent the next seventeen months as a prisoner of war. That was the only plausible outcome in 1961 as no search-and-rescue units yet operated within Southeast Asia. The situation changed drastically during the opening years of the Vietnam War. Entire squadrons existed solely for rescue missions. When an aircraft went down helicopters and escort planes were dispatched within hours to look for missing airmen. These rescue missions often met with success. Had he gone down later, Major Bailey might also have been rescued. Had he gone down later, Colonel Robert Wilke might have been the one to find him.

Robert "Bob" Wilke was born September 14, 1925, the eldest son of Herbert and Marie Wilke. He and his brother, Donald, and sister, Joan, grew up in Milwaukee. Herbert, a dentist, died unexpectedly when Bob was 14 years old. Afterward, Marie worked as a secretary to support the family.

Two years later, on December 7, 1941, the Japanese attacked Pearl Harbor, launching the United States into World War II. Bob joined the fight in May 1943 at age 17. He enlisted with the Naval Reserves, volunteering where he thought he would see the most action. It was a trend that continued throughout his life.

Four months later Bob was accepted into the Naval Aviation Cadet Program. Naval aviation was a top military priority during World War II. The German Luftwaffe had demonstrated the need for a strong air defense during their initial assaults on Poland and France. In 1940 the Luftwaffe and the British Royal Air Force (RAF) fought for air superiority during the Battle of Britain, and the RAF's victory forestalled a German invasion. In the United States, the Air Force did not yet exist, and the Navy and Marine Corps had only about two thousand pilots between them.[1]

The Aviation Cadet Act, created in 1935 and revised in 1938, established a pilot training program for Naval and Marine Reserves. The program worked as intended, increasing the number of pilots by mid–1941 to more than four thousand. By 1943 the program had established a goal of twenty thousand graduates annually. Initially, the Naval Aviation Cadet Program required applicants to be between the ages of 18 and 28 and to have two year's college education. This was later changed to a high school diploma, enabling Bob to join at age 18.

Bob left the program in August 1944. He remained in the Naval Reserves until September 1945 to pursue a college education. He enrolled at the University of Wisconsin–Madison, which he attended until February 1948.[2]

After Bob left the UW he returned to the military, although not to the Navy. He turned to an Aviation Cadet Program within the newly created U.S. Air Force. Bob's training took place at Reese Air Force Base in Lubbock, Texas, the first of many times he would be assigned to the Lone Star State over the next two decades. On June 23, 1950, Bob was one of twenty-six aviation cadets to receive their Wings and commissions as second lieutenants. He was, however, the only member of his class to be commissioned into the Regular Air Force; the others joined the Reserves.

Not long after graduation, Bob received an assignment with the 370th Bomb Squadron at MacDill Air Force Base, Florida. The unit did not remain in the United States for long. The month Bob joined the 370th was the same month the Korean War began, and the squadron relocated to Kadena Air Base in Okinawa, from which they flew combat missions for the remainder of the fighting. Bob served with the 370th in Korea until March 1951, flying the Boeing B-29 Superfortress. For someone motivated to enlist by the heroics in World War II, Bob must have appreciated the opportunity to fly the same type of aircraft that had dropped the atomic bombs to end the war with Japan in 1945.

After completing his overseas tour, Bob returned to the United States. He continued to fly the B-29 as a pilot with the 364th Bomb Squadron until that summer, when he transitioned to the Boeing KC-97 Stratotanker. The KC-97 was introduced in 1950, making it a relatively new aircraft when Bob began flying it. A modified version of an earlier Boeing aircraft, the KC-97 used the "flying boom" system for inflight refueling. The boom was a long tube that extended from the KC-97 to the fueling area of an aircraft flying slightly below the Stratotanker, a system still used by the Air Force today.[3] When Bob joined the 305th Air Refueling Squadron in September 1951, he was among the pioneers for this new system.

Bob returned to the B-29 after several months with the 305th Squadron and attended aviation observer school in San Antonio.[4] Aerial observers performed visual reconnaissance during flights, gathered information from the ground, directed attacks, and recorded their results. It signaled a new direction in Bob's career, but Texas also triggered a new direction in Bob's personal life.

Bob during his first tour in Vietnam, standing in front of a Cessna O-1 Birddog aerial observation aircraft. Courtesy the Wilke family.

Bob Wilke married Janet Christie in Houston on October 4, 1952. It was a quiet ceremony, so quiet, in fact, that most of their families didn't know the wedding had taken place until the couple visited relatives several months later. When Bob's friends in Milwaukee heard the news, one issued a playful press release, announcing the loss of one of the city's best-known bachelors. "Tears flooded the downtown streets as the news came," the entertaining notice reads. "Meanwhile, the male element has been enjoying raucous parties in celebration over elimination from competition."

Although they never had children, Bob and Janet had plenty of nieces and nephews to dote on. "I remember him coming to visit us when I was really small," says Mary Wilke, the daughter of Bob's brother, "and he and my father playfully tossing me back and forth like a football."

The couple saw the children whenever possible, but they often did not live close by. Their first house together was in North Highlands, California, but they lived all over the country, traveling to Bob's various assignments. Janet was no stranger to the Air Force life. Before their marriage, she volunteered with the service as a nurse, treating children in Central America. After honeymooning in California, Bob was assigned to the 51st Bomb Squadron at Lake Charles Air Force Base in Lake Charles, Louisiana, again flying the B-29.

In August 1953 Bob took on another new aircraft, the Boeing B-47 Stratojet. The B-47 was a groundbreaking achievement in the history of aviation. Its design, based on secret records taken from a German lab following World War II, was the first to place the engines beneath the wings and use swept-wing technology.[5] As a result, the jet broke a number of records when it first flew in 1949. Faster than any jet of its era, the B-47 needed no defensive weapons in the front because nothing could keep up. Training lasted from August to November 1953. What followed was one of Bob's longest-lasting assignments, flying B-47s with the 52nd Bomb Squadron at Lake Charles AFB from December 1953 to May 1958. Perhaps anticipating the longevity, Bob and Janet moved to Louisiana in the spring of 1954.

Bob flew with three units at Lake Charles[6]: the 52nd Bomb Squadron, 51st Bomb Squadron, and 657th Bomb Squadron. In December 1959 Bob left Louisiana after six years, and he and Janet returned to Texas. Although his next assignment made use of his observational training, it would to be unlike anything he had done before.

In 1954 the Soviet Union introduced the Myasishchev M-4 "Hammer," a long-range jet bomber whose capabilities posed a threat to the United States. One year prior the USSR claimed it had built and tested a hydrogen bomb. Although the United States was winning the nuclear arms race, President Dwight Eisenhower and the National Security Council deemed the need for aerial reconnaissance over the Soviet Union as a pressing and immediate concern. They selected the Lockheed Corporation to design and build an undetectable espionage aircraft. Lockheed was given eight months to produce such a plane. Working under great pressure and secrecy, Lockheed did just that.

The Lockheed U2 "Dragon Lady" was long and light, which allowed it to fly up to three thousand miles while carrying seven hundred pounds of photoreconnaissance equipment. In early flights, the aircraft reached record heights of 65,000 feet, and eventually soared as high as 70,000. The record could not be announced, of course, because the plane and its purpose were entirely covert. Flying over the Soviet Union and photographing their nuclear capacities violated international law, but provided critical knowledge to the United States military throughout the Cold War.[7]

Flying the U2 was difficult, and the screening process for pilots was intense. Bob passed. Starting in December 1959 Bob flew U2 spy planes out of Laughlin Air Force Base, Del Rio, Texas, with the 4028th Strategic Reconnaissance Squadron (SRS), a part of the 4080th Strategic Reconnaissance Wing. His first solo flight took place in early 1960. By the time the Cuban Missile Crisis began on October 14, 1962, he'd had plenty of experience.

In early 1960, as the Communist dictator of Cuba, Fidel Castro, turned to the Soviet Union for economic and military aid, the American CIA directed U2 flights out of Laughlin AFB to conduct photoreconnaissance over Cuba. In June 1962 the flights revealed the first photographs of a Soviet medium range missile installation on the island. Despite security concerns the 4080th Strategic Reconnaissance Wing continued to provide photographic evidence throughout the summer and during the thirteen-day crisis in the fall. By that time Bob and the rest of the 4028th SRS were operating out of the Strategic Wing Air Force Base in Hawaii.

Janet remained in Del Rio while Bob was in Hawaii, but after Bob returned in September 1963 the two would not be separated for some time. Bob's time with the 4028th SRS ended and he enrolled in the Air Force Institute of Technology at the University of Texas A&M in pursuit of his Master's Degree in computer science. He graduated

Just as Bob enjoyed spending time with his nieces and nephews, he made friends with some of the children near his base in South Vietnam. Courtesy the Wilke family.

from the program in July 1965 and began flying the Cessna O-1 Birddog, a light forward air control aircraft used to support ground troops and mark targets. For the first time since Korea, Bob was given a permanent overseas assignment. He served with three units: the 6250th Support Squadron, the 505th Tactical Control Group, and the 19th Tactical Air Support Squadron. All three were in Vietnam.[8]

Bob completed his tour in Southeast Asia in July 1966. He returned home to Janet and took a job as an Air Force liaison officer to the Civil Air Patrol. Overseas, though, the Vietnam War was far from slowing down. Many of the men now in the Air Force had limited experience and were facing war for the first time in the deadliest year of conflict thus far. The young pilots could benefit greatly from the guidance of more senior officers like Bob Wilke.

Bob volunteered for the assignment. He was senior enough that he could easily have kept a desk job in the United States if that was what he'd wanted. By May 1967 Bob had been in the military for twenty-four years. He had served longer than the Air Force had existed. He'd fought in Korea and had already served one tour in Vietnam. Bob could have stayed out of the conflict—was perhaps *expected* to remain out of it— but he chose to return. Not everyone in the family agreed with his decision, but he said it was his job and he was going to go.

He would once again fly a new plane, the Douglas A-1 Skyraider. Bob spent the summer of 1967 training, during which time his nieces, Mary and Susie Wilke, visited him and Janet. They drove to San Francisco, from where Bob would depart in August to join the 602nd Fighter Commando Squadron at Udorn Royal Thai Air Force Base in Thailand.

The A-1 Skyraider was an attack and close air support plane, but the 602nd used it in a different capacity. The squadron performed search-and-rescue operations, called "Sandy" flights.[9] In 1962 only three officers and three enlisted men at Tan Son Nhut Air Base, South Vietnam made up the official American search-and-rescue unit. As the war continued, the Air Rescue Service (ARS) developed a formal procedure to rescue downed airmen, involving combat search-and-rescue teams, multiple helicopters,[10] and an escort plane. For many years the A-1 was ideally suited for this purpose: It carried small armaments for defense, provided extra armor around the pilot, and could fly eight hours without refueling.[11] The ARS also formed squadrons dedicated to search-and-rescue operations, including the 602nd.

Bob's mission on January 17, 1968, was like that of any other rescue. The previous day two McDonnell Douglas F-4 Phantoms had gone down in North Vietnam, approximately ninety miles from the base in Thailand.[12] All four crewmen were on the ground. It was established via radio contact that the pilot, Thomas Moe, was on top of a mountain. Colonel Wilke set out to find him. The area was cloaked in clouds by the time Bob arrived. He contacted Thomas Moe, who told him the clouds reached all the way to the ground and that he should go home. Bob wouldn't hear of it; he said he knew the area and would try to find him.

Bob radioed his wingman to say that he was going below the clouds. Having completed that maneuver, he radioed that he was near a large, heavily populated valley, above a major road and a river. That was the last the wingman heard from him.

One of the other downed airmen nearby heard the same report, then the rumble of a plane overhead, followed by weapons firing, after which time the rumbling ceased. Thomas Moe felt the mountain shake as Bob Wilke's plane collided with it.

Janet Wilke was in Thailand. Bob's overseas assignment hadn't kept them apart. She received a late-night phone call before a major and a chaplain arrived at her door. She was whisked out of Thailand and back to the United States. If Bob had survived and been taken prisoner, they did not want Janet to become a target used to make Bob talk.

When the telephone rang in New York, Mary Wilke answered and greeted her aunt. She woke up her father, Bob's brother, and listened as he received the news.

The military changed Bob's status from missing in action to killed in action on May 5, 1978. A monument in Arlington National Cemetery stands tribute to his sacrifice. When Janet died in 2012 she was buried in Arlington as well. For his actions on January 16 and 17, Robert Wilke was awarded the Air Force Cross, the Air Force's highest decoration after the Medal of Honor.

The American ARS was enormously successful. They rescued 4,120 servicemen over the course of the war. They lost 71 of their own personnel. Colonel Robert Wilke had a long, accomplished military career. The goal of his final mission was the rescue of four downed airmen. Thomas Moe was captured and taken to a prisoner of war camp, but survived the war. The other three men were rescued, and Bob's radio contact was essential in locating them. In the end, he exemplified the ARS's motto as few others could: "That Others May Live."

Major James Alan Ketterer
United States Air Force,
disappeared January 20, 1968

"My brother, when he wanted something, he went after it. In everything he did.... He was a hard worker. Ethical. That was very important to him. Honesty. Anything that he did, he wanted to do well."—Jeanne (Ketterer) Wallrath

"He just was a really neat person. We've always wondered over the years what it would have been like had he lived and what kind of life he would have had.... When someone dies when they are 25 years old, that's the age they always are in your mind. You can't imagine them fast forwarded to what they would look like, even."—Karel (Ketterer) Bretsch

Jim Ketterer loved to compete and, when he competed, he loved to win. "When he went to some of these contests, he said, 'I'm going to win this,'" remembers his sister, Karel. "And Mother said, 'You might not.' And he said, 'Nope, I'm going to win.'" It was hard to argue with Jim. A sense of dogged determination, coupled with an intense work ethic, drove him throughout much of his life. Jim did nothing halfway and, if he wanted something, he would find a way to get it.

Jim didn't plan to go to Vietnam. When orders came, though, Jim responded as he had to every challenge in his life: He met it head-on with everything he had.

James Alan Ketterer was born in Milwaukee on December 18, 1942. He was four years younger than his sister, Karel, and four years older than his sister, Jeanne. He was baptized into the Lutheran Church and remained active in the church throughout his life. Jim's father died when he was 9 years old, leaving his mother, Norma, a single working mother. Jim stepped up immediately. "He kind of became the head of the house," remembers Jeanne, "and he was very protective."

He was especially protective toward his little sister, a quality that defined their relationship throughout his life. "He was a wonderful older brother," she remembers. "He was not perfect, but he was a great brother."

Despite the age difference, Jim and Jeanne spent a lot of time together, ice skating and sledding during Wisconsin's winters and double dating when Jim was in college. More than once, Jim set Jeanne up with a friend of his, only to tag along and remind her date, "That's my little sister. Don't touch her." Jim liked to tease her, but he never failed to look out for her or do something special for her either. Jim worked at Hobby Horse in Milwaukee's Capitol Court Shopping Center throughout high school and made Jeanne a doll wardrobe and furniture.

Jim had always liked building and woodworking. He was in Cub Scouts and Boy Scouts during elementary and middle school, and began making model planes when he was 8 years old. By age 11, he was designing and building the planes from scratch. Soon after he was competing with them across the nation. In 1959 and 1960 Jim was the Wisconsin Model Airplane Youth Champion. He traveled to Naval Air Station Los Alamitos, California,[1] and then to Hensley Field at the Dallas Naval Air Station, Texas, to compete on the national level. Jim competed in the speed division—the faster, the better. "He wanted to win," says Jeanne. "He *never* wanted to lose."

Jim applied that same work ethic in school. "He was an A student," Jeanne says. "He skipped a grade because he was bored." Jim was on the National Honor Society all four years at Milwaukee's Custer High School. He was in the German Club and the Drama Club. He acted and he sang; he had a leading role in the school's production of *Annie Get Your Gun*. Jim played tennis and he golfed. He loved to watch the Green Bay Packers.

After he graduated from high school in 1960 at age 17, Jim attended the University of Wisconsin–Milwaukee. He joined the Alpha Kappa Psi fraternity; Jeanne's dates were usually one of his fraternity brothers. Jim was a business major, graduating with a Bachelor of Science degree in January 1965.

Within days, his draft notice arrived in the mailbox.

Although the United States had had a military presence in South Vietnam for nearly a decade, from the public's perspective the war in Vietnam was only beginning. Jim's post graduation plans had not included the military, but if he was going to serve—and the draft notice in his hand said he was—he was going to serve in the Air Force. Years later, his sisters can't quite remember how he managed it. He might have talked to a congressman, or an alderman, but Jim convinced *someone* to petition on his behalf to release him from the draft so he could enlist in the U.S. Air Force.

Once enlisted his first stop was Lackland Air Force Base in San Antonio for basic training. Jim then attended pilot training at Vance Air Force Base in Enid, Oklahoma. Two important events occurred at Vance AFB: First, Jim met Diane, who quickly became his girlfriend. Second, Jim graduated at the top of his flight class so he was given one of the top choices of assignments. He could have gone to Europe or stayed in the United States as an instructor, but what Jim wanted was to fly the fastest jet ever built, the McDonnell F-4C Phantom II.

Although designed for the Navy, the multipurpose Phantom was so efficient and versatile that it was quickly adopted by the Air Force and the Marines, becoming the first aircraft to be used by the three fighting forces concurrently. Flying at twice the speed of sound, the jet held sixteen world records, including altitude, speed, and time-to-climb. Jim couldn't let the opportunity to pilot such a jet pass him by.

Jet training took place at MacDill Air Force Base in Tampa. Jim was no longer an underclassman, but an Air Force officer. When Jeanne visited him for a week that spring, she compared him to Tom Cruise from *Top Gun*: cocky and self-assured. "To fly a plane, you had to have that edge," she says. "And he had that edge."

Jim lived in an off-base apartment complex with several other guys. While he was still completing flight training during Jeanne's visit, he had time to show her around on her first trip outside Wisconsin. He took her out to dinner and to a dance at the officer's club. Several underclassmen approached Jeanne, but Jim stood watch over her like a drill sergeant. "This is my little sister," he warned them all. "You better take care of her."

Partway through Jeanne's visit, Jim's girlfriend, Diane, joined them from Oklahoma. One morning after she arrived, as Jim left for classes, he gave the girls his car keys and asked them to come to the base. He gave them a specific time to be there and a specific place to park. When they got there, they sat at the end of the runway as Jim flew a jet directly over their heads.

Before the week was through, Jim proposed to Diane, and she said yes. With training at MacDill nearing an end, Diane wanted to get married before Jim left for Vietnam. Jim, though, wanted to wait until he returned home. The couple remained engaged as she went back to Oklahoma.

After graduating from flight school, Jim went to Fairchild Air Force Base, outside Spokane, Washington, for survival training, stopping in Nebraska for Thanksgiving with Karel and her husband. The last stage of Jim's training was jungle survival school at Clarke Air Force Base in the Philippines in the fall of 1967. In September he left the Philippines as part of the 389th Tactical Fighter Squadron, then based at Da Nang Air Base, South Vietnam.

The 389th, 390th, and 480th fighter squadrons made up the 366th Tactical Fighter Wing. Squadron enlistments lasted either one year or 100 missions, whichever came first, and in late 1967 and early 1968 there was no shortage of missions. In 1967 the Air Force carried out 54,316 sorties in North Vietnam alone, and 41,507 more would be flown in 1968. By contrast, in 1969, missions fell to only 213.[2] Pilots vied for missions over North Vietnam; often called "counters," such missions served as a means to get home sooner.

Most pilots flew every other day, sometimes more. Jim flew an aggressive flight schedule. North Vietnam was divided into six bombing quadrants, or "packages." Jeanne now has Jim's mission calendar from his tour. In it, she can see exactly where and when he conducted missions. In the ten-day stretch before he was shot down, Jim flew every day, sometimes twice. After seeing the intense schedule in early 1968, the empty pages in the calendar after January 20 are a sudden and sad reminder of his fate.

Chip High, an intelligence officer in the 366th Tactical Wing, briefed Jim and the flight commander, Major Tilden "Til" Holley, on their mission for January 20, 1968. Chip had gone through much of his training with Til and knew Jim from the Da Nang officers' open mess, where Jim was a regular at the bar. Til and Jim were well acquainted, too; they had lived together in the off-base apartment in Tampa. First Lieutenant James Ketterer was the pilot in the lead ship of a two-ship night-armed reconnaissance mission over North Vietnam. Major Tilden Holley was his aircraft commander.[3]

That night's target was Quảng Khê Ferry in Quảng Bình Province, the southern part of North Vietnam. The ferry, crossing the Gianh River and emptying into the Gulf of Tonkin, was considered a "choke point," a point at which the North Vietnamese had to gather and which was a frequent target of the 366th Wing's bombing missions. "The river comes down to the sea," explains Chip. "And inland is all jungle and fairly rough mountain ranges, so the most convenient way was right down the coast. [The NVA] always had to cross the ferry at that point, and we were always waiting for them as much as we could."

At around 10:02 p.m., the two-ship formation departed Da Nang Air Base. The weather was not optimal for a bombing mission: Cloud tops were at 4,000–4,500 feet with ragged bottoms from 1,000 to 1,500 feet. Regardless, Jim and Til dropped their flares. While

James Ketterer prepared for flight in South Vietnam. Courtesy Jeanne Wallrath.

dropping their ordnance afterward, the second aircraft noticed antiaircraft artillery in the area. Til radioed for them to hold back while he and Jim observed the site before the flares went out.

At roughly 10:37 p.m., the second aircraft's crew saw a sudden streak of orange in the sky. They immediately radioed the lead aircraft, but received no response. They had not seen any parachutes, but within thirty seconds of seeing the streak, thought they'd heard an emergency beeper. The signal was gone within two or three seconds, though, and could not be homed in on. The second aircraft stayed in the area for twenty minutes, hoping to receive some communication from the downed plane before returning to the air base due to fuel shortage. Another aircraft was diverted to the area and remained for about an hour, searching for a signal, but no communication was established. It was too dark to see the downed plane that night and too hostile in subsequent days to conduct an organized ground search.

Jeanne was home with her mother when an officer came to their door to tell them Jim was missing. The news was devastating enough, but the officer had more to tell them: "The hard part was we were kind of instructed not to talk about it," Jeanne remembers. "That only lasted so long, and then my mother did talk about it."

Norma became active in the National League of POW/MIA American Families. In addition to leading letter-writing campaigns to Hanoi to release American prisoners and searching for answers in MIA cases, the league became a support group for those involved. Especially within Wisconsin, the MIA's and POW's families grew close, and Norma's positive outlook was a source of comfort to many in the group.

"I always thought, maybe in her lifetime, we would have found something out," says Karel, but they never did. "The not knowing part is the part that's always been hard all these years. You surmise that this is what happened, but you don't know.... It's kind of like they're frozen in time." Eight years after Jim disappeared at age 25, the family requested that his status be changed from missing in action to presumed dead, and they held a memorial service in his honor.

"He was just a very determined, very bright person," say Jeanne. "Just very outgoing,

Left to right: Charles "Jerry" Huneycutt Jr., Tilden "Til" Holley, and Jim Ketterer. Jim and Til were lost and declared MIA after the same mission on January 20, 1968; Jerry went MIA after his plane was lost on a mission on November 10, 1967. Courtesy Jeanne Wallrath.

very hard worker. Anything he did, he did it to the best he could. And he wanted to fly the fastest jet he could, and that's what he did. Under the circumstances, he would not have enlisted in the Air Force, but if he had to go, and he did, that's what he wanted to do.

"He did what he loved."

Chief Petty Officer
Donald Louis Gallagher

United States Navy,
disappeared February 6, 1968

"He was so proud of his service and the plane and the crew."
"He just loved his service."
"And we loved him."—Nancy (Gallagher) Roehre and Lynn (Gallagher)
Schmitt

During his two terms, President Harry S. Truman kept a sign on his desk with the phrase "The Buck Stops Here." The words served as his personal motto. They constituted a promise to the people he governed that he, and he alone, would take responsibility for the decisions and actions of his administration. When President Truman left the White House in 1953, taking his sign with him, another group adopted the phrase.

"The buck stops here" quickly summarizes the role and mentality of a chief petty officer (E-7) in the United States Navy. He is a disciplinarian, a supervisor, and an expert in his field. He is charged not only with ensuring that the men who work under him are properly trained and militarily competent, but also that they are fed and housed appropriately, that their morale is high, and that they trust each other and their commanding officer. He is their leader and their advocate. "Ask the chief" is a phrase heard time and again in the Navy, and when the chief is consulted, his word is law.

Prior to 1958, chief petty officer was the highest noncommissioned rating a sailor could achieve. It required a recommendation from a commanding officer and qualifying scores on the chief petty officer examination.[1] Not everyone achieved the coveted rating, and even those who did often worked toward it for twelve or more years. Some managed it in fewer.

Chief Petty Officer Donald Gallagher was one of them. He did it in nine.

Don never brought much attention to his accomplishment. "He was very proud of having made chief petty officer at his age," remembers his sister, Nancy, but he was "very self-effacing.... He was never a braggart."

Donald Gallagher, born March 2, 1938, was the second of John and Rose Gallagher's four children. Called Donnie growing up in Sheboygan Falls, Wisconsin, he was known for his kindness, his mellow attitude, and his good sense of humor. "He had a quick wit," recalls Nancy. "He was just very funny." His youngest sister, Lynn, agrees, calling him a joker.

The jokes he played were seldom solely his own. With only thirteen months separating them, Don and his older brother, Jack, were the best of friends. "It was always said, 'Where's Jack?' 'Well, wherever Don is,'" Lynn explains. "'Where's Don?' 'Wherever Jack is.'"

The boys did everything together. They hunted, once shooting a deer and hanging it outside Lynn and Nancy's bedroom window to greet them in the morning. They fixed old cars (Don had a Model T Ford) and built a go-kart together. They took their little sisters ice-skating in the winter and to an outdoor amphitheater in the summer. They played night games in the boulevard in front of their house with the neighborhood kids, and once taught Lynn how to attract bats by tying a small stone in a white hanky and throwing it in the air for them to catch. When trucks from the local canning factory came by in need of extra workers, the brothers jumped on board at 6 in the morning and spent the day picking beans in the field.

Together the Gallagher boys worked a paper route, while Don held additional jobs at a local grocery store and an automobile dealership. He served in a peer-nominated position on Sheboygan Falls High School's student council. "People liked Don," says Nancy. "Kind of gravitated when he was around." Don's sense of humor rubbed off on others, and his jokes weren't limited to his home. He and his school friends were well known to be playful and mischievous.

With blue eyes and blonde hair, Don was the only one of the four Gallagher kids to take after his mother. Courtesy Lynn Schmitt.

The Gallagher kids walked the few blocks to school each day. When Jack graduated, Don and Nancy made the trip alone.[2] When Nancy ran late, Don threatened to leave without her, but he never did. She always found him standing outside the garage waiting for her. In addition to everything else, he was also a good big brother.

Sixty-five students graduated in Don's high school class of 1957. In the yearbook, beneath a photograph of a young man with curly blond hair in a suit and tie, Don's senior quote reads: "My brilliant career has not yet begun; until then, I'll just have fun!"

How true that proved to be.

Don enlisted in the United States Navy in the fall of 1957 and trained at Great Lakes Naval Station in Great Lakes, Illinois.[3] The family came down to visit him once during training, but for the rest of his career, it was usually the other way around.

Over the next few years Don received further training in the fields of sonar, mechanics, and radar. His main base was Brunswick, Maine, but as his career advanced, it took him all over the world, including England, Iceland, Italy, and the Philippines. Don sent back gifts from wherever he was stationed and wrote often, maintaining a regular correspondence with Lynn throughout his time in the Navy.

He returned to Wisconsin two or three times a year, homecomings that were eagerly anticipated by the rest of the family. "When he did come home, we gathered," says Nancy. "As soon as Donnie was home, *we* were home.... He was the nucleus of our family." Nancy learned to make lemon meringue pie—Don's favorite food—for him each time he visited. (She later learned that his base served the same dessert regularly, but Don never told her that.) A visit in July 1965 was particularly special for Lynn when he returned for her wedding.

At the same time Don thoroughly enjoyed life in the Navy. Contrary to most Naval men, Don was never stationed aboard a ship. For much of his career, Don served with Patrol Squadron 26 (VP-26) of Patrol Wing Eleven. Activated in 1944, VP-26 provided intelligence and support around the world, starting in World War II, when six squadron airplanes flew during the Normandy invasion.[4] A VP-26 aircraft was the first publicized downed aircraft of the Korean War after it was intercepted by several Soviet planes over the Baltic Sea on April 8, 1950.[5] In 1952, the squadron became the first to operate from the newly opened Naval Air Station Brunswick, Maine, which remained their primary operating base until 2010. The "Tridents" flew in support of the Cuban Missile Crisis during the fall of 1962 and, in 1965, were the Navy's first squadron to fly the Lockheed Martin P-3B "Orion."

VP-26 conducted maritime patrol reconnaissance, and the Orion, designed to fly at low altitudes and slow speeds for long stretches of time, was perfectly suited for such missions. Equipped with magnetic anomaly detection, which tracked changes in the earth's magnetic field, the aircraft could easily detect the presence of submarines beneath the ocean's surface.

On board, Don worked in ordnance, serving as the aircraft's weapons specialist. After nine years of service, he was promoted to chief petty officer.[6] Then Don was charged not only with the care and maintenance of the plane's armaments, but also of his men. "Your entire way of life has now been changed," reads the Navy's Chief Petty Officer's Creed. "More will be expected of you, more will be demanded of you.... You have joined an exclusive fraternity, and as in all fraternities, you have a responsibility to your brothers, even as they have a responsibility to you."[7]

It was a responsibility he fully embraced. VP-26 was made of several individual crews who trained and flew missions together. While people in the squadron interacted, each crew was a close-knit family unto itself. They stuck together, and Don's unit, Combat Aircrew 8, was important to him.

"He told me one time that if he ever had to go," Lynn says, "he wants to go with his crew."

Don and his crew were in the United States in late 1967, and Don was in Wisconsin on leave when he found out that Combat Aircrew 8 would soon deploy to U-Tapao

Royal Thai Naval Air Base in Thailand. It was November, shortly before Thanksgiving, and his mother was disappointed he would be leaving before the holidays again. He'd missed the last few Christmases. He told her, "Mom, I promise I'll be home for Christmas."

"I can still hear him saying it," says Lynn.

"I went with Mom and Dad when they took him to the plane the last time he left," Nancy remembers of that November:

> We took him down. I remember standing there.... It was raining and it was dark. We were waiting at the gate, like behind the fence. In those times, it was different, you could walk right up there. Milwaukee. And I remember standing back, and Mom was standing at that fence in the rain in the dark, watching. That's in my mind. That would have been the last time she saw him.

VP-26 deployed for Southeast Asia in November 1967. Some crews remained at Naval Air Station Sangley Point in the Philippines and others, like Don's, continued to Thailand to take part in ongoing Operation Market Time. Named after the native boats used for fishing and trading, Operation Market Time began in 1965 tasked with patrolling and securing the twelve hundred miles of South Vietnam's coast against North Vietnamese infiltrators. The responsibilities were shared among the U.S. Navy and Coast Guard as well as South Vietnamese naval forces.

On the P-3 Orion Don's crew flew photoreconnaissance missions over the South China Sea, using radar and high-powered searchlights to spot supply ships along the southern coastlines. "Don said they would fly so low that they could just see the young

men on the decks of the ships," remembers Nancy. He also told her that if their aircraft were ever hit, flying below 1,000 feet as it did, the crew would not have time to parachute.

Combat Aircrew 8 departed in the late hours of February 5, 1968, for a typical photoreconnaissance mission, but they failed to file their scheduled position at 4:00 a.m. on February 6. Search-and-rescue units were dispatched two hours later and spotted debris from the aircraft and two bodies in the Gulf of Thailand. Search-and-rescue operations were concluded at sundown on February 7, while salvage operations continued to recover pieces of the plane for over a month. All twelve men aboard were lost on the morning of February 6, 1968.[8]

The other crews of VP-26 held a memorial service at Sangley Point. "The personnel of crew 8 were superb and dedicated men," it is noted in a unit newsletter days after the crash. "Their loss is irreplaceable to the country, the Navy, and the squadron as well as to their families."

Chief Petty Officer Donald Gallagher served eleven years in the Navy. Courtesy Lynn Schmitt.

The Gallagher family were told Don was missing, but the Navy changed his status to killed in

Don Gallagher's aircraft, a P-3 Orion. The symbol of the VP-26 "Tridents" can be seen on the tail. Courtesy Lynn Schmitt.

action, body not recovered before the end of the month. He was 29 years old, with eleven years of Naval service. The family held a ceremony at which they distributed memorial cards with the words of St. Ambrose printed on them: "We have loved him in life, let us not forget him in death."

They never did.

Don was Sheboygan Falls's first Vietnam death. A year later, his former classmates dedicated a lectern with his name on it for the high school's new auditorium. He is the only member of their class to be killed in the war, and former classmates continue to talk about him with each other and the family today.

Decades later Don's niece, who never knew him, noticed a silver bracelet around her boss's wrist with the name Donald L. Gallagher written on it.[9] Her boss had worn the MIA bracelet for twenty years, always wondering who he was. The family was all too happy to tell her.

"I just think of him all the time," Lynn says. "We're proud of our Don and, as you can tell, we loved him very dearly."

Lieutenant (Junior Grade)
Roy Arthur Huss

United States Navy,
disappeared February 6, 1968

"Roy was a great guy. He was kind of quiet and shy, but he was a super person. Everybody liked him. You couldn't help but like him."—Richard Bunkelman

"He was fairly quiet.... He was a straight-A student. He was a pretty smart kid."—Richard Voelker

"He was just a wonderful person.... He loved flying, and he was always happy-go-lucky. He was very cheerful all the time. He was easy to get along with."—Bob Brown

Abbotsford, a small town in central Wisconsin, occupies 2.71 square miles of land, with pieces in both Clark and Marathon counties. The town owes its founding in large part to the Wisconsin Central Railroad Company. In the 1870s the company surveyed the land and cleared it of forests to build a set of railroad tracks that stretched north to Ashland, south to Chicago, and west to St. Paul and Minneapolis. Many young men in the small town worked on the railways, but from an early age Roy Huss dreamed of a different frontier.

"He always talked about getting to the moon," says a friend, Jerry Weideman. "That was his goal. He was always trying to figure out how to make a rocket ship. That was third or fourth grade."

Roy was born in Abbotsford on July 29, 1943, the youngest of three children. In the '50s and '60s, Abbotsford had a population of a little over one thousand. Most children, including Roy, attended a two-room primary school before entering Abbotsford High School, where an average class size was around thirty or forty students. The school provided plenty of extracurricular activities. During his senior year Roy was a member of "A" Club, served on the student council, and played center on the football team.

Football was an important part of Abbotsford life, not least because the team was very good. "We lost like two or three games in two years," remembers Richard Bunkelman, Roy's teammate. Abbotsford won the state championship in 1959. In his final season the team went undefeated until losing in the conference title game to its rival, Colby.

In school Roy was at the top of the class. "He was a smart kid. Very smart," Richard says. "Just down-to-earth, didn't say a lot."

Outside of school Roy's was the life of many from small towns in Wisconsin. "Those days you'd run around at night and go to the dairy bar and get a malt," Jerry explains. "It was the 50s.... He was one of my best buddies. Sometimes we had to walk home, and he lived one way and I lived the other, and sometimes we walked both ways."

Like many in Abbotsford, Jerry lived on a farm. When he had chores to do, Roy often waited for him at his house so they could go out afterward. It was on one such occasion that Roy met Jerry's cousin, Judy, visiting from out of town. Roy hadn't had a steady girlfriend during high school and had shown little interest in dating—until Judy.

They married on June 26, 1965. Jerry served as Roy's best man. By then Roy was finishing his final semester at the University of Wisconsin–Eau Claire. He graduated that summer with a degree in biology. On January 5, 1966, he enrolled in the Aviation Officer Candidate School, Naval Air Station Pensacola, Florida.

Roy was the first in his family to serve in the military. His goal was not simply to serve, but to fly. He wanted to be a pilot and had first considered joining the Air Force. The glasses he wore limited his options within that branch. Different vision requirements meant that there were opportunities for Roy to fly with the Navy.

He was commissioned an officer in the United States Navy on April 14, 1966. By then Roy was a father. While his wife and daughter remained in Abbotsford, Roy continued his training. After several more months he qualified as a Naval flight officer (NFO)[1] and was assigned to Patrol Squadron 26 (VP-26).

VP-26 was one of several active maritime patrol squadrons whose main role was to survey sea-based operations and acquire necessary intelligence on potential enemy threats. The squadron was composed of individual crews of twelve men who operated a Lockheed Martin P-3B Orion. Roy's NFO status qualified him to navigate as well as run the antisubmarine warfare operations in the aircraft. Roy flew with both Combat Aircrew (CAC) 1 and, later, CAC 8.

The squadron's main station in the United States was Naval Air

Roy and Judy Huss were married in Abbottsford on June 26, 1965. Courtesy Bob Brown.

Station Brunswick, Maine. While he was there Roy's sister and brother-in-law, Ethel and Bob Brown, visited him on base. Bob remembers:

> He'd just come back from a flight. The admiral sent him to Nova Scotia to pick up lobsters for dinner. That was his last mission before he went overseas. He took us through his plane and he was so proud of it. He was younger than my wife and when I had visited his home, his room was decorated with model planes.

That was the last time the Browns saw Roy. In November 1967, the 300 men of VP-26 deployed overseas to Southeast Asia, joining thousands of others in fighting the Vietnam War.

Theirs was a split deployment. The squadron was stationed at Naval Station Sangley Point in the Philippines, while missions were flown out of U-Tapao Royal Thai Navy Airfield in Thailand. The crews rotated, each spending about six to eight weeks in Thailand before returning to the Philippines. Overall, the crews spent about one-third of their deployment conducting surveillance out of U-Tapao.

Being stationed at either location was exciting and fun. At Sangley Point the hot and humid weather did little to detract sailors from venturing to the active downtown scene in Cavite City. Roy enjoyed the area, writing to Jerry Weideman in Wisconsin that he should consider coming over.

"I don't know a single person, a guy especially, who was doing something more exciting than hanging out in a drug store [in the United States]," William Young of VP-26 reflects. "The guys in-country, that was a different story.... It was exciting to be on a crew. You were flying and doing things, not just sitting at a desk."

When stationed at U-Tapao, life was busy in an entirely different way. Crews flew every two to three days, allowing for one day of rest between flights before going on call again. Because it usually took two to three hours of flying to reach the coast they were intended to patrol, surveillance missions lasted fourteen to sixteen hours at a time.

Aboard the P-3B Orion the crews carried various books of languages, which were used to identify any writing observed aboard ships in the areas they patrolled. Many of the ships were Soviet, Chinese, Cambodian, and Laotian. VP-26 was an observation squadron and it photographed enemy ships when spotted. At night, when it was too dark to take pictures, the crews had another way to identify friend from foe: When they spotted a ship in the water, they sent the ship a code over the radio. If the ship sent an incorrect code in response, the crews knew there were enemies in the area.

VP-26's missions were part of Operation Market Time, an ongoing effort to prevent troops and supplies from North Vietnam and their Communist allies from reaching North Vietnamese units in South Vietnam. Although the Orion flew low and slow, the aircraft carried no armaments. "When flying over sea, you didn't really expect to get shot because you didn't think they'd come out that far," explains Jack Karstens, another member of VP-26.

On the morning of February 5, 1968, the twelve-man crew of Combat Aircrew 8 departed Thailand to conduct surveillance operations along the coast in the Gulf of Thailand. What happened in subsequent hours is unknown. The crew failed to report its position at 4:00 a.m. on February 6, and search-and-rescue commenced shortly afterward.

Search-and-rescue eventually became search-and-salvage. Wreckage of the P-3B

Orion was located forty miles from the coast of South Vietnam. The bodies of two crewmembers were found in the water on February 7. There were no survivors. Twenty-four-year-old Lieutenant (Junior Grade) Roy Huss was among those missing.[2]

The military determined the official cause of the crash was "unknown." There may have been a technical malfunction or pilot error, but other patrol squadron members think that unlikely. "The ship [they were inspecting] would have seen it and radioed for help," explains Larry Moore, whose VP-40 was stationed at Sangley Point and U-Tapao after VP-26 left. "But since there was no contact by anyone I suspect it was shot down.... Those Navy pilots were incredible."

Donald Tiedt was a member of Combat Aircrew 6, the crew on ready alert, prepared to take over

Roy Huss was commissioned an officer in the United States Navy on April 14, 1966. Courtesy Bob Brown.

Crew 8's mission after it went down. He heard the search-and-rescue efforts over the radio: "I know officially the 'accident' cause is unknown, but as we listened on the radios a swift boat crew picked up a door and stated it looked like 50-caliber holes in it."

Further supporting the theory that enemy action brought down the Orion, VP-26's Crew 1 was lost to confirmed antiaircraft fire on April 1, 1968, while patrolling the same area as Crew 8. As with the earlier crash, there were no survivors.[3]

VP-26 returned to the United States in the first week of June 1968, after six months overseas.[4] The unit was acutely aware of the twenty-four men who did not come home. Their deployment cruise book is dedicated "to the officers and men of Patrol Squadron Twenty-Six who deployed with us and will not return, for they have given their lives so that others might live, in the very highest of Naval traditions."

Roy Huss's absence is a poignant memory in the small town of Abbotsford. "Everybody knew everybody," Richard Bunkelman reflects. "That made it harder, too, when they were gone so fast."

A small plaque in the Abbotsford cemetery memorializes Roy Huss. Beneath his name, his rank, and the casualty date are inscribed the words: "Lost at sea."

Petty Officer Second Class
John Francis Hartzheim
United States Navy,
disappeared February 27, 1968

"Although the memories are clear, it is difficult to put into words the impact a leader like John has on a young kid looking for his place in a new world.... He was genuine. He was sincere. That's the John Hartzheim I was blessed to know for a brief period in time."—David Weber

"Fine young man—a credit to the state of Wisconsin, to his family, and to the Navy."—John Driver

Naval Observation Squadron 67 (VO-67) operated for 500 days in 1967 and 1968. Nicknamed "The Ghost Squadron," the unit performed top-secret intelligence-gathering operations along the Ho Chi Minh Trail at the height of the Vietnam War before the squad was decommissioned. The accomplishments made during this time remained classified for decades. For the men who served with VO-67, this meant years of silence regarding what they had done in the war. For the families of the twenty men of VO-67 who did not come home, it meant years of questions. For the family of Petty Officer John Hartzheim, answers finally came in 1999.

John Francis Hartzheim, born November 25, 1945, came from a large family; he was one of five boys and seven girls in the Appleton, Wisconsin, household. Being one of many certainly didn't diminish his personality. Even as a kid John had a certain swagger about him. He was something of a ringleader for the junior high and high school kids living along Owaissa Street so when he brought new-to-town David Weber into their group, David was immediately accepted into the neighborhood circle. "John went from stranger to big brother in a matter of days," David remembers.

John had a big grin and a playful spirit and he extended his friendship to anyone in town. During the day, the Owaissa Street kids went their separate ways, attending either the parochial or, like John, the public school nearby. Evenings and weekends were prime time for games and mischief. At least twice a week they gathered to raid a neighbor's yard for apples. "I swear [he] knew we were coming and enjoyed watching our stealth escapades," David says. The gang divided the spoils behind the Hartzheim's house afterward. John led at least one raid a week.

Other nights were more laidback. "John would give us new ideas we had not heard of—technology and science what-ifs he somehow knew a lot about, and other things that were probably utter BS," says David.

Rarely could John not find something fun to do, whether it was hunting, fishing, or doing handstands with his best friend, Bob Woldt, in the middle of an intersection. Bob enlisted in the Navy in 1964. John followed suit in March 1965.[1]

John completed basic training at Naval Training Center San Diego and performed strongly enough to advance to the Naval Air Technical Training Center (NATTC) in Millington, Tennessee. A highly selective and rigorous training school for aviation technicians, the NATTC accepted only the top 5 percent of its applicants. To John Driver it was no surprise that John Harzhiem qualified. "He was a very bright young man," Driver says. "You had to be very bright."

John Driver met John Hartzheim after graduation from NATTC, when John worked under Driver in Sunnyvale, California. Their unit was part of the Military Airlift Command, which was run by the Air Force, but employed many Naval personnel. "We were ahead of the Air Force guys at that time," John Driver explains. "We were closer to being engineers than technicians."

John Driver was the unit's radar chief, and John Hartzheim was one of his avionics technicians at a time when avionics technology was the Navy's number-one priority. Technicians maintained and operated all radar, communications, and navigational equipment. The requirements for such a job were the highest of any position in the Navy. John's happy-go-lucky personality helped keep things lighthearted in the shop despite the seriousness of their work. John managed to be "not overly serious but certainly very capable," remembers Driver.

In February 1967 John began training for a top-secret assignment as a member of Observation Squadron 67. When he completed his training, he joined the squadron at Naval Air Station Alameda in California.

John Hartzheim in his flight suit. John's unit, Observation Squadron 67, performed important intelligence gathering during its short existence. Their work remained classified for decades. Courtesy Vietnam Veterans Memorial Fund.

John and the rest of the squadron departed for Nakhon Phanom Royal Thai Air Force Base in Thailand in November 1967. Before leaving, John returned to Appleton to get married.

Observation Squadron 67 (VO-67) came into existence in February 1967 and was decommissioned in July 1968. It was not publicly recognized for thirty years. Nor were the men allowed to discuss their wartime duties during or after their service. "We were told to keep quiet and not talk about it, or else," remembers Ed Maubach, a member of VO-67. The "67" designated the year of the squadron's inception, but the "observation" term was intentionally misleading, masking their different, highly classified, mission: intelligence gathering over the Ho Chi Minh Trail.

The use of aircraft for intelligence gathering was not new. The Navy had used anti-submarine sonobuoys (acoustic devices capable of detecting, localizing, identifying, and tracking submarines) many times before. The sonobuoys were modified to act as tracking devices on land rather than the sea, and VO-67 was first tasked with releasing this new technology, called acoubuoys. When released, a small parachute opened and ensnared the acoubuoys in the treetops above the trail. The release activated sensors, which worked for approximately forty seconds to record all sounds within roughly thirty feet of the device.[2]

When VO-67 began testing the devices in November 1967, the acoubuoys worked almost too well, picking up the sounds of nearby animals as well as enemy activity. By December, they'd been improved so that they recorded primarily personnel and trucks, which were then targeted by American aircraft nearby. The method was successful, and reduced truck activity along the Ho Chi Minh Trail by an estimated 70 percent.

Before being deployed, VO-67's crews were given extensive training to fly and operate the squadron's twelve P-2E Neptune planes. The twin-engine Neptunes, designed during World War II for antisubmarine patrols, had been heavily modified for VO-67 and fitted with Norden bombsights.[3] The aircraft's original gray and white colors were covered with an innocuous green, camouflaging the planes as they flew low above the jungles along the Ho Chi Minh Trail.

On February 27, 1968, the nine members of Crew 7, including Petty Officer John Hartzheim, departed from Thailand for an intelligence-gathering mission over Kham-mouane Province in Laos. On reaching their assigned target, the underside of their aircraft was hit with an artillery round from 37mm antiaircraft artillery. The artillery passed through the radar well, setting the bomb bay on fire and mortally wounding Petty Officer Hartzheim. As the aircraft filled with smoke, the plane's copilot, Commander Paul Milius, ordered the crew to bail out.[4]

After the aircraft crashed, some crew members thought Commander Milius had jumped as well, but when Crew 7 was rescued, Petty Officer John Hartzheim and Commander Paul Milius were not among them.[5] Both men were listed as missing in action. Commander Milius was 40 years old, with twenty years of military service. Petty Officer Hartzheim was 22.

When VO-67 was decommissioned, the squadron had lost three planes and twenty men, all members of Crews 2 and 5, and two members of Crew 7.[6] For the self-proclaimed band of brothers, the losses were still too high. When the unit was deactivated, the members scattered. They were prohibited from communicating with one another or telling anyone what had happened to their fallen comrades.

John Hartzheim's family was given the news of his death, and little else. "Details on circumstances surrounding Hartzheim's death have not been divulged by the Navy," wrote his hometown newspaper. This remained the status quo for decades. When it finally changed, it changed quickly.

In 1998 Observation Squadron 67 was declassified, and its members permitted to talk about their service and to communicate with each other for the first time in thirty years. The squadron members quickly found one another, and details about the fatal flight of Crew 7 were made known to the public.

On February 19, 1999, John Hartzheim's remains were identified. He was buried in Winneconne, Wisconsin, that August. Once his squadron members detailed the nature and extent of his service, John was awarded the Air Medal with the First Strike/Flight Award. Observation Squadron 67 was awarded the Presidential Unit Citation for the "extraordinary heroism and outstanding performance of duty" of its members during its short lifespan. Although John Hartzheim was not present for the ceremony, his heroism was no less extraordinary.

"He did his duty," says John Driver, "and his family and the state of Wisconsin should be very, very proud of him."

Private First Class
Thomas Joseph Blackman

*United States Marine Corps,
disappeared May 10, 1968*

*"Tom was a quiet and humble person, and the recollection of his kindness
and calm demeanor is still an influence on me today."—Randall Smith*

"He was a very courageous man."—Tim Brown

Someone once told him he looked a bit like Tom Sawyer, without the freckles. They even shared a first name, but quiet, hard-working, and humble, Tom Blackman's personality bore little resemblance to that of the literary Tom. If there were ever an easy path for him to follow, he didn't take it. Tom didn't do things halfway. He pushed himself, not for any external praise, but for an internal sense of accomplishment. He knew how to make the right choice. The hard choice.

The brave choice.

Thomas Joseph Blackman was the second of seven children in the Blackman family. Tom was born in Davenport, Iowa, on February 22, 1949, but the family moved to Wisconsin when he was young. Tom attended St. Catherine's High School, a Catholic school in Racine well known for its athletic program.[1] Tom played tennis for the Angels, but most of his time was devoted to the cross country and track teams. The school's often-crowded locker room was shared among the sports teams, and a portion of the room was reserved exclusively for seniors. Tom's class was particularly strong athletically: The boy's baseball team competed in the state championship their senior year, and their cross country and track runners consistently placed at the top in competitions.

Tom was never the star of the team. He placed—usually between third and sixth—and he lettered in the sport as an underclassman, but the impact he made was not something that could be recorded in newspapers or on score sheets.

"He wasn't somebody with exceptional talent, but he was a person with an exceptionally big heart," Tom's former coach, Bill Greiten, was quoted as saying in 2005[2]:

He was one of these kids who, no matter what you asked him to do, he did. There wasn't a workout that he wouldn't complete. He had a real positive attitude towards country, towards dedication, towards hard work, towards responsibility.... Oh, I can picture him right now. He was one of these silent

114

leaders who you respected as a coach. He was always will-ing to put himself out for everybody else and for the team.

Tom not only challenged himself to be the best that *he* could be, he encouraged other runners to do the same. Randall Smith lived in Tom's neigh-borhood, but he competed on a rival school's track team. Despite being opponents on the field, the boys trained together outside of school. "Tom was faster than me, but I wore him down a couple of times on our longer runs. We were great training partners," he remembers. "We liked to push each other and compare our performances in meets."

Today, the school continues to remember Tom's exceptional drive by offering a cross country and track trophy in his name. It's not awarded every year, but is reserved for the occasions when a runner demonstrates Tom's exceptional commit-ment and dedication.

Tom's drive extended beyond the track field. After his high school graduation, Tom biked to his birthplace of Davenport. He biked alone simply because he wanted to make the trip before starting the next phase of his life.

Tom planned to attend college, but he enlisted

Tom Blackman graduated from St. Catherine's High School in 1967. The school continues to give a cross coun-try and track award in his honor today. Courtesy St. Catherine's High School.

instead in the United States Marine Corps on Sep-tember 12, 1967, hoping to continue his education on the GI Bill after his service. Not for the first time, and not for the last, Tom took the harder route.

Boot camp began on September 18 at Marine Corps Recruiting Depot, San Diego. Within the larger training battalion, Tom was assigned to a platoon of seventy men. He was one of the quieter platoon members, remembers Terry Campbell, who trained alongside him. That was perhaps due in part to Tom's natural disposition and in part due to the intense nature of boot camp.

"Boot camp focused on physical conditioning, two weeks on the range, and classes on history, organization, arms, military code of conduct, [and other military subjects]," Terry recalls. The first few days were the hardest, as everyone accustomed themselves to the rigor and discipline of military life. The most difficult task for the battalion was learning close order drill—marching in total synchronization. "We put in countless hours on the 'grinder,'" he says, "and won first place in our series."

The battalion graduated from boot camp on November 20. Then followed two weeks of infantry training with the Basic Infantry Training Battalion, of the Second Infantry Training Division, at Camp Horno, located at Camp Pendleton, California. The men studied and practiced combat tactics and familiarized themselves with a vari-ety of weapons. "Every Marine is considered a rifleman first and foremost," explains Terry, "though most are assigned to other jobs."

After infantry training, the Marines who had completed recruit training and basic infantry training together parted ways, returning home for Christmas before continuing with advanced training in their military occupational specialty (MOS). Tom's MOS was fire artillery control operating in the Fire Direction Center (FDC) as part of an artillery battery. Following advanced training, he was assigned to Delta Battery, 2nd Battalion, 13th Marines (D/2/13), the artillery battery supporting the 1st Battalion, 27th Marines (1/27), part of the 5th Marine Division. D/2/13 was then performing routine field training exercises in Hawaii. Tom joined the unit only a few days before it shipped out on what team members believed to be a Pacific cruise. It wasn't until they had already departed that they were informed of their real destination: South Vietnam.

In late January 1968 the North Vietnamese launched a series of coordinated attacks on major South Vietnamese cities in what would come to be known as the Tet Offensive. The attacks caught the Americans by surprise.[3] As tours ended and men were lost, the Marines were in dire need of replacements. To make up for some of the losses the 5th Marine Division gave operational control of both 1/27 and the artillery batteries of D/2/13 to the 1st Marine Division.

Tom arrived in South Vietnam on February 28, 1968, six days after his nineteenth birthday. The unit was temporarily stationed at a base just south of the major city of Danang. In April D/2/13 transferred to Kham Duc, a Special Forces base near the Laotian border and the last standing border-surveillance camp in I Corps.[4] The unit waited on the airstrip for several hours on the day of their departure for Kham Duc. There was a chapel on the airstrip. Tom and another unit member, Tim Brown, took advantage of the idle time by attending a Catholic mass, going to confession, and receiving Communion before their flight.

Kham Duc turned out to be another temporary stop for D/2/13. Within days Delta Battery's X-Ray Detachment, consisting of about forty Marines, was sent roughly four miles away to a former French outpost called Ngok Tavak.[5] They brought with them two of Delta Battery's six 105mm howitzers. Additional Marines, including Tom, made their way to Ngok Tavak on May 4.

Ngok Tavak was an encampment set atop a hill, named after a nearby mountain. Built by the French in the 1950s, Ngok Tavak had been manned inconsistently since 1963. The outpost was roughly the size of a football field and was nearly engulfed by the surrounding jungle. Australian Captain John White commanded Ngok Tavak, and under his authority were several members of the Australian Army Training Team Vietnam (AATTV) and about one hundred twenty Nungs.[6]

Approximately 20 to 30 members of the Civilian Irregular Defense Group (CIDG), U.S.-trained South Vietnamese forces, were also stationed at the outpost. The Marines' arrival in early May brought Ngok Tavak's total defense to 210 men.[7]

The outpost was located near Route 14. More a jungle trail than a road, Route 14 ran north and south near the outpost. Traveling north led to Kham Duc, and local North Vietnamese Army units had been cutting through the jungle for months to connect with the route. Captain White and his forces regularly patrolled the area, and the Delta Battery Marines were sent to provide artillery support with two 105mm howitzers.

An artillery team has three components: forward observers, cannoneers, and FDC, Tom's MOS. To successfully complete a fire mission required the coordinated efforts of all three components. The forward observers searched for targets and radioed specific target coordinates back to the FDC team. The FDC team converted the coordinates into settings for elevation, direction, and explosive charge for the howitzers. The cannoneers altered their weapons accordingly and fired artillery rounds on the target.

The howitzers were powerful, indirect fire artillery weapons if used under the right circumstances. A small hill, where any conflict would likely be close and would require short-range weapons, was not the proper place for a gun designed to fire at targets several miles away. Many in the unit felt the howitzers' presence on the hill was a tactical mistake.

In addition to the artillery, resupply issues plagued the Marines. The nearest road was unusable. The hill was steep, making it difficult for large sup-

The hill of Ngok Tavak, circa May 1968. The block on the right is the landing zone and the rectangle on the left is the former French fort, estimated to be the size of a football field. The entire encampment is engulfed in triple canopy jungle. Courtesy Bob Adams.

plies to travel upward, but relying too heavily on the nearby airstrip could alert the NVA regulars of a troop deployment in the area. There was also a problem of support. A report made in early May predicted that, if attacked, the soonest reinforcements could reach them in their isolated location would be 2 and a half hours.

The NVA 2nd Division, however, was already aware that the outpost was in use again. NVA units had been working for several months to clear a path to Route 14. To gain full control of the strategic supply route, they needed to travel north, attack, and overpower Kham Duc. This placed Ngok Tavak directly in the line of fire. U.S. intelligence was monitoring the position of the NVA 2nd Division and believed an attack on Kham Duc to be in the works.[8]

The attack came just before 3:00 a.m. on May 10, 1968, from a reinforced battalion of between 500 and 600 North Vietnamese.[9] Many of the 210 defenders at Ngok Tavak awoke to the sounds of gunfire. One sleeping Marine, Private Charles Reeder, was awakened by Tom Blackman, alerting him to the attack. The two Marines, along with Private Barry Hempel, made their way out of their bunker and toward the perimeter.

Tom's MOS was fire directional control, but every Marine is a rifleman. Amid a

storm of grenades and enemy fire, Tom grabbed
his M-16 rifle and ran to the berm at the edge
of the outpost. Rather than firing from behind
it, Tom stood upright and fired over the protective barrier, delivering, in the words of one witness, "a devastating accurate fire upon the
enemy." Private Thomas Blackman held the
position for roughly thirty minutes before he
was hit.

Eleven Marines, including Tom, and one
Army Special Forces officer were killed at Ngok
Tavak. As the fighting continued, the survivors
made an arduous, but mostly successful evacuation from the outpost, although one Special
Forces medic was lost along the way.[10] Unfortu-
nately, they had no choice but to leave behind
those who had fallen during the battle. After the
evacuation Americans bombed the hill, and the
North Vietnamese overran Kham Duc. Because
their bodies could not be recovered, the American servicemen were classified as missing in
action.

For the families, this indicated a possibility
their loved ones could still be alive. Adding to
this belief was a false version of the events at

In school and in the Marines, Private
Thomas Blackman was known for his
dedication and humility. Courtesy
Nancy Konkol.

Ngok Tavak that persist to this day. Survivors of Ngok Tavak took it upon themselves
to make the truth known. More than that, though, many returned to the hill and recovered the bodies of those killed that morning.[11] The remains of the eleven Marines and
one Special Forces soldier killed on the hill were recovered, and five were positively
identified and given private burials. 19-year-old Private Thomas Blackman was among
the seven buried in a group grave in Arlington National Cemetery in 2005. His family
received his dog tags and gained closure.

According to a witness statement made three days after the attack on Ngok Tavak,
Tom's charge at the berm was a "definitive factor" in the defense of the perimeter. The
witness continues, saying "Through his example of great personal courage, he provided
us with the determination to hold our position." Tom Blackman was posthumously
awarded a Silver Star for his actions on May 10, the third-highest medal of valor given
in the United States Armed Forces.

Lance Corporal
Raymond Thomas Heyne

United States Marine Corps, disappeared May 10, 1968

"His sense of humor.... I don't know how to put it into words. He would just be funny saying ordinary things."—Tim Brown

"He was very quiet. He loved being on machines. He liked his bike. He was a quiet person."—Janice (Heyne) Kostello

In Arlington, Virginia, row after row of white marble gravestones line the green grass cemetery. It is the final resting place of more than four hundred thousand servicemen and -women and their families, who have made great sacrifices for their country since the Civil War. Arlington National Cemetery is massive, covering 624 acres near Washington, D.C. On a hill overlooking the city stands the Tomb of the Unknown Soldier, a tribute to all the dead whose bodies have never been recovered. For decades, the twelve men lost at the small outpost at Ngok Tavak on May 10, 1968, were among those it represented. That changed in October 2005, when remains of the men were found and returned to the United States for burial. Now, in Section 60, stands a monument with the names of those eleven Marines and one Army Special Forces soldier.

The remains of seven are buried beneath the monument. Unable to be identified by DNA, they were buried together. Four of the five whose remains could be positively identified were buried in their hometowns.

For the fifth, there is an additional, smaller grave at Arlington. Raymond Heyne had been with those men for thirty-seven years. His two living sisters and their families decided he should remain with them. His remains are buried beside the larger monument, giving him the honor of burial at Arlington National Cemetery.

Raymond Heyne was born July 15, 1947. After losing his parents at a young age, he was cared for by his grandmother, Mary Heyne, with the help of his sisters, Fay, Janice, Sonya, and Dawn. He later lived with Janice on a 344-acre dairy farm near Benoit, Wisconsin. He loved being on the farm, and Janice and her husband, John, loved having him there. They also appreciated his help with the many farm chores. He later moved to South St. Paul, Minnesota, to experience city life with Sonya and her family, then returned to the farm to attend high school.

Raymond was called "Butch" by his family, but went by his preferred nickname of Ray in school. He attended Ondossagon High School in the town of Barksdale, about seventeen miles from the farm. Ray rode the school bus every day and enjoyed the ride as it meant time with his girlfriend, Karen. Ray was a good student, particularly enjoying several carpentry classes. He also discovered another passion: the United States Marine Corps.

Officers came to the school on occasion to speak about the service, and Ray's interest was piqued immediately. "Before he even graduated he was talking about the Marine Corps," Janice says. Ray didn't change his mind after graduation. Janice and John half-heartedly supported him when he enlisted in 1966.

Following training, Ray and several other Marines were given orders aboard the USS *Shadwell* (LSD-15).[1] Named after Thomas Jefferson's birthplace, the *Shadwell* was commissioned on June 24, 1944, survived a Japanese torpedo six months later, and returned to fight in the Pacific before decommissioning in 1947. Returning to action in 1950, the ship made several voyages to the Arctic Circle and, in 1959, became the first dock landing ship capable of transporting helicopters. In March 1967, with Ray on board,[2] the *Shadwell* began its eighth deployment to the Mediterranean. The ship made numerous stops in Italy and surrounding countries, giving Ray the opportunity to see a bit of the world. "He liked the Marines a lot," says Janice. He wrote often; not a week went by when she didn't receive a letter.

The *Shadwell* returned to the United States later that year, and Ray took his leave at home before joining a new unit: Delta Battery, 2nd Battalion, 13th Marines (D/2/13) in Hawaii. The artillery battery would soon be called on to support the 1st Battalion, 27th Marines, which was forming and training at Camp Pendleton, California. Both were part of the 5th Marine Division, which was being reactivated in response to the Marine Corps's growing commitment in the Vietnam War.[3] Delta Battery was performing routine training drills in Hawaii when Ray joined. The training increased in January after the unit was informed that it would shortly be departing for a cruise to the Philippines, Okinawa, and Japan. They departed Hawaii in mid–February. Several days into the cruise, the unit learned its destination was South Vietnam. While Ray had been overseas before, he had never been in Southeast Asia. For some in Delta for whom this would be their second tour in Vietnam, the news came as an unpleasant surprise.

The Marines arrived first at a base just south of Danang. In early April they were sent southeast to a Special Forces base at Kham Duc, but this did not become their permanent base either. Less than a month after arriving at Kham Duc, the X-ray Detachment of the Battery, roughly forty men and two 105mm howitzers, was sent about four miles away, to an old French outpost called Ngok Tavak. Ray Heyne joined them at the outpost on May 4.

The outpost was located in an isolated area near the Laotian border. The outpost's commander, Australian Captain John White, and his forces frequently patrolled the nearby Route 14, running north and south parallel to the Laotian border. Traveling north on the road led to Kham Duc. A primary purpose of Captain White's patrols was to determine if the NVA was looking to connect with the route and, if so, which way it wanted to travel along it. Delta Battery was providing fire support for the patrols in early May. As an artillery unit, operating the 105mm howitzers was the Marines' main purpose at the outpost.

The Marines first set up the howitzers in a triangle along Route 14. Ray worked as part of a team that operated the guns. The gun crew consisted of "powder monkeys," who put the shells together; loaders, who pushed the shell into the breech; and gunners, who fired the gun. Ray could have held any of these jobs, all of which were vital to putting rounds down range and on target. "Work was extremely hard," says Joe Jackson, who spent time as an artillery crewman with Echo 2/13, another 105mm battery. "Lots of shells to move around. Tension was high during missions because you knew guys were depending on you. Speed and accuracy mattered extremely."

Growing up on the farm, Ray knew how to work hard and loved operating machinery. His work in Vietnam suited him. He was quiet, remembers Tim Brown, a D/2/13 Marine stationed at Ngok Tavak. "I wouldn't say shy, but reserved.... He was a typical farm boy." Of both Ray and Tom Blackman, also from Wisconsin, Tim states, "They were playful sort of guys when it was time to be playful and deadly serious when it was time to be Marines."

Conditions were serious in May 1968. The 2nd NVA Division's patrols along Route 14 were on the increase. Captain White decided to move the guns away from the road and to the fort atop of the hill nearer the main encampment.[4] Ngok Tavak was steep, covered by the thick jungle canopy, and each howitzer had to be transported separately so one would always be operational.

"We thought we would tie it to a truck, but that didn't work," says Bob Adams, Delta Battery's executive officer. "We had to take it apart completely." The Marines disassembled the massive guns and pushed them up into the fort. Transporting the howitzers inch-by-inch up the hill one at a time was a long, arduous task, but both were operating again by May 9. "Not that it did any good," adds Bob.

Tim Brown elaborates:

> You have to understand, artillery is designed to be used to fire at targets 2, 3, 4, 5 miles out from where you are. We were dropped into this rugged mountain range, where the only effective fire was high-angle fire, like the mortar. You shoot way high and it comes down close. Putting that type of artillery ... it was a mistake.

The howitzers were heavy artillery and powerful weapons. However, the rugged terrain and steep hills surrounding Ngok Tavak made the howitzers unsuitable for that kind of environment. The Marines worked with what they had.

The Marines had been on the outpost less than two weeks when a reinforced regiment from the 2nd North Vietnamese Division attacked Ngok Tavak. The attack began just after 3:00 a.m. on May 10, 1968. The Marines and Captain John White's 11th Company of Australians, U.S. Special Forces, South Vietnamese, and Nungs[5] combined for a defense of 210 men against an estimated force of 500 to 600 North Vietnamese. The battle raged for nine hours. Amid the chaos, Raymond Heyne was shot and killed. He was just shy of his twenty-first birthday.

Over an hour into the battle, a gunship arrived to provide air support. This helped end the main assault, and the main NVA force continued north toward Kham Duc.[6] Captain White was assured reinforcements were coming, but his remaining men were

Both photographs: Ray Heyne knew he wanted to join the Marines even before he graduated from high school. He loved the travel involved and wrote home often. Courtesy the Virtual Vietnam Memorial Fund.

still faced with incoming grenades and sporadic gunfire. Medevac helicopters evacuated thirteen of the wounded, but two helicopters were shot down during the Medevac operation. Captain White decided to take no chances: They needed to get off the hill and they needed to take with them as much valuable equipment as they could to prevent it from falling into enemy hands.[7]

They could not, however, bring out their dead. Before evacuating the outpost, the Marines gathered some of the bodies and placed them behind Captain John White's bunker; others were left where they died. Eleven Marines and one Army Special Forces sergeant were killed in the battle. One Special Forces medic was lost in the escape.[8]

In the following years all the men would be listed as missing in action. Many of the relatives were given a false account of what occurred on May 10. What's more, the story left open the possibility that the Marines and Special Forces soldier were still alive. The survivors of Ngok Tavak knew the truth: The men had died valiantly on the hill. That they remained there was a constant source of distress to those who had escaped.

"When you're in a situation like that you have to depend on others for your very survival and one of your basic fears is being left behind," says Tim Brown. "You not only have this code of conduct ingrained in you in the Marine Corps, but you have the knowledge that, for the sake of each other, for your wives and parents and girlfriends, we're gonna get you home."

Efforts to remedy the situation began with Tim Brown, who first heard the false story several years after the battle. Tim, who had been evacuated before the attack due to pneumonia, dedicated himself to locating and bringing back the men still at Ngok Tavak.

He began his work in the 1970s by locating families and providing them with accurate information. He organized a team of veterans, and they discussed the possibility of locating the missing men. Tim brought the issue to the attention of the Vietnam Veterans of America (VVA), and they negotiated with the Vietnamese government to return to the hill. "It was very bureaucratic," Tim Brown says, as he recalls the process. "Everything there had to go from the central government, to the province, to the district." Additionally, Ngok Tavak was closed off, littered with unexploded mines and ordnance, as well as the natural dangers such as snakes. In 1994, though, Tim and a team of others traveled to Ngok Tavak.

The hill, they found, had been largely untouched in the decades since the battle. It was overgrown, covered by jungle, but nearly everything was left just as it had been on May 10, 1968. The hood of the truck the Marines had used to try hauling the howitzers up the hill was still there, "USMC" clearly visible directly beneath an unexploded mortar round sitting atop it.

The conditions at Ngok Tavak provided a convincing argument that the bodies of the fallen men could be recovered, and the VVA set to work organizing a larger team for a return trip in 1995, including, among others, Delta's executive officer, Bob Adams, and Captain John White. The Americans and Australians met with the commanding officers of the North Vietnamese forces they had fought in 1968. The two sides walked through the battlefield, exchanging battle notes and memories, while being monitored closely by officials from the American and Vietnamese governments. Perhaps most

The Ngok Tavak monument (right) and Raymond Heyne's grave marker (left) at Arlington National Cemetery. The names of all the individuals killed during the battle at Ngok Tavak are on the group memorial, and all unidentified remains are buried beneath it. Ray Heyne's identified remains are buried beneath his grave marker. Photograph by the author.

important, the North Vietnamese told the Americans that they had not removed any bodies. "There was a reasonably good chance that some of the remains could be identified and recovered," says Tim. At that point, the VVA began to pressure the U.S. government to recover the fallen men.

The recovery began in 1998. Veterans from the battle supplied hand-drawn maps and directions to aid the Joint POW/MIA Accounting Command in their search. The excavation was very thorough and continued into 1999.

The families and Ngok Tavak survivors did not learn of the results until 2004: The excavation had been successful. The dig had uncovered enough evidence—bones, dog tags, wallets—to identify all eleven missing Marines and the one Army Special Forces soldier.[9] DNA positively identified five men, including Ray Heyne.[10] The twelve men made up the largest single group of MIAs recovered since the war had ended.

Across the country, four families buried their boys in local cemeteries: Donald Mitchell, Thomas Fritsch, Gerald King, and Joseph Cook had also been definitively identified by DNA. In October 2005 all unidentified remains were buried beneath a memorial that bore the names of each of the twelve men lost at Ngok Tavak.

Raymond Heyne's identified remains were buried beside the memorial gravesite.

"We don't leave our men behind. Period," says Tim Brown. "Sometimes you can't do it right away. For us it took thirty-seven years, but no one ever forgot them. In the end, we succeeded in bringing them home."

Sergeant Paul Reid Frazier

United States Army,
disappeared September 3, 1968

"Paul Frazier was just one of those very steady, very dedicated, very focused, hard-working patriotic guys. He never complained. He did the job and he did it beautifully. His aircraft was always impeccable. He was above reproach."—Victor Milford

"This guy was always a pro."—John Falcon

"He was just business. He wasn't trying to control your life or anything. I don't remember him ever telling me what I had to do. Unless there was a reason, like flight schedule or platoon meetings, he wasn't going to mess with you."—August Kraemer

In military slang, STRAC stands for "Strategic, Tough, and Ready Around the Clock." "Real shiny, real straight," explains John Falcon. "Uniform was clean, shined his boots. Commands his men very professionally." It's high praise and the sign of a well-respected leader. For the men of the 191st Assault Helicopter Company, it was one way to describe Assistant Platoon Sergeant Paul Frazier.

Born March 11, 1949, Paul grew up in Milwaukee, the fourth of Myron and Donna Frazier's five children. He attended Custer High School, where students fell into one of two main groups: the "collegiates," who were more studious students, and "the hoods," whose main interests were along the lines of parties, dancing, and girls. Paul fell into the latter category.[1]

While Paul was still in high school, his older brother, Myron, enlisted in the United States Army. Paul followed on June 13, 1966, while only 17 years old. He completed basic and advanced training, then attended further training in helicopter maintenance.

Some soldiers trained exclusively as helicopter repairmen. It was an important job; one hour of flight in Southeast Asia was often followed by two to four hours of repairs. Other soldiers trained as crew chiefs. Although crew chiefs were trained to fix minor repairs, they differed from repairmen in that repairmen remained on the ground, while crew chiefs took part in aerial operations and were responsible for what happened in the aircraft while it was airborne. Paul Frazier was a crew chief, and while most crew chiefs were specialists, Paul was a sergeant.

After earning his Wings as a crew chief, Paul was assigned to the 135th Assault Helicopter Company (AHC), stationed at Robert Gray Army Airfield at Fort Hood, Texas. There, he met Robert Walker and Joe Clancy. "The three of us were the best of friends," remembers Robert.

The 135th AHC attended lectures and gained classroom knowledge at Fort Hood, but were also given more hands-on experience in the helicopter. "We probably did about one hundred hours of flying time," says August Kraemer, another member of the 135th. "Sometimes, we went to a range at Fort Hood where they had the big armor divisions so you could hear them firing their weapons."

They were also put in the odd position of being on call for a brief time during their training. From June 5 through 10, 1967 the unit was prepared to deploy if needed as the Six-Day War unfolded in the Middle East. In the end, nothing came of it; indeed, some members did not know they had been put on notice at all.

Their training was nearing an end. "We were forming a company there," explains Robert. "We were training to work together as an aviation company."

The entire company deployed to Vietnam together. Paul's first day in-country was October 2, 1967. Coincidentally, Myron Frazier's first tour ended at the same time. "I believe that our planes passed one another," he says. "Me, on the way home; him, just arriving."

On reaching their destination, some men found they had been selected for an infusion program and would be transferred to another unit. This program assigned men who were new in-country and placed them with an established company to avoid a situation where an entire company's enlistments ran out at the same time. Those infused were chosen randomly and were not all sent over at the same time. By chance, Robert, Joe, and Paul all joined the 191st Assault Helicopter Company at Bearcat Base, South Vietnam, outside Saigon.

The 191st had not been in Vietnam much longer than Paul. In fact, so new was the unit that its first members were charged with helping build the base. It was an ongoing project. They had constructed the mess hall, but when Paul, Robert, and Joe arrived at Bearcat, the men were still living in tents. Over the course of their enlistment, however, a set of ventilated two-story barracks were constructed. There were no windows, but the walls kept everything a bit cleaner when compared to their life in the tents.

In the center of the base ran a long airstrip. The helicopters operated by the 191st were flown in support of the 9th Infantry Division, which was also headquartered at Bearcat. The 191st had about twenty-one "slicks" (troop-carrying helicopters) and eight gunships. Four gunships, called lead ships, were armed with rocket pods on both sides and a grenade-launching cannon. The other four helicopters—wing ships—had smaller rocket pods and mini guns for protection. A typical 191st mission involved insertions or extractions of members of the 9th Infantry and nearby South Vietnamese soldiers. During missions, two gunships escorted slicks and then remained nearby for protection. Paul most often flew as the crew chief on a lead gunship, but could also serve as door gunner.

The unit was required to send up one lead ship, ten slicks, and four gunships a day, says Jerry Kahn of the 191st. They usually managed to do so. "We had a proud tradition of always having our ships ready and up no matter how badly we were shot up." And there were days when they were shot up badly. He remembers starting a day with fifteen helicopters and ending with only one operational. The ships often required lengthy repairs after missions, but the 191st's ships were nicknamed the Boomerangs—they always came back.

"Gunships and flight teams were volunteers as long as they could be," says August Kraemer, who was also infused to the 191st from the 135th. "We eventually had a shortage of people who wanted to fly because we had so many casualties."

"It was getting so bad—we were flying so much—we had no days off," adds Robert. "Christmas Day was the only scheduled day off.... They were supposed to let us stay down on Thanksgiving, but we ended up getting called into combat."

The men of the 191st had very little downtime while on base, so when an opportunity for an R&R to Bangkok was offered, Paul, Robert, and Joe jumped at the chance. Men were allowed one leave during their tour. The three friends had already chosen their preferred R&R destinations elsewhere, but they were told that the plane leaving for Bangkok had empty seats that needed to be filled, and they could take the trip in addition to the one they had previously selected. They found out later that the rules had changed and Bangkok would be their only R&R.

It was a five-day reprieve from the war, a three-hour flight there and back, and three full days off, but they couldn't escape entirely. Their R&R began at the end of January 1968, just as the North Vietnamese launched the Tet Offensive, a series of massive, coordinated strikes on major South Vietnamese cities throughout the country, including Saigon. Paul, Joe, and Robert watched the start of the Tet Offensive on a television in the Bangkok airport, and wondered if they would be able to reenter Vietnam. The airport to Saigon had closed. If it didn't reopen, they wondered how they would be able to afford to stay in Bangkok any longer than they had planned.

They didn't dwell on those problems. Bangkok was huge, loud, and busy, and the men had plenty to do. They initially planned a bus trip to the Bridge over the River Kwai, but the trip would have taken an entire day. Rather than waste a day on a bus, they just hung out in Bangkok. They saw a movie and they drank beer that wasn't good, but was cold, a luxury they didn't often have on base.

The day of their scheduled return was the day Saigon's airport reopened so the three returned to Vietnam without any trouble. The trouble, of course, was *in* Vietnam. The Tet Offensive was raging, and American servicemen across the country were busier than ever. "Our platoon was very reactive," says Jerry Kahn. Saigon was only one of several nearby cities under attack, and the unit supported many of the locations affected by the Tet Offensive.

In addition to his role as a crew chief, Paul was the assistant platoon sergeant. He was responsible for his helicopter crew during operations and for ensuring that all platoon members carried out their orders. "If we were busy," Jerry says, "he was very, very busy."

Paul was good at his job. *All* his jobs. "You could ask him to do something, and he'd do it," remembers Clifford Walls, his platoon sergeant. "You'd never have to go back and check it." He took his role seriously, and the men respected him for it. August Kraemer remembers that he wasn't the type of leader to yell at his men or badger them needlessly; the unit performed well too, and he knew it. As long as they did their work, he left them alone. He led by example.

The 191st weathered the Tet Offensive. For those who had transferred from the 135th, their tours were nearly up in the fall of 1968. Most men stopped flying about ten days before they were scheduled to go home; for Paul, that would have meant the end of September.

Paul volunteered for the mission on September 3, 1968, flying as the crew chief in the lead gunship in support of a combat operation near Rach Kein, south of Saigon. Before he left, Paul stopped by Robert's room to borrow a uniform shirt; none of his were clean.

The ship's pilot that morning was Captain David Burch.[2] Warrant Officer Ronald Cederlund[3] was the copilot, and Specialist Fourth Class Ed Davis completed the crew as the door gunner.

Paul in front of one the 191st Assault Helicopter Company's helicopters in Vietnam. As a crew chief, he was responsible for the helicopter crew during operations. Courtesy Jeff "Doc" Dentice.

Weeks later, in the Burns Ward at a hospital in San Antonio, Ed Davis told recently discharged Victor Milford, another member of the 191st, what happened on that mission. Victor recounts the conversation:

> Ed said, "We had Charlie. They were in spider holes, and we were trying to root them out. I was laying down on a spider hole, and my gun jams. I'm trying to clear the jam and I look up briefly to see the Charlie come out with an Alaska-47. He fired."

The first shot killed the pilot, Captain Burch, and sent the helicopter crashing. It hit the ground and rolled on its left side, where Paul would have been standing directly above the helicopter's large rocket pods. Each pod contained between twenty and thirty rockets. The rockets exploded.

A search-and-rescue team arrived at the scene within eight hours. Robert Walker was on the team. Of the four men, only Ed Davis survived, severely burned.[4] Of the three killed, two bodies were recovered and identified. Nineteen-year-old Paul Frazier was listed as missing in action.

Today, the crash site has been turned into a lake. As Myron Frazier points out, Paul will remain MIA.

"He was just a kid," Robert reflects. "He was a good guy."

Jerry agrees. "He was a very good man."

"Wisconsin lost a wonderful guy," says Victor. "America lost a super guy."

Captain Paul David Derby

United States Marine Corps,
disappeared November 17, 1968

"I can't put him in a few words.... It would not be an easy thing to do."—
Dorothy Derby Franczyk

Dorothy Derby Franczyk keeps a beautiful scrapbook. In alternating pages of red and blue, in pictures and letters, in certificates and telegrams, the book tells the story of Paul Derby, the man she married before college graduation, and the man whose memorial she attended three years later.

A picture of Captain Paul David Derby fills the first page. He wears his dress uniform, his Wings of Gold pinned to his chest.[1] But before he was a captain with Marine Fighter-Attack Squadron 115, he was the oldest of Charles and Ramona Derby's four children. Born in Green Bay, Wisconsin, on January 4, 1943, Paul graduated from Columbus Catholic High School in 1961 and attended Stout State College,[2] where he studied industrial technology.

Paul was president of the Stout Society of Industrial Technology and was also active in the Chi Lambda fraternity. During the school's annual winter carnival, Chi Lambda competed in what can only be described as "bumper cars on ice" on nearby Lake Menomin. They took an old car, donated by one of the members, decorated it in the fraternity's colors, and raced it against other campus fraternities across the frozen lake. Paul had driven stock cars before, so thought he would make a good candidate to drive during the competition in 1963, but the Chi Lambda president claimed the right that year. "Some of the guys were mad," Dorothy remembers with a laugh. "And Paul was one of those guys."

She and Paul were dating by then, although their first date hadn't gone as planned. Actually, it hadn't gone at all. Paul and Dorothy were introduced by mutual friends in his fraternity and her sorority. They planned their first date for Saturday, November 23, 1963. The Friday before, though, President John F. Kennedy had been assassinated in Dallas. In shock, most of the campus returned home that weekend, Dorothy included. "He always teased me about breaking our first date," Dorothy says. They rescheduled, and the relationship progressed quickly after that.

Paul was already on his way to becoming a Marine officer when he met Dorothy.

He'd spent the summer of 1963 at Quantico, Virginia, at Officer Training School, and would spend the subsequent summer of 1964 there as well. Dorothy can tell when a photo was taken by the length of Paul's hair: wavy in the months away from Quantico, short just after his return from training.

When Paul and Dorothy returned to Stout in the fall of 1964 for their senior year, they had plans to marry soon after graduation. Those plans changed fast. They had spent enough time apart, and they married during winter break.

Come graduation, it was Paul's wife and mother who pinned his bars onto his uniform. Images of Paul's commissioning in the United State Marine Corps fill several pages of Dorothy's scrapbook. The lighting is dim in some of the photos; when the family chose a room at random in the Student Union to prepare for the ceremony, they hadn't realized it was also the room in which the ceremony would take place. Paul was the only man commissioned that day at Stout State College in 1965.

That summer the couple moved to Pensacola, Florida, as Paul began his pre-flight training. The house they rented was owned by a large family who ran a furniture store, so the house was spacious and well furnished. It was more than enough for a young couple expecting a baby. The house was so large, in fact, that they briefly shared it with another family, on Paul's invitation. Not long after they arrived in Pensacola, Paul returned from training with a classmate, his wife, and their infant daughter. Like the Derby's, they had come from Wisconsin, but unlike Paul and Dorothy they had not yet found a house. "Stay with us," Paul said. "He was always bringing people home," Dorothy remembers. "Meeting people was not a problem, ever."

The first page of Dorothy's scrapbook, memorializing her husband, Captain Paul Derby. Courtesy Dorothy Franczyk.

The next few pages of Dorothy's scrapbook are filled with certificates of achievement. Most are for Paul, but there is one for her as well. Shortly after arriving in Pensacola, the commanding officer's wife invited the wives of all the new arrivals to her home for brunch and conversation. She sent them home with a certificate for successful completion of the "Wives' Indoctrination Tour."

Around the same time, Paul received his pre-flight training certificate. He completed his first solo flight on February 8, 1966, although the landing, he admitted to Dorothy, was a little bumpy.

They left Pensacola briefly and rented an apartment in Meridian, Mississippi, where Paul began jet training, then returned to Pensacola for carrier qualification—taking off and landing on an ocean aircraft carrier. Pilots jokingly referred to ships as "postage stamps" because of the limited space they provided for takeoffs and landings. It was certainly one of the more difficult requirements, but Paul successfully completed his "postage stamp" qualification on August 15, 1966.

After Pensacola and carriers came Kingsville, Texas, and advanced jet training. It was there that Paul qualified as an official Marine Corps aviator. The certificate documenting this achievement, dated February 17, 1967, is among those in Dorothy's scrapbook. She has no pictures of the event, though. Paul simply came home one day with his Naval Aviator Wings of Gold pinned to his chest. A similar situation would occur several months later when Paul was promoted to captain. That day, he planned to surprise Dorothy with the news, but she had already received a call informing her of his promotion. Instead, she and their son, Scott, surprised Paul by waiting eagerly in their driveway to congratulate him.

After Paul earned his wings, the Derbys returned to Wisconsin to visit family. Also on leave was Paul's younger brother, Chuck, who enlisted in the Air Force after his high school graduation and would soon report for duty with the 6417th Combat Support Group in Taiwan. The family had a military history. Their father, Charles Sr., was a sergeant in World War II.[3] Their mother placed the two Derby brothers side-by-side, each in his dress uniform, and took their photo. It's in Dorothy's book.[4]

After their visit, Paul, Dorothy, and Scott moved to Marine Corps Air Station Cherry Point, North Carolina, where they would remain until Paul left for Vietnam. There, Paul completed the Survival, Evasion, Resistance, and Escape (SERE) School, a survival exercise on land and sea that lasted several days and ended in a mock prisoner of war camp. The assumption was that a good Marine would function best when prepared for the worst. Paul completed this rigorous exercise on July 13, 1967.

At Cherry Point, Paul liked to wake early and watch the morning colors ceremony each day. Dorothy and Scott often rose with him, and together they would walk to the base flagpole to hear the Base Band play the National Anthem and watch the Color Detail raise the National Flag. "He loved the Marine Corps, that's for sure," Dorothy says. "I don't think he wanted to be anywhere else." She adds, though, "He had hoped he could fly for the British Royal Air Force someday." He'd told her that just before he left for Vietnam in July 1968. Dorothy, Scott, and their infant daughter, Pam, returned to Wisconsin.

The following pages in her scrapbook are filled with photos, most taken by Paul. Paul's unit, Marine Fighter Attack Squadron 115 (VMFA-115), nicknamed "the Silver Eagles," was stationed at Chu Lai, South Vietnam. He sent home pictures of his hooch (a large, metallic structure with a rounded roof and two wooden doors and surrounded by sandbags), his room (a small, cluttered space with a bed just out of sight of the camera), and his view from his front door (sand, sandbags, distant mountains). There is a picture of his squadron lined up in front of a McDonnell Douglas F-4 Phantom. Paul stands just beneath the star on the plane's wing. Another photo is a close-up of Paul and other flight crew members. There are many copies of this photo (two in Dorothy's scrapbook alone), and the men signed them all, brief messages, scrawled across their uniforms and the plane, wishing the others luck.

There are more pictures; the men loved to take photos of themselves and each other in their planes. She has one such photo of Paul, out of sight in the cockpit, thousands of feet above the ground. That was what it was about for him, Dorothy says. Paul loved to fly. He was "always cutting out pictures of planes and building models." Paul flew more than one hundred missions out of Chu Lai.

Captain Paul Derby was flying a close air support mission[5] over Quảng Ngãi province on November 17, 1968, when his plane was hit by antiaircraft artillery. After a week of searching, the body of 1st Lieutenant Thomas A. Reich, also in the plane, was found, but Paul was not.

Charles "Chuck" and Paul Derby, early 1967, posing in their uniforms at their mother's request. Chuck enlisted in the Air Force in September 1966. He was killed in a car crash while stationed in Germany in 1983. Courtesy Dorothy Franczyk, digitized by Jerry D. Swanson.

Dorothy called off the search. She did not want daily phone calls from officers, telling her that nothing had changed, nor did she want anyone hurt searching in a hostile area. "If we can't have all of Paul," she decided. "I don't need what they could give me."

In Dorothy's scrapbook is the telegram informing her of Paul's death. The next pages contain newspaper articles and the obituary. She has a copy of the sermon that was read at the memorial and a letter from Paul's college recruiting officer, offering condolences and advice. There are pictures of Paul's grave marker, placed in 1969 at Rock Island National Cemetery, Illinois. One of the pictures shows just the kids at the marker: Paul's son, Scott, kneeling on the left, Paul's daughter, Pam, kneeling on the right, and Cheryl, Dorothy's daughter from her second marriage, standing behind the marker with her hands placed protectively atop it.

Paul's name is inscribed on the Vietnam Veterans Memorial Wall: panel 39W, line 007. He is also memorialized in the Courts of the Missing, Court A, in the Honolulu Memorial.[6] A memorial stone at the Veteran's Memorial in Reedsburg, Wisconsin, bears Paul's name. A stone in his honor was place at the Highground Veterans Memorial in Neillsville, Wisconsin, next to similar memorials to his father and his brother.

The Neillsville memorial also has a sculpture, titled "Fragments," dedicated exclusively to Wisconsin's Vietnam servicemen. On the back of the sculpture are bronze wind chimes, each bearing the name of a man lost during the war. The names are not meant to be read individually, but spoken collectively as the wind blows. When Dorothy's family visited, though, the first name they saw was Paul Derby.

Paul was 25 years old when he died. He was a son, a brother, a husband, a father, a pilot, and a Marine. The scrapbook pages commemorating the years of his life that he spent flying are filled with tremendous accomplishments and wonderful memories. It's a short book, but it's beautiful.

1969–1973

Captain Edwin James Fickler
*United States Marine Corps,
disappeared January 17, 1969*

*"He was a guy that everybody liked. He was a good pilot and a good stu-
dent. And I know that he longed to become a pilot, and he did."—Bob
Nelson*

*"I can still picture him with that infectious grin of his.... A nice guy; very
friendly."—John Hawkins*

*"I considered Jim a friend of mine, and he made the United States and
the Marine Corps proud."—Arnold Husser*

If you want something, you've got to work for it. That was Jim Fickler's motto, and
he lived it. He dreamed big and worked hard, and nowhere is this more evident than
in his drive to become a Marine aviator. An ambitious goal for any Marine, Jim had his
own set of unique challenges to overcome. Surprising no one who knew him, Jim con-
quered them all.

Jim, Jimmy, Fick—he had several nicknames, but few called him Edwin, the name
he shared with both his father and grandfather. Edwin James Fickler was born May 4,
1943, the second of four Fickler children, two boys and two girls. He grew up in West
Bend, Wisconsin, then Kewaskum, Wisconsin, on the east side of the Milwaukee River.
Jim spent much of his time outdoors, building rafts or fishing.

As a kid Jim was "top dog among his peers," remembers an elementary school classmate, Frank Schoenbeck. This statement was true for Jim throughout much of his life.
He participated in a variety of activities at Kewaskum High School. He was a member
of the drama club, Spanish club, and operetta, took part in the variety show, served on
the prom committee and as prom royalty, and was twice elected class president. He
played football for three years, and baseball and basketball for two. All this, despite an
accident freshman year that nearly cost him his life.

Lake Seven, a fishing and boating lake outside Kewaskum, was a popular hangout.
There was a slide in the lake the kids liked to go down on their stomachs and belly flop
into the water. While the lake was twenty-five feet at its deepest, the slide was set in
the shallow end. Climbing the steps on the slide one day, Jim's foot slipped and he tum-

bled headfirst into the lake. His friends managed to get him into a car and stabilize him on the drive to the doctor, where they discovered he had a hairline fracture in his neck. Jim spent nearly six months in a full-body cast.

It wasn't the first close call he'd had. At age 6, Jim had survived a bout of spinal meningitis, defying the doctor's prognosis. Once his neck fracture healed, it was business as usual for Jim. He lettered in two sports and received All-Conference honorable mention as a center in football. He graduated from Kewaskum High School in spring 1961, and attended the University of Wisconsin–Stevens Point in the fall. Inspired by his love of the outdoors, he majored in biology and minored in conservation, with plans to become a game warden. Jim was a member of Sigma Phi Epsilon fraternity and was selected as their candidate for the 1965 Winter Carnival king.

In early 1965, Jim met with a Marine Corps recruiter on campus and applied for the service. While still in school, Jim took a series of tests, including flight tests in Minneapolis. When he graduated from Stevens Point in the spring, he had already qualified for the Marine Corps aviation program. When he began training at the Officer

Edwin "Jim" Fickler's senior photo at the University of Wisconsin–Stevens Point. It was during college that Jim made the decision to pursue the Marine Corps. Courtesy the University of Wisconsin–Stevens Point Archives.

Candidate School (OCS) in Quantico, Virginia, later that year, he went through the program as an aviation officer candidate.

"That was his desire right off the bat," say Rich Baxter, who went through recruiting and OCS alongside Jim. "He knew right off the bat that he had qualified for the AOC program."

Jim was one of some six hundred fifty young men beginning the 38th Officer Candidate Course (38-OCC) on October 10, 1965. Most were recent college graduates, although some were enlisted Marines who aimed to become officers by completing the program.

Completing OCS was by no means guaranteed, and those who stayed with the program for its entirety were physically and mentally pushed to the limit.

"We're all thinking, 'What the hell are we doing here? Why did we sign up for this?'" remembers Bob Nelson, a member of 38-OCC. "Every minute of every day there's just something going on, so there's a lot of stress for everybody."

John Admire, another 38-OCC graduate, agrees: "That was the most hell I think I've gone through except combat."

The men were divided into platoons of forty to forty-five men upon arrival. Jim was assigned to C-3. Two drill sergeants ran each platoon and they stuck with their platoon from the moment the candidates woke in the morning until they were allowed to fall into bed at night. "Drill instructors were just mean and nasty, but at the same time, they had a job to do and we understood," says John. "They were preparing us to be leaders and they knew that every one of us, within the next six or seven months, were probably going to Vietnam."

There were three main components to the training. The first element, physical fitness, involved general calisthenics, daily runs, twenty-mile hikes, and a variety of physical tests. Like high school pre-season football workouts, the exercises took place two or three times a day and were always exhausting and demanding. At the same time, they were arguably the most important part of the training. John Admire explains:

> If you're on a three-mile run or a twenty-mile hike and you get done and you have to take a break or, God forbid, quit (quit was never in the equation) and you fall back and you're not with the pack, naturally your leadership's going to be of concern because your peers are going to think, "If you can't keep up, you can't lead." Then mentally and emotionally you're distracted and your academics go to hell. If you were physically fit and could do what was expected, you were going to be okay. Most people were rejected by the Marine Corps because of the physical fitness.

Jim completed some of this training with boots that did not fit properly. Likely leftovers from the Korean War, the boots left his ankles chafed and bloody. The condition worsened each week, but Jim refused to drop out and wore them until the end of the program anyway.

Leadership skills were the second component taught and evaluated at OCS. Candidates rotated among various jobs within the platoon, which allowed them to be evaluated at different tasks. Sometimes their jobs placed them in charge of four people; sometimes they involved leading the entire platoon of forty.

The final part of training consisted of academic work. Since most of the men already had college degrees behind them, this was often the least taxing portion of the program.

There was little downtime. The men were several days into the program before they were allowed a one-minute phone call home to inform their families that they'd arrived safely. They had one weekend off during the ten weeks, and most of them went to Washington, D.C. At Quantico they lived in old World War II–type barracks. One squad bay consisted of two rows of iron bunk beds with two-inch spring mattresses. They each had one wall locker for their uniforms and one foot locker for nonclothing items. Jim's bunkmate, Bob Nelson, knew Jim to be "a really, really nice fellow" and a good student. Across the squad bay from them was Arnold Husser, whom Jim taught to play cribbage.

"I never ever heard him utter a foul word," says Arnold, "and [he] was totally gung-ho."[1]

On December 17, 1965, 511 members of 38-OCC graduated as 2nd lieutenants in the Marine Corps.[2] The Marines departed from Quantico the next day for a brief respite at home before continuing their training in early January. Some would return to Quantico and attend The Basic School (TBS) before going into the Marine infantry. Others would travel to Pensacola, Florida, with hopes of becoming a Naval aviator. Jim, who had qualified for aviation before beginning OCS, was among the 106 graduates destined for pre-flight training at Naval Air Station Pensacola.

Regardless of the destination, the Marines were no longer mere candidates, but officers, and they were treated with the respect that came with their rank. The work was still hard, but there was more time to relax and enjoy themselves. Jim and a fellow Marine, Mike Forney, spent much of their free time on Pensacola Bay, fishing for sea trout and channel catfish. Jim also ventured up to Mobile, Alabama, one weekend and picked up his red Corvette.

At Pensacola Jim lived in bachelor officer's quarters, where he kept a picture of a jet plane pinned up to his wall as a reminder of his goal. Although he'd made it through OCS and into flight school, it was not guaranteed that he would be assigned to jets. Some of the men would be assigned to helicopters or fixed-wing transport planes instead. Others wouldn't pass the training and would be sent back to TBS or reassigned.

Pre-flight concluded at the end of February, and ground training followed at Saufley Field, also in Pensacola. It was at Saufley where pilots flew solo for the first time, and where they were assigned to jets, helicopters, or transport planes. In 1966 many wanted jets, but Training Command allotted only three graduates a week to receive such an assignment. The rest were sent to helicopters or transport aircraft, regardless of their preferences. Whether a Marine was sent to basic jet at Meridian, Mississippi, was often a matter of how many other candidates completed their training the same week and where their scores ranked. For example, during weeks with poor weather, when it was difficult to fly, only three students might graduate. If they wanted, all three could go to basic jet. Other weeks, when more flying could be done, seven students might complete their training, but still only three would be assigned to jets.

"Jim Fickler, I am sure," notes Jim Garvey, who also trained at Pensacola, "graduated on a wonderful weather week and because of his high grades in ground school and superior performance with the T-34,[3] he got his desired assignment—Meridian."

Jim spent the summer of 1966 at basic jet training in Meridian, flying the North American T2-A Buckeye, a training aircraft designed to prepare Naval aviators for jet flying. Over the summer he would accumulate approximately one hundred twenty-five hours of flight time, including cross-country, night flying, and basic navigation practice. Training culminated with four landings on the aircraft carrier the USS *Lexington*.

Advanced jet training followed at Naval Air Station Kingsville, Texas, with more carrier landing qualifications, instrument training, and formation and night flights in the Grumman TF-9J Cougar. As at Pensacola the training allowed for downtime, and Jim and his buddy, Mike Forney, used it for hunting jackrabbits and cooking hasenpfeffer (marinated rabbit served in a hot stew), using a recipe Jim wanted to try. "It was so bad we [threw] it out," Mike notes, before adding that, despite all, Jim was a good cook.

Jim received his Wings of Gold in April 1967, a 1st lieutenant and a Naval aviator. He also received his first assignment: Marine Air Group (MAG) 14. Based at Marine Corps Air Station Cherry Point, North Carolina, Jim flew the Grumman A-6 Intruder, an all-weather, twin-engine, two-seat jet plane.[4]

Just before shipping out to Vietnam, it came to the attention of a Marine doctor that years earlier Jim had fractured and nearly broken his neck. The doctor declared him ineligible to fly. Jim refused to accept such a diagnosis and sought the opinions of three other doctors so he could remain a pilot. With much persistence, he won that battle, and left for Vietnam on April 9, 1968.

Jim was first assigned to Marine Attack Squadron 242 [VMA(AW) 242] then to Headquarters and Maintenance Squadron 11, MAG 11. The squadron was stationed at

Da Nang Air Base and performed close air support and direct air support missions. Nine months into his tour Jim was scheduled for an evening mission on January 17, 1969, departing at 11:40 p.m. The unit's command chronology shows that Jim's mission was switched with that of another pilot within the unit. His new mission was direct air support over the A Shau Valley, near the western border of Laos, east of Hamburger Hill. Captain Edwin James Fickler and his bombardier/navigator, 1st Lieutenant Robert Kuhlman, departed Da Nang Air Base at approximately 8:40 p.m. and were shortly advised by forward air control (FAC) of antiaircraft artillery in the area. Fifteen minutes after that initial report, FAC identified a target and passed its coordinates to Captain Fickler. Not long afterward FAC saw two explosions. The FAC pilot first believed them to be the result of the bombs released by Jim's plane. However, when he attempted to contact the aircraft with another target, he was unable to get a response. He later concluded that one explosion might have been the aircraft itself.

Jim's plane did not return to Da Nang, nor did it land at any of the surrounding airfields. Search-and-rescue efforts were launched the night of the mission and continued for five days, but the aircraft was never located. Jim's status listed him as missing in action. It would remain so for more than five years, until after America's role in Vietnam had ended. The Department of Defense changed his status to killed in action on February 4, 1974.

Jim Fickler was one month shy of completing his tour of duty when his aircraft disappeared that January 17, 1969. He was 25 years old. In his nine months overseas flying the A-6 Intruder, Jim accrued fourteen Air Medals. It was an accomplishment that could not be prevented by bloodied feet or a broken neck, and it stands as a testament to Jim's skill as an aviator, his passion, and his unstoppable determination.

"He was one of the good guys," Mike Forney reflects, "and would have made a positive contribution in today's world."

Sergeant William Anthony Evans

United States Army,
disappeared March 2, 1969

William Anthony Evans was born October 4, 1948.[1] He grew up in Milwaukee. After high school, William enlisted in the United States Army. He later reenlisted as a member of Military Assistance Command, Vietnam, Studies and Observation Group (MACV-SOG), 5th Special Forces Group, B 50, Reconnaissance Team Plumb.

The title "Studies and Observation Group" was, almost certainly, an intentional misnomer. The name implies highly intelligent men analyzing reports brought back from the field. The men of MACV-SOG were, indeed, highly intelligent, but they were also specially trained to undertake covert missions so cloaked in secrecy that only senior officers like General William Westmoreland knew of its doings. Special operations group, the organization's original name, more closely describes the group's activities during the Vietnam War.

The history of the special operations group began years before Sergeant Evans joined. The first group of Americans in Vietnam in the 1950s, the Military Assistance Advisory Group (MAAG), provided support to the French in their fight against what was then Indochina. After the French defeat at Dien Bien Phu in 1954, the United States began training South Vietnamese troops through MAAG. In 1955 MAAG's role expanded further when it began advising the South Vietnamese President Ngô Đình Diệm.

In November 1961 President John F. Kennedy changed the course of the war when he called for increasing the number of American military personnel in Vietnam and expanded their role. Such an expansion required a headquarters, separate from MAAG, responsible for military operations. Military Assistance Command, Vietnam, was activated February 8, 1962.

Although it had a staff of only 216, MACV symbolized America's renewed effort in Southeast Asia. Its Saigon headquarters was responsible for Air Force, Army, Navy, and Marine units in Vietnam. It was also tasked with advising the South Vietnamese government and military. Although in 1964 MACV was subordinate to the Commander in Chief of Pacific Command (CINCPAC), it grew to surpass and engulf MAAG and formed suborganizations of its own, including the Studies and Observations Group.

SOG was intended to perform reconnaissance and psychological warfare in North

Vietnam. Originally comprising only 99 military servicemen and 31 civilians, SOG eventually increased to 2,500 Americans and 7,000 Southeast Asians. As its membership expanded so, too, did its purpose.

The group's work spread beyond North Vietnam, into Laos and Cambodia. SOG included members of nearly every branch of the military as well as the CIA. SOG operated more or less under its own jurisdiction. To maintain its secrecy, the group avoided MACV as much as possible. It received orders from General Westmoreland, who in turn received his orders from the State Department, the Defense Department, or the White House. There were times, too, that SOG activities bypassed Westmoreland altogether.

SOG's volunteer members were sworn to secrecy under threat of twenty years' imprisonment. SOG files were only declassified in 1995. As a result, Sergeant Evans's final mission is documented thoroughly by Lieutenant Colonel Fred Lindsey in his book, *Secret Green Beret Commandos in Cambodia*.[2]

On March 2, 1969, Sergeant Evans led a team that included Specialist Fifth Class Michael May and six "indigenous" members, heading to a known NVA rest-and-recuperation area along the Ho Chi Minh Trail in southeastern Cambodia. Almost immediately upon landing, they met with hostile fire from a battalion-sized NVA unit. The team established a defensive position. William radioed for air support.

Helicopter gunships arrived to help the team stave off the first round of attacks, but after forty-five minutes, they were redeployed. The NVA resumed its assault after the gunships departed. Soon after a B-40 rocket grenade exploded above the SOG team. 22-year-old Sergeant William Evans died instantly. SP5 May succumbed to his wounds roughly half an hour later.

Three team members survived the fight and were extracted from a different location the next day. Due to the intensity of the fighting, the survivors were unable to return for the bodies of the fallen. The men were listed as missing in action.

In 2001, SOG received the Presidential Unit Citation. The citation praises SOG and its members for "extraordinary heroism, great combat achievement and unwavering fidelity."

Major Richard Lee Bowers

*United States Army,
disappeared March 24, 1969*

"He was very personable, very courteous, and hard working. He could relate well to people his own age, and people older, and did so.... He was a great big brother."—Cindy (Bowers) Schmitz

During the Vietnam War, commanding officers filled out thousands of casualty reports. Often, they supplied relatively little information: a man's name, his birthdate, his physical stature, and the date of the incident that led to the status of killed in action or missing in action. However, the commanding officer who filled in the report for then–Lieutenant Richard Bowers was thorough. He noted a slight stagger in Richard's walk and suggested this was from a history of athletics. He noted that Richard was in "very good" physical condition and that he wore jungle fatigues and boots the last time he was seen. He called Richard a "very friendly person," who "got along well with every-one." And in a box marked "Commander's Estimate of Individual's Physical and Moral Courage," Richard's commander wrote that Richard "displayed a degree of courage which would suggest that he would definitely resist the enemy in all ways possible."

The commanding officer, it seems, assessed Richard Bowers well.

"He was very protective," says his sister, Cindy. From a young age, Richard took it upon himself to care for his family: for his parents, Roy and Ann; for Carol, older than he by a year and a day; for his two younger brothers, David and Mike; and for Cindy, fourteen years his junior. From middle school on, Richard worked all sorts of odd jobs in Lake Mills, Wisconsin. One of the longest lasting was his paper route, which began with thirty houses and eventually grew to more than one hundred. "He was so popular on that route with the older people," Cindy says. "He was so conscientious about always having the paper there by 6:00 a.m."

Richard recruited his brothers to work the route with him. The boys received their pay at the beginning of the week, but it didn't always last until the weekend. When that happened, they turned to Carol for a loan. "The three boys were really close," Cindy says, "And so I remember they did everything together." They spent much of their summers on the beach or fixing old cars. On Saturday mornings Richard, David, and Mike sought out Carol to teach them new dances from the hit TV show *American Bandstand*.

Growing up, Cindy referred to her brothers as "The Handsome One," "The Strong One," and "The Smart One." She can't remember now who was who, but it hardly matters. "It was kind of like The Three Stooges," she explains. "You got one, you got them all."

At Lake Mills High School, Richard was on the wrestling team and worked on the yearbook staff, but he didn't have much time for extracurricular activities in high school. Working took up much of his free time. After graduation, he took several classes at a correspondence school. A year later he enlisted in the Army. It was 1966.

The family wasn't surprised. They were very patriotic. Their father, Roy, had fought with the Marine Corps at the Battle of Midway during World War II and belonged to the local VFW and American Legion. Ann was frequently an officer of the Women's Auxiliary, and both Carol and Cindy were members of the Junior Auxiliary. All three boys eventually enlisted or were drafted into the Army.

After Basic Training and Advanced Infantry Training, Richard was accepted into Army Officer Candidate School (OCS) at Fort Benning, Georgia. He arrived in August 1966 and was assigned to Class 14–67.[1] OCS was a twenty-five-week-long program divided into three phases: Introductory (Basic), Intermediate (Black), and Senior (Blue).[2] If they graduated, the men would be commissioned as 2nd lieutenants. Officer status meant they would receive roughly five times the paycheck of a private, but also committed them to serving one year more than draftees. Richard was one in

Richard Bowers's senior photo for Lake Mills High School, circa 1965. Courtesy Cindy Schmitz.

a class of roughly two hundred forty[3] candidates undergoing six months of training at OCS.

Days began at 5:00 a.m., when a tactical officer awakened the men by beating on an empty metal garbage can. Within ten minutes the men were outside, running the track around the Airborne towers and performing calisthenics before breakfast.

The day was filled with physical training, classroom lectures, and leadership activities. Men were not allowed off base during the introductory phase. When outdoors they were required to run everywhere they went until they reached the senior phase. If an officer or a senior candidate caught them walking, the candidates could be subjected to push-ups—any place, any time.

"This extreme disciplinary atmosphere that was created was again done for very legitimate reasons," says Brian Smith, a member of Class 14–67.

> I think that most of my classmates would agree that the lessons taught were simple but effective. If you did something wrong, there was a cost. Simple. Understand that if you did something wrong in a different situation, the cost may be in blood and lives. We grew to recognize these life-and-death lessons.

Not everyone could handle the pressure. Some dropped out; some were kicked out because they weren't considered officer material; some were held back to repeat the experience. On their first day at Fort Benning, a tactical officer told them, "Candidates, look to the man on your left and look to the man on your right. One of you will not be here when we graduate." For the Class of 14–67, the "two out of three" statistic was almost exactly right. On March 7, 1967, 169 of the original 250 men were commissioned as 2nd lieutenants.[4] As they filed out of Wigle Hall, they received their first salute from their company's 1st sergeant. Per tradition the man receiving the salute had to pay the man doing the saluting one dollar, which they all did, proudly.

Before Richard left for Vietnam, he spoke with Carol and made sure all his finances were in order. He wanted to ensure the family would be cared for should anything happen to him. He also made a deal with Cindy: For every "A" she earned in school, he would pay her five dollars. "That was a lot of money back then," Cindy remembers. "But I think that was his way to make sure I had a college fund." Then, in the fall of 1967, he departed for Vietnam.

Richard joined Mobile Advisory Team (MAT) IV-49. MATs were composed of three to five men paired with a Vietnamese interpreter. The teams worked with Vietnamese regional and Popular Forces as military advisors and were supported by a Military Assistance Command, Vietnam (MACV) Advisory Team in the district in which they operated; for Richard, this was Advisory Team 71. Richard was assigned to an outpost at Tam Soc in the Thuận Hóa District, one of six districts in the southern province of Ba Xuyên within the Mekong Delta.[5] The outpost at Tam Soc was "out in no man's land," says John Baum, a member of Team 71. Few American troops operated at such outposts; instead, the MATs assigned there trained Vietnamese troops to defend themselves.

Because Richard was often "off the grid," letters home were scarce. It made the letters the family received all the more special. In those letters Richard told his family not to worry about him: "I'm going to be up in the trees, watching the war go by," he wrote. In truth, though, Richard's job was a dangerous one. MATs could be considered scaled-down versions of the Special Forces. In addition to training Vietnamese, they planned and accompanied the Vietnamese soldiers on missions. Night ambushes and operations often kept them away from the outpost for days at a time. "It was a scary job," states Pres Funkhouser, a member of Richard's OCS class. "They were way out on the pointy end of the stick." John Baum agrees: "These were not jobs for the faint of heart."

Richard was never gung-ho about the war, Cindy recalls:

> But once he got over there and got to meet the people, and he saw how the war and the communists were destroying their lifestyle.... He said they're really sweet people and everything, and I think he could see that aspect of it, then.... He was doing some good for them.

MAT members were thoroughly immersed in Vietnamese daily life. They were familiar with, lived, and worked with the local population. Richard liked the Vietnamese people and wrote home about them whenever he had the chance. He often included pictures of the local children for Cindy. "I used to ask their names and stuff," she says. "My guess is he probably didn't know some, or a lot, of them, but he would make up names or something because he always answered my questions.... He also bought me a Vietnamese women's outfit."

The protectiveness Richard had always shown to his family extended to the Vietnamese at the outpost, especially the local interpreter, who worked alongside him. As the area grew more hostile, Richard worried about what would happen to the interpreter and the other people at Tam Soc once he left for home. He also worried about his brother, David, a Green Beret, who would soon be sent to Vietnam. David was married and expecting a baby. Knowing that his brother would not be deployed while Richard was overseas and that he could remain with the Vietnamese he knew at the outpost, Richard extended his tour six months when his initial tour ended in the fall of 1968.

He didn't tell his family immediately. Carol was getting married in California in September 1968 and had chosen the date specifically so Richard would be home to attend the ceremony. It was only afterward that he told everyone that he would be going back to Vietnam. "Mom had a really hard time with it, and said she wished he hadn't done that," Cindy remembers. "But at the same time ... she understood his reason for it."

After the wedding, Cindy and her parents stayed in California, while Richard and Mike went back to Wisconsin.[6] Their mother despaired over what would happen to the house with the boys there by themselves, but it was still standing when the rest of the family returned. Shortly thereafter Richard departed for six more months in Vietnam.

Richard served as the team's senior advisor throughout 1969. As his second tour neared its end, Richard prepared to return to civilian life. He had a job arranged in Wisconsin and a car waiting for him in the lot. Ten days before his scheduled departure the outpost at Tam Soc was attacked by a battalion of Vietcong, reinforced by a heavy-weapons platoon. The post was "very vulnerable," says John Baum. Only several Vietnamese villagers and a few American military personnel, all in advisory roles, defended it. Sóc Trăng Army Airfield was roughly ten miles from Tam Soc. During an attack, it was possible to call in air strikes in hopes of defending the post, but help could not always arrive in sufficient time to drive the enemy away.

Richard was last heard on the radio on the morning of March 24, 1969, calling for reinforcements. When the relief force arrived, the Vietnamese defenders were dead, as were two Americans: Staff Sergeant Darrell Anderson and Staff Sergeant Jimmy Freeman. First Lieutenant Richard Bowers and Staff Sergeant Gerasimo Arroyo-Baez, the team medic, were nowhere to be found.

Cindy was in third grade when her sister-in-law picked her up from school in tears. When Cindy arrived home,

Richard at the Army outpost at Tam Soc. As a MAT member, Richard spent much of his time working with the local Vietnamese population. His loyalty to the village and friendship with his team's interpreter were part of his motivation to extend his tour. Courtesy Cindy Schmitz.

her parents told her that an officer had come to their door and informed them that Richard was missing. A telegram a few days later confirmed it. "I remember thinking, 'How could we not feel it, if something bad had happened to him?'" Cindy says.

It was a hard time for the family and a hard time for the town. Two other local boys had died in Vietnam. John Imrie, Carol's classmate, was killed in August 1967.[7] Jeff Netzow, Richard's classmate and the son of the Bowers's family doctor, died in May 1968. In such a small town the losses touched everyone. "Richard's was a little different in that they still had a little hope for a while," Cindy says.

In 1973 Hanoi released 591 prisoners. Their return was broadcast live across the country. Cindy remembers that day:

> We had ... aunts and uncles over to watch TV, and they just watched and watched, and I could tell when I came in that, you know, Richard's name wasn't mentioned. And they had a hard time with that. You know, you've waited all these years to hear something and then, poof. You think, "This is going to be it," and then nothing.

Richard was declared killed in action in 1978. The Bowers held a memorial service, with no one to bury and few answers as to why. It was a long time before they learned the real story, and even then, they were never sure exactly what happened.

Local Vietnamese interviewed in the early 1970s provided some details. Witnesses claimed to have seen Richard and Gerasimo Arroyo-Baez taken into the jungle; another account suggested their Vietnamese interpreter was captured as well. The Americans escaped when a helicopter gunship strike scattered the Vietcong, but they were recaptured. In a fit of anger, one of their captors shot and killed Richard. The Vietcong deposited his body in a nearby river. Staff Sergeant Arroyo-Baez died in captivity on August 22, 1972. His remains were returned to the United States in 1985. The interpreter escaped the prisoner of war camp in October 1971.

No sign of Richard was ever found. In 1972 a Joint Personnel Recovery Center team investigated the area where Richard's body had supposedly been discarded. In a striking coincidence, Pres Funkhouser, of Richard's OCS platoon, was the main provincial intelligence advisor on the mission. They found no evidence that Richard had been there, but Pres says this is not surprising, nor does it mean that the reports were false. The river's waters fluctuate ten to twelve feet a day and move swiftly downstream to the sea, less than twenty miles away.

Richard's casualty form states that he died March 24, 1969. It gives his rank 1st lieutenant, although he was posthumously promoted to major. It indicates that his birthdate was July 20, 1946, making him 22 years old when he was killed. And in the last box on page three, it states that, based on the accounts of Vietnamese personnel on the ground, "Bowers had made it to safety, but returned to the scene of the battle to aid Arroyo who had been wounded."

Richard died just as he had lived: protective and displaying a high degree of courage.

Chief Warrant Officer
William Cooper Pierson III

United States Army, disappeared April 13, 1969

"Bill (Biff) Pierson was funny to be around. He was always willing to do anything at any time. He was a practical joker and would always try to do something funny.... Biff was a good friend."—Phil Van Treese

"A very nice guy who was very intelligent and always had a smile on his face."—Terry Koelbl

In December 1969, Representative Roger Zion[1] arrived in Paris with a letter signed by 406 members of Congress, demanding humane treatment for American prisoners of war held in Vietnam. He returned to the United States with a film showing healthy-looking POWs attending a religious service for Christmas.[2] The film was shown to families of known POWs in early 1970 and then broadcast on national television in September. Analysts counted 75 faces in the film, including 20 whose names had not previously appeared on any United States POW list. The Department of Defense beseeched families of missing in action servicemen to contact them if they believed that they saw their son, their husband, their brother, or their father among those men. Darlene Pierson contacted the Defense Department, which begs the question: Was her husband, William Pierson III, in that film?

Growing up in Wisconsin, William was hard to miss. He was born December 23, 1947. At a young age he acquired the nickname "Biff" and a reputation for being adventurous and a bit wild. "Biff was always a little crazy in a good way," remembers his schoolmate, Phil Van Treese.

Phil wasn't William's only friend to feel this way. "When he grinned at you, he looked like a little Grinch," says Dave Phipps. Together, William and Dave got into all sorts of mischief at Lourdes High School,[3] a Catholic high school in Oshkosh, Wisconsin. They were notorious pranksters and often had to be separated in classes to prevent hijinks and distractions. It rarely worked. One teacher, determined to keep the boys as far apart as possible, placed William in a desk in the front right corner of the room and Dave in the rear left. When the teacher's back was turned, they still managed to make the class laugh.

William and Dave both had jobs washing dishes in the school cafeteria during their senior year. Because they worked during the normal lunch hour, the boys were allowed to leave class early to eat before their shifts began. The time they were supposed to leave was 11:10. Several weeks into the school year, they questioned whether anyone paid attention to when they left, so they left one minute early—11:09.

The next day, they left at 11:08.

They were leaving at 10:50 by the time they were caught. Two weeks later, they tried again, making it to 11:00.

The boys' hijinks extended beyond the classroom. William always had something of a playful glint in his eye. One Fourth of July, Dave made the mistake of falling asleep, and William put a firecracker by his legs and set it off. When William dozed off later that day, Dave returned the favor. Instead of merely going off, though, the firecracker fizzled and set William's pants on fire.

"We ran around doing stuff we shouldn't have been doing," laughs Dave. Dave had a driver's license their senior year and a '57 Ford convertible so the two went all over town chasing girls. William had a moped, which he could pedal or turn the motor on. "He would go riding down the street with his motor until he saw a cop, then he'd pedal like hell."

William rode the bus to and from school. Lourdes was on the opposite side of the Fox River from where he lived, and the city buses were the easiest way to get home. To keep entertained on the bus ride back, Phil Van Treese remembers making jokes just to rile William up. "It was fun to get him started because he was high strung," says Phil. "We'd have a blast seeing him turn red."

At the same time, William had a quiet and responsible side, one that makes his classmate Steve Schumerth remember him as "a real gentleman." At Lourdes, he was a member of the Boys Science Club and a religious organization called Benildus.[4] At home, William was the man of the house. His parents were divorced, and he lived with his mother and two younger sisters.[5] He shouldered the responsibilities with a "wonderful demeanor," says Steve. It was this side of him, coupled with his desire for adventure, his wish to see the world, and his love for his country and family, that led him to enlist in the United States Army after graduation from Lourdes in 1965.[6]

It almost wasn't possible. When William told Phil he wanted to join the army, Phil didn't believe him. Not because of any lack of desire or courage on William's part, but for a lack of fingers. It was the result of another high school adventure—a

"Biff" Pierson's high school graduation photo from Lourdes Academy. Today, his classmates remember him for his great smile and sense of humor. Courtesy Karen Boehm.

practical joke gone awry. The boys were making pencil top rockets by cutting off match heads and sticking them into pencil tops, lighting a fuse, and letting them shoot off. But William stuck one match too hard, and it exploded in his hand. He lost two fingers in the accident.

The injury didn't hinder him, though, because William enlisted and trained at Fort Jackson, South Carolina,[7] becoming a member of the Army Reserves.

From there he moved to Chicago and took a job working for Braniff Airways at Midway Airport. Dave Phipps and a friend visited him one weekend in early 1968, and said that while they had a good time, William's work schedule kept him busy. It was around this time that William married Darlene. They had one son.

By June 1968 William's job was once again with the Army, where he was training at Fort Hood, Texas, with B Packet of the 2nd Squadron of the 17th Cavalry in the 101st Airborne Division.[8] Constituted during World War II, the "Screaming Eagles" used to parachute ground forces out of airplanes or gliders into enemy territory. But because there were few parachute operations in Vietnam in 1968, the 101st was transitioning from an airborne to an airmobile division. Their new purpose was air mobile helicopter operations.

At Fort Hood, the 210 men of B Packet received their assigned twenty-eight helicopters, a combination of the Bell UH-1 Iroquois (Huey), Bell AH-1 Cobra, and Hughes OH-6 Cayuse.[9] While at Fort Hood, the soldiers were also divided into helicopter crews, infantry platoons, maintenance components, and support personnel, and given their equipment. "We were a fully functional and self-sustaining unit," says Jim Matthews, a member of B Packet. He explains their training further:

> Training consisted of going to the personal weapons range so the personnel could qualify with their assigned weapons. It also included other military subjects like escape and evasion (how to avoid the enemy if shot down) map reading, military combat tactics, trips to the Vietnam Village (a training area set up like a village to expose us to what it was like, etc.). The infantry platoon honed their combat tactics, the maintenance personnel perfected their mechanic[al] abilities, and the pilots practiced combat flying tactics, aerial gunnery ranges for our attack helicopters, plus numerous trips to the field (going out and living and performing your jobs in the wide open spaces for three to five days at a time).

Training ended in December 1968. From Texas the unit flew its aircraft to California to be dismantled and transported via boat to Vietnam. In February 1969, the entire unit was packed onto buses and returned to Texas, waiting at Bergstrom Air Force Base for their departure to Vietnam. They were to join the newly expanded 2/17th Cavalry.

William did not remain with B Troop for long. After arriving in Thừa Thiên Province, many of the unit's pilots were exchanged for more experienced flyers, and William was in one of the first groups of pilots to be reassigned. He remained in the 101st Division, but was now a member of D Troop, 1st Squadron, 1st Cavalry.

On April 13, 1969, Chief Warrant Officer William Pierson III was the copilot of an AH-1 Cobra attack helicopter flying a visual reconnaissance mission. The helicopter's pilot was Captain Alvie Ledford, Jr. Flying alongside them was an OH-6 LOH. At approximately 12:30 p.m., the LOH pilot informed Captain Ledford they were above several enemy huts and advised an attack. The Cobra dove. At 500 feet above ground level, the helicopter burst into flames. The LOH pilot saw the Cobra's pilot's compartment break off from the rest of the aircraft and disintegrate as it fell.

The LOH pilot flew to the crash site immediately and spotted one body on the ground, identified one week later as Captain Alvie Ledford, Jr. There was no sign of 21-year-old William Pierson III.

Then, in 1970, Representative Zion's POW film reel was shown to families of MIAs across the country. Darlene Pierson sent multiple photos of William to the Department of Defense, and two technicians studied the photos separately, looking for any resemblance to the POWs in the film. The report filed on February 9, 1971, listed three possible results from the analysis:

1. In the view of the similarity in general appearance and significant number of similar features, ____ could be the subject of the questioned photos.
2. In the view of the significant number of differences in distinguishable features, ____ probably is not the subject of the questioned photographs.
3. In the view of the quality of photography and the small number of distinguishable features which could be compared, no conclusions can be reached.

The last option was circled.

After the American POWs returned to the U.S. in 1973, they were questioned about others who might have been held in captivity and not returned. This included William Pierson. One returnee, Norris Charles, believed the name Pierson sounded familiar. Charles stated that he may have seen it on a note passed in camp in early 1972. Another POW, James Mulligan, recalled hearing the name but could not remember when or why. The same report that includes these witness statements noted that there were four individuals named either Pierson or the closely-related Pearson, but there was no evidence suggesting any of the four were prisoners of war. The results were, again, not enough to affirm whether William Pierson had ever been a POW. In 2017 he remains MIA.

It's hard to imagine that any prisoner could have met William and not remembered him. Equal parts mischievous and responsible, adventurous and dedicated, he had a one-of-a-kind personality, one that those who knew him attest was impossible to forget.

Major Norman Karl Billipp

*United States Marine Corps,
disappeared May 6, 1969*

"Norm was the epitome of a Marine's Marine. He was a jut-jawed, spit-and-shine guy. He took being a Marine seriously.... He would literally do anything for you. He might rag you about it for a while, but if I were ever in a fight, I would want to make sure Norm was on one side of me or the other."—Steve Beers

"He was what you would call a consummate Marine.... He was a gentle giant and he was very, very passionate about the Marines and serving his country."—Jack Freckman

"It's a damn shame that he didn't have a chance to come back because he would have been a good dad and he would have made a success of his life, whatever he would have done."—Ken Hurst

"Ever seen the movie *The Great Santini*?" asks Steve Beers, a member of the University of Wisconsin–Madison NROTC program, class of 1967. "It's about a Marine Corps pilot who turns his family into a Marine Corps unit. He was very tough and very vigorous. That's the way I saw Norm."

When his fellow midshipmen look back on their UW years, they can't help but agree with Steve's assessment.[1] Ross Annable describes Norman Billipp as a "gung-ho Marine," while Duncan Hoffman says, "He was very serious about NROTC, but he was a gregarious and fun guy." Norm's larger-than-life disposition suited his rugby player–like physique. With an affinity for risk taking and the confidence to go along with it, Norm seemed the personification of a Naval aviator.

It was a career path he'd long intended to follow. Born March 14, 1945, in Schenectady, New York, to Betty and Gordon Billipp, Norm was the eldest of four sons. His father, a salesman and sales manager for Armstrong Cork Company, was a World War II veteran, having served as a lieutenant (junior grade) in the Navy aboard the destroyer escort USS *Howard F. Clark*. During Gordon's Armstrong sales career, the Billipp family moved frequently. Norm spent his childhood in Hingham, Massachusetts; East Aurora, New York; and Chagrin Falls, Ohio; and his teenage years in Lancaster, Pennsylvania. In Lancaster, Norm graduated from Manheim Township High School, where he lettered in baseball and swimming and helped lead the Blue Streak swimming team to a district championship. He also participated in Press Club as a senior and served as the president of the German Club. In their yearbook, members of the graduating class of 1962 included their post–high school career plans beside their photographs. Norm's stated "Naval career."

The University of Wisconsin–Madison's Naval ROTC program was the first step toward achieving that goal. Norm attended as an NROTC scholarship student, committing to at least four years of active duty in either the Marine Corps or the Navy after graduating from the program.[2] Outside of the NROTC, Norm played on the UW club rugby team, was a member of the Kappa Sigma fraternity, and worked in a school cafeteria.

The NROTC held classes three days a week in a brick building on University Avenue. Freshman and sophomore years were filled with classes on naval science and the history of warfare, while junior and senior year courses were more specific, focusing on weapons and engineering.

For the first two years, the midshipmen followed the same curriculum regardless of whether they were destined for the Navy or the Marines. They selected their service branch before their junior year.

Scholarship students participated in cruises each summer to different training locales. Norm (known as Blip during college) spent the summer of 1963 aboard the USS *Essex*, an Atlantic fleet aircraft carrier from the Second World War era. While onboard the midshipmen were exposed to nearly every aspect of Naval life. They worked in the boiler room and engine room and on the flight deck, the hangar deck, and the bridge. On occasion, they were even given the opportunity to take the helm.

One day that summer Norm noticed two young seamen aboard the *Essex* struggling with a monkey wrench while repairing a steam line. He asked if he could try, then proceeded to remove the tightened coupling by himself. "Norm was a big bruiser–type guy," explains Jack Freckman. "He could crush you in a heartbeat if he wanted to." Not that he would. According to fellow Midshipman Ken Hurst, Norm was "a bear of a guy.... He was a big teddy bear."

Norm's size was not always an advantage. Midshipmen underwent a series of physical tests during their four years, one of which required them to float for twenty minutes. It seemed simple enough, but Norm would enter the pool and just sink. "He was really scared for a while that they were going to wash him out because he couldn't float," Ken Hurst remembers with a laugh. The NROTC officers eventually waived that portion of the test for him, conceding that the former high school long distance swimmer could probably tread water as long as needed.

The summer after Norm's sophomore year, the cruise was split between amphibious assault training at Little Creek, Virginia, and Naval Aviation Command at Corpus Christi, Texas. This was Norm's introduction to flight training, and he loved it. On returning to Madison as a junior, he decided to opt for the Marine route in the NROTC program and set his sights on becoming a Naval aviator.

There was plenty of friendly competition between the members of the two Naval services. "Norm would always talk and joke around," remembers Jack, who chose the Navy path. "And he was always saying how good the Marines were. We'd be telling him, 'Yeah, but the Navy is the one who is going to take you where you need to go.'"

The NROTC offered Norm a chance to earn his private pilot's license through the Civil Air Patrol. The program required forty classroom hours and forty hours of flight and helped the Navy determine which candidates were best qualified to fly, and whether subsequent flight training would be a worthwhile investment. For Norm, it was. "I flew as a passenger with him, before he had his license, even though that was taboo," recalls Ross Annable, "and saw firsthand his joy and love of flying."

Norm's final summer cruise took him to Quantico, Virginia, for the Naval midshipmen's equivalent of Marine Officer Candidate School, focusing predominantly on testing the physical toughness of the men. While there were courses on leadership, weapons, problem-solving, team building, and strategy, one of the main goals was to replicate the physical and mental exhaustion of war and see how each man handled the situation.

Under ordinary circumstances, returning to the University of Wisconsin as a senior should have meant that Norm knew all there was to know about campus life, but the fall of 1965 was unlike any other time in recent memory. It was a difficult time for young military recruits on the Madison campus. As the Vietnam War was expanding overseas, the opposition at home was growing. "It was the start of the hippie movement on campus," explains Ken Hurst. "They all carried a cloth, green book bag with a drawstring on campus."

Along with the University of California, Berkley, Madison led the country in campus protests and antiwar activism. One of the earliest protests, a faculty-led "teach-in" about Vietnam at the Social Science building, had been held the previous spring. With approximately fifteen hundred students in attendance, the peaceful antiwar seminar was not indicative of the violent protests that would later take place on campus.[3]

"It got to the point where we were called baby killers and stuff like that," says Ken. "We were officially supposed to be nice, but we weren't as politically correct as people today."

Norm was proud of what he was doing. He took his commitment to NROTC seriously and was far from apologetic about it. In the spring of 1966 the midshipmen attended an annual military ball at the Memorial Union (student union) around the same time that the Students for a Democratic Society (SDS) was

Norm Billipp with a South Vietnamese boy at a school near Chu Lai Marine Air Station during the first part of his tour. Friends and family remember Norm as a gentle giant. Courtesy Andy Billipp.

becoming more aggressive in its protests. As the midshipmen and their dates arrived at the ball, SDS members threw tomatoes and eggs at them. There was no physical violence, no rioting, but the midshipmen were understandably insulted and hurt. They continued with their evening, and many attended after parties. Norm, though, had left the ball early.

Nearby, the Elvehjem Museum of Art[4] was under construction, and the sidewalk was covered with large boards that blocked off the site. The morning after the military ball, the campus awoke to find the words "Do Antiwar Protesters Have Balls?" painted across the boards. Among his fellow midshipmen there was no doubt where and how Norm had spent the remainder of his evening.

The protests continued. Every Tuesday the midshipmen dressed in full uniform and marched to Camp Randall Stadium for drill exercises. It got to the point, remembers Donald Bruss, another 1966 graduate, where they were walking through armed guards on both sides of the streets, helmets and guns raised in case of violence. "The campus itself was really uptight," he says.

With mounting concerns about the potential for violence, university authorities asked the NROTC officers if they would rather not wear their uniforms on campus to avoid the catcalls and unwanted attention. Everyone in command, including Norm, the battalion commander, said they would continue to wear their uniforms, symbolic of their commitment to the service. The University then asked if some NROTC members would be willing to participate in a question-and-answer session with the protesters. They agreed.

The well-attended session was held in a campus lecture hall. Norm was among the officers taking questions. "When they started asking about the war and service, Norm was really eloquent," Steve Beers remembers. "I don't know if he changed the ideas there, but he, as a person, got their attention. Afterwards, people came up to me and said they understood."

After graduating from the UW in 1966 with a Bachelor of Science degree in bacteriology, Norm attended The Basic School (TBS) at Quantico, Virginia, for more Marine officer training. While his first stint at Quantico had focused heavily on the physical demands of a Marine, TBS was more about shaping the young men into officers and giving them the skills that infantry officers needed to lead a platoon of Marines in combat. The Marine Corps orthodoxy was "every Marine a rifleman—every Marine officer an infantry officer."

Following TBS, the men received their military occupational specialties (MOS). They submitted their top three choices and were given their assignments based primarily on their Basic School class standing.[5] MOS training schools were scattered throughout the country, but anyone selected for Naval/Marine aviation went first to Naval Air Station Pensacola.

"At that point in time, those that went from TBS to Pensacola were at the very top of their class," says Duncan Hoffman. "You couldn't go to Pensacola unless you were really good."

Norm was assigned to Pensacola.

He returned home on a brief leave to visit his family in December 1966, who were then living in Milwaukee. Now an alumnus, Norm ventured back to the UW campus to assist in officer candidate recruitment and to help staff a recruiting table at the Memorial Union. The antiwar protests had increased since his graduation. Not surprisingly, the recruiters' presence that day garnered attention. A team of cameras and reporters stood nearby for three hours to capture any confrontations. Some shoving and insults were exchanged among the students and reporters, but the three Marines at the table weren't involved. The crowd reached an estimated one hundred twenty-five people, carrying signs that read, "Recruitment for Killers Has No Place in Our University." However, the *Wisconsin State Journal* reported that the Marines "kept their cool." Captain Ron Losee, who worked alongside Norm that day, sarcastically commented to the protesters that he was anxious to receive his transfer from the "combat zone" and go to Vietnam.

That was exactly where Norm was heading. Following primary and advanced jet training, Norm received his Wings of Gold on a cold March day in 1968. Shortly thereafter he received his first operational assignment to VMA-214 to gain combat flight proficiency in the McDonnell Douglas A-4E Skyhawk, a single-seat jet attack aircraft. The unit was stationed at Marine Corps Air Station El Toro, California.

In August 1968 he joined VMA-211, stationed at MCAS Chu Lai, South Vietnam. Norm flew combat missions in the A-4 Skyhawk with VMA-211 for the first seven months of his tour, then transferred to Marine Observation Squadron 6 (VMO-6) at

VMA 211 squadron pilots in early spring 1969. Norm is kneeling, third from left in the front row. In April, Norm transferred to Marine Observation Squadron 6. Courtesy Andy Billipp.

Quảng Trị in April 1969. Such transfers were not made frequently, although Norm's fellow squadron mate, Jim Lawrence, made the same transition a few months earlier.[6]

VMO-6 was composed largely of volunteers. The primary mission of pilots flying the Cessna O-1 Birddog was as forward air controllers (FACs). Their job was to seek out enemy troops and other targets in a designated area and to direct and control attack and fighter aircraft in dropping ordnance. FAC pilots often flew with a Marine infantry or artillery officer in the back seat as an aerial observer (AO) who could help spot and mark targets. The AO also coordinated with infantry on the ground to ensure that they were clear of the strike zone before the O-1 pilot authorized the attacks by the fighters.[7] Sometimes, when FAC pilots flew alone, they controlled both air and ground artillery attacks.

A primary justification and motivation for having seasoned attack jet pilots flying the O-1 FAC mission were because these pilots knew the capabilities of the attack and fighter aircrafts and their respective ordnance. It was a major transition, however, to switch from a fast fighter jet to the much slower O-1 Birddog. Since the O-1 was not typically armed, the pilots and AOs carried their own weapons, reasoning that if they were shot at it was only fair to shoot back. They dropped smoke grenades and fired handheld "Willie Pete" smoke rockets out the aircraft's small side windows to mark targets. The windows were left open so the AOs could hear and pinpoint where the enemy was shooting from. Carrying personal weapons was primarily for defending themselves if they were shot down. Simply flying the aircraft was a challenge as well because the O-1 was a light taildragger, which could easily be tossed around in the heavy winds common in Quảng Trị. The O-1 was designed to fly incredibly low and slow. This provided an easy target for ground fire.

"We thought, 'Why go into battle at 600 miles per hour when you could go into battle at 120?'" Jim Lawrence recalls. "What could possibly go wrong?"

Why would a pilot voluntarily make the transition? "We used to do crazy things," Jim says. The O-1 might have had a certain appeal for Norm, who flew and enjoyed a similar plane as a civilian. Norm also had a penchant for risk taking; the dangers that came along with the assignment may have enticed him as well.

By May 6, 1969, Norm had been with VMO-6 for roughly five weeks. That morning, then–1st Lieutenant Norman Billipp and Aerial Observer 1st Lieutenant John Hagan departed Quảng Trị and performed visual reconnaissance of several sites in support of the 3rd Marine Division. They briefly returned to the base before departing on their second mission shortly after noon. This mission took them west into Laos to provide visual reconnaissance of possible NVA troop movements and other enemy targets along the Ho Chi Minh Trail.

While Norm and John Hagan were airborne, the entire area was engulfed in a powerful thunderstorm. When the aircraft failed to return by 4:30 p.m., search-and-rescue efforts began immediately. One of the men sent to look for the aircraft was Jim Lawrence. He was unaware that he was searching for two of his friends. Active search efforts continued for three days. They did not find the plane or any indication of Norm or John Hagan's whereabouts.

While serving more than eight months in South Vietnam, Norm flew more than two hundred sixty-five combat missions, was awarded two Distinguished Flying Crosses,

Today, Jim Lawrence pilots his own O-1 Birddog, identical to those that Norm Billipp flew with VMO-6. It is a flying memorial, with the names of all his fallen squadron members painted along the side, including Norm Billipp and Bob Hagan. Courtesy Jim Lawrence.

the Bronze Star, twenty-two Air Medals, and the Purple Heart. While listed as missing in action, he was promoted to captain, then major, before being declared killed in action in 1976.

The Department of Defense asked the Billipp family for photographs of Norm to compare with pictures of prisoners of war being held by the North Vietnamese in Hanoi, but none proved positive. Even after the DOD's presumptive finding of death in 1976, rumors persisted that Norm might have survived the plane crash, but no evidence or substantive reports ever followed. It would be another twenty years before the Billipp family would learn more of Norm's fate: that he had almost certainly died at age 24 in the crash of his O-1, alongside John Hagan.

In 1995 records from NVA archives in Hanoi led to a crash site approximately twenty miles from the Vietnam border inside Laos. A full excavation in early 1996 uncovered minimal remains of both men. Norman Billipp and John Hagan were buried in Arlington National Cemetery in 1997. Their burial sites and their names on the Wall have been visited many times by their family and friends and serve as permanent reminders of the character and courage of both men.

"When I think back to those days.... Norm is always one of the people who pops up in my mind," says Jack. "If you ever met Norm, you would absolutely never forget the guy."

In 2010 Norm's three younger brothers, Andy, Jim, and Peter, traveled to Vietnam together. They visited Chu Lai and Quảng Trị, where Norm had been stationed forty-one years earlier, in what was then South Vietnam. Most important, using data provided by the U.S. government and with the help of a Laotian guide, an interpreter, and local villagers, Norm's brothers visited the crash site in Laos to fulfill their long-standing objective of paying their final respects to their oldest brother and his fellow Marine.

Each year in April, on the evening of the annual University of Wisconsin NROTC Spring Ball in Madison, a Marine officer's dress uniform sword is given by the Billipp family to the most distinguished NROTC Marine-option graduating senior in honor and remembrance of Norm. The Major Norman K. Billipp Memorial Sword continues to be a coveted award within the NROTC.

Aviation Boatswain
Mate Third Class
William Dale Gorsuch

United States Navy, disappeared October 2, 1969

"He was a really likeable guy.... He was brave and he wanted to fight for his country. He was in the service. And he was a good brother to have. I mean, that I can remember, I could talk to him all the time. Just a good guy all around."—Duane Gorsuch

In the 1960s the Cambria High School football team's field partially overlapped with the baseball diamond. It was in a park on a slight hill. There were no lights. They played their games during the day, like every other team in their conference, so the players could see the ball and the fans could see the players. In a small town like Cambria, with a population of fewer than six hundred, support was never lacking, and weekly fall football games were a popular pastime.

In 1970 when the school installed a true scoreboard, the team and the town were proud. No longer would they need to manually flip numbers to keep score. With a new football field behind the high school and lights for evening games, Cambria High School had one of the most impressive football stadiums in mid-state Wisconsin. The other schools caught up eventually, but one feature has always set Cambria's field apart. Emblazoned across the top of the scoreboard, the words "In Memory of William 'Dale' Gorsuch" overlook the football field, a reminder to all of Cambria of the young man they lost.

Anyone who knew William Gorsuch knew him by his middle name, Dale. Born March 20, 1948, Dale was well known at Cambria High School.[1] A three-sport letterman, Dale played football, baseball, and his favorite, basketball. Although the team never won any championships, Dale, a point guard, excelled on the court. He was awarded the Kiwanis Athletic Award as the senior athlete of the year his final year of high school.

Dale was a typical All-American teenager. In addition to sports, he sang in the school chorus and played trombone in the school band. A younger girl had beaten him for first chair in band, a fact he kidded her about during practice. One of Dale's teachers was also his aunt, which meant that his academics remained a priority alongside his extracurricular activities.

Dale had two younger brothers, Dennis and Duane. When Dale went out with friends or a girlfriend, his youngest brother sometimes accompanied him.

"I'd want to go with him, and he wouldn't want me to go, and I remember my mom would say, 'Oh, just take him along. You're home; just take him along with you. Let him go with you.' So I got to go with him," says Duane, who was ten years old when Dale was eighteen. "Not all the time, but I tried to sneak along somehow. Because I wanted to be with him."

When Duane managed to tag along, Dale usually had suitable retribution prepared. "We'd go over a bridge … and he'd be going real fast, and the car would feel like it's going airborne," says Duane. Other times, Dale would make sharp turns around ditches or by light posts to get a rise out of his brother. And, Duane admits, it usually worked, but it didn't stop him from going with Dale.

On winter weekends they went skiing on a hill outside of town. There was a towrope to climb the hill and a small heated building with a wood-burning fire for when it got too cold. Dale liked to hunt. In the summer, he enjoyed Cambria's swimming pool and fishing pond. It was the typical Wisconsin small town, friendly and fun.

Dale worked, too. His father, also named William, owned a trucking business for livestock hauling, and sometimes Dale helped there, but he held a separate job at a local canning factory, harvesting peas. Dale worked on a pea mower at a farm outside Cambria, riding twelve to fourteen hours along the pea field. They were long days, and often hot, but Duane, who worked the job years later, says, "You could almost fall asleep driving it" once you learned what to do.

When Dale graduated from high school in 1966, he didn't want to go into the trucking business with his father or remain with the canning factory. Instead, on October 24 he enlisted in the United States Navy.

The Gorsuch family had a history of Naval service. William Sr.'s younger brothers, Emerson and Emery, were both Naval veterans of the Korean War, serving aboard the USS *Salem*. Another brother, John, was a World War II veteran who survived two Japanese kamikaze attacks on the USS *Bunker Hill* aircraft carrier in 1945 by jumping from the flight deck into the open water. William, himself a World War II vet, served in the Navy on a diesel submarine, sleeping, he would say, directly over the torpedoes.

Dale followed the family tradition. At that time, it was almost certain that had he not joined willingly, he would have been drafted. He didn't

William "Dale" Gorsuch's senior photo from Cambria High School, circa 1966. Courtesy Duane Gorsuch.

want to leave it to chance. The Navy was his choice. There was also, he thought, a certain security in being aboard an aircraft carrier. So many men were dying on land, in the Army and the Marines, that being in the ocean seemed a better prospect.

Dale attended basic training at the Great Lakes Naval Station just north of Chicago and received further training in aviation handling before being assigned to Cecil Field in Jacksonville, Florida, where he would remain for two years.

Cecil Field was built in 1941 as a training base for the nearby Naval Air Station (NAS) Jacksonville. In the 1950s it was selected as one of four Naval Master Jet Bases for carrier-based jet aircraft and expanded to accommodate a growing number of recruits. When Dale arrived it was operating as an airport and training station on its own.[2]

At NAS Cecil Field Dale served as an aviation boatswain mate, handling (ABH3). ABH3s controlled all movement on the flight line, guiding aircraft into and out of their assigned ramp slots. He was trained to handle fires on deck and to prepare the foam formula used to quench the flames. He was stationed aboard the USS *Ticonderoga* at times during his two years and went to sea aboard it when it made one of its cruises to the Gulf of Tonkin. In October 1968 Dale was named "Sailor of the Month."

While he likely didn't intend to make a career of the Navy, Dale liked life in the service. He had most weekends off, and played on a softball team on base. He also returned home about every six months for a short leave. He came by train; Duane remembers him once arriving in the early hours of the morning, and the long night his family spent tracking Dale down to drive him home. In the summer of 1969 Duane, a cousin, and an uncle flew to Cecil Field to drive Dale back to Wisconsin. Dale surprised them by inviting several friends from the base along for the ride.

Dale wouldn't return to Florida. He'd been assigned to the USS *Constellation* (CVA-64), then operating out of the Gulf of Tonkin. When the end of his leave approached, Dale grabbed a small sea bag full of the few possessions he could bring with him, said goodbye, and left for the USS *Constellation*.

En route to the USS *Constellation*, Dale had layovers in California, Alaska, and Naval Air Station Cubi Point, Republic of the Philippines. On the morning of October 2, 1969, within twenty-five miles of the *Constellation*, the aircraft—a Grumman Greyhound Transport Aircraft (C-2A)—disappeared.

The *Constellation*, which had been in radio contact with the Grumman and had been tracking the plane's progress along a radar screen, received no distress calls. Within minutes of the aircraft's disappearance, the ship launched search-and-rescue operations. They located aircraft debris in the water but none of the twenty-six individuals aboard the plane.[3] The cause of the crash remains unknown.

Back in Cambria, it was Duane's thirteenth birthday. He was sitting on the porch, having just finished pumping up his football, when a gray car pulled into the driveway. It resembled an old-time taxi, and he watched as two Navy officers stepped out, along with the reverend from the Presbyterian Church and his father, who was crying. William Gorsuch asked him to come inside, where he told Duane and Betty that Dale had been killed.

Because his body had not been recovered after the crash, Dale was listed as missing in action, and the family initially had their doubts. "I think my mom and my dad kind of thought, 'Well, he's not really dead.' You know, they have second thoughts. I'm sure everybody does," says Duane. "They thought, 'Well, maybe he never got on the plane. Maybe he's still in Alaska some place.'"

They had a funeral, nonetheless, on October 11, 1969. All military rites were performed, but there was no casket, only an American flag draped over a table. The same reverend who had exited the car with William performed the service, and a family friend sang *When They Ring the Golden Bells* and *Face to Face.* When it was over, the family was left with a gravestone and a flag.

At home the objects of his life became precious mementoes. Betty Gorsuch saved everything from

Dale Gorsuch at Naval Air Station Cecil Field, May 11, 1968. Courtesy Duane Gorsuch.

when the boys were little, and overnight, everything that had been Dale's was all the more important. Clippings from his first haircut as a baby. Old combs and wallets left behind. His letters. All the clothes he couldn't take with him to sea, still in his closet. "When something like that happens, you try to get everything together," Duane says. "What else? You don't have anything else."

They had a lot of support. In a small town, where everyone knew everyone else, the Gorsuch family was never alone in their grief. The young girl who had played first trombone in the school band sent the family a letter several pages long with her memories of Dale and her condolences. Eventually, they gave Dale's American flag to the American Legion, and it still flies over the cemetery every Memorial Day. For decades friends and neighbors approached Dennis and Duane's own children to tell them how much they looked or acted like their Uncle Dale.

And forty-five years later, when

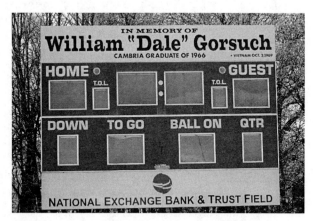

The current scoreboard above the Cambria-Friesland football field. Photograph by the author.

the lights turn on over the Cambria-Friesland football field, the scoreboard is illuminated. It's not the original one, presented to the high school by William and Betty Gorsuch in October 1970; it's bigger, more high tech. But on the top, the same words stand out above the field: "In Memory of William 'Dale' Gorsuch."

Because in a small town like Cambria, no one is ever forgotten.

Chief Master Sergeant
Charles Richard Fellenz

United States Air Force
disappeared November 24, 1969

"What was he like as a person? Happy."
"Friendly."
"Caring."
"Handsome."
"Caring."
"Oh, very handsome."
"A good family man."
"And he had a sense of humor."
—*Sue (Fellenz) Adler, Vivian Fellenz, and Cheryl (Fellenz) Clancy*

Dear Folks ...

He began his last letter much like he always had. Since enlisting in the Air Force on February 3, 1959, Charles Fellenz wrote home regularly of his kids, of his duties on base, of the weather, of football. And for over a decade Herbert and Ann Fellenz received and replied to their son's letters. The last letter was different. The last letter was delivered after the news that their son's plane had gone down. When they received Charles's last letter, he was already missing in action.

> Well, I guess I messed up on one of my letters. My mail box at Naha is 601. The one I had in Korea was 701. Here in Thailand I have no mail Box they just put all our mail by al[ph]abet in C-130 boxes in the mail room. So while I'm here at Thailand my mail will come to the above address. I'll be leaving here around 28 of Dec. so mail should stop coming here.[1]

For most of his life Charles Richard Fellenz went by his nickname, Chuck. He was the second of four children, born October 20, 1939, in Marshfield, Wisconsin. His youngest sister, Sue, describes him as a "very helpful, caring, and fun loving person."

Growing up, Chuck served as an altar boy at the nearby church and sang in the middle school boys choir at St. John's Parochial School. Chuck was known as Chaz at Columbus High School, where he started on both the varsity football and basketball teams. He also played on summer baseball leagues and actively followed the Wisconsin Badgers football team. After high school Chuck worked briefly as a delivery boy for a local bakery before enlisting in the United States Air Force in 1959.

The Fellenz family photo, circa 1968. Left to right: Chuck, Vivian, Cheryl (on Vivian's lap), Tommy, and Terry. Courtesy Sue Adler.

Chuck's letters home began that year. Chuck trained at Lackland Air Force Base and Amarillo Air Force Base in Texas before receiving his first overseas assignment to Osan Air Base in Pyeongtaek, South Korea. He followed his high school football team and the Wisconsin Badgers from afar. "Tonight in the show they had the Wisc. and Northwestern game in the news reel," he wrote home. "They missed tackles like mad on the touchdown Northwestern made." He worried that Wisconsin might not win the upcoming Rose Bowl game. (He was right.) The weather was foggy and wet in San Antonio, he added, and all he was hoping for was snow. He missed the cold.

Chuck was a long way from a typical Wisconsin winter in December 1960 as he was based in Okinawa. He spent Christmas at an orphanage in what Sue remembers as "the most memorable experience" of his military career. "The little kids just adored the men, and he enjoyed every moment of playing with them and giving them food," she recalls.

> I work 12 hrs a day. I really enjoy it because what I'm doing I can always see the finish product. Getting the planes off the ground. The weather here the last two days have been real hot. Today it feels like its about 90° so, mom, there is no snow here in Thailand.

Chuck returned to the United States in January 1961. He was assigned to the 74th Air Defense Missile Squadron at Duluth Air National Guard Base in Duluth, Minnesota. There, he met Vivian Klug, a college student in nursing school. They married on May 19, 1961, and their first son, Thomas, was born in Minnesota in 1963. Their son Terrence (Terry) and daughter Cheryl were born during Chuck's next overseas appointment at Wiesbaden Army Airfield, Germany.[2]

Chuck was next assigned to Grissom Air Force Base[3] in Indiana. After Indiana he was assigned to the 41st Tactical Airlift Squadron, part of the 374th Tactical Airlift Wing. His was one of several squadrons that rotated between Naha Air Base, Okinawa, and Ubon Air Base in eastern Thailand. The squadrons flew missions from the latter location, spending about sixty days at a time in Thailand before heading back to

Okinawa. Vivian and the kids moved to California, near her parents, when Chuck departed overseas again. His daughter, Cheryl, remembers a Gentle Ben teddy bear he sent her while he was away; she could pull its strings to make it talk.[4]

Chuck continued to write his parents. In August 1969 he told them that his baseball team on base was in second place. He was in Okinawa, as he had been almost a decade earlier, and he was again working with the local children. In early November, Chuck's squadron departed for Thailand.

> I think I'll enjoy my 52 days here because a person is kept busy all the time so we can make our missions for that nite. Received a bible from Viv and the kids have been real good.

In 1969 the Air Force had six large bases in Thailand. The U.S. and Thailand had friendly relations, and this location allowed the U.S. easy access to Cambodia and Laos. Although the U.S. was not officially operating in either country in 1969, the Ho Chi Minh Trail ran through both, and the trail was the target of most missions out of Ubon.

Construction on the Ho Chi Minh Trail began in 1959. The North Vietnamese continued to expand it until the war against South Vietnam ended in 1975. The trail, which was composed of a string of complex paths through the jungle, provided passage to the thousands of North Vietnamese soldiers who traversed it for access to South Vietnam. In addition to troops, supplies and machinery were also shipped down the trail.

The number of U.S. airstrikes along the trail increased each year after 1964, but the Ho Chi Minh Trail continued to be the most effective route for the NVA to enter the South. "Laos is some of the most rugged terrain in the world," remembers Shelton Bembry, assigned to Ubon in November 1969. "It's jungle-mountains, which is the worst of everything." It was a grueling journey, but one that members of the NVA continued to make. In all of 1964 roughly ten thousand North Vietnamese infiltrated the country this way; by 1968, however, nearly twenty thousand soldiers a month traversed the trail.

> The Captain I came with went back to Naha Saturday. So the little shop is all mine. That's why I got called out this afternoon because the boys aren't supply people and there not sure of a lot of things. Therefore I call them now and then and if problems arise I go to work.

Chuck's squadron conducted visual reconnaissance out of Ubon. Missions began just after sundown. Men used star scopes[5] aboard the Lockheed C-130 Hercules aircraft to look for soldiers and material traveling down the trail. Almost immediately after takeoff, the crew lowered a ramp and put a platform in place that held tubes about four to five inches in diameter and three to four feet long. They loaded flares containing phosphorus into the tubes. Once someone spotted something on the trail below, the flares were released. They suspended in the air on a parachute for several seconds before bursting into flames and emitting "an intense amount of light," recalls Shelton. "You would be surprised by how much light these things would put out." Crews then called in another aircraft to hit the moving targets the flares had marked. While essential to the mission, the phosphorus was also a danger to the crew should it ever catch fire before being released.

Planes flew at a relatively low altitude, about twenty-five hundred to three thousand feet above ground level—and much closer to the mountains—in an effort to spot truck headlights. The planes flew with their lights off, the flaps of their wings partially extended, and at a speed of only about one hundred eighty miles an hour. A big concern for the crews, says Shelton, was midair collisions. Another threat to flying so low and slow along the trail was antiaircraft artillery. Aircraft tried to determine where this artillery was located and avoid those areas whenever possible.

> Today I started to listen to the Ohio, Purdue game and it really, as you know, a walk away on Ohio's part. I sure wish Ohio could go to the Rose Bowl. Next week Ohio plays Michigan Guess they'll send Michigan to the Bowl since they haven't been there lately.

Staff Sergeant Charles Fellenz was not assigned to fly on the evening of November 24, 1969. One member of the eight-man crew[6] scheduled for the night's mission was unable to fly, and Chuck volunteered as the crew's illuminator. It was his job to release the flares. At approximately 9:07 p.m., while flying over the target area in Laos, the aircraft pilot was informed of nearby antiaircraft artillery. He turned the plane and again was informed of enemy fire. Seconds later, the aircraft was hit.

There were no signals or radio contact made as the plane went down. "It wasn't like you reported everything you did," says Shelton. "You were out there by yourself. You were in radio contact with your command base or other aircrafts, but ... they didn't have a play-by-play of what was going on.... You either came back in one piece, or you didn't come back."

Shelton remembers the status update on base regarding the C-130A. It simply read, "Plane Missing."

Chuck was 30 years old. His children were 6, 5, and 3.

> When the Captain left he told me I'd be going to Vietnam after I left here in Dec. I told him he was crazy.... A full bird colonel wanted to make me PCS[7] here but the captain said no. I agree especially if it gets this darn hot here during the summer.

When the news reached the Fellenz family in Marshfield, Herbert Fellenz swore to raise the American flag on his porch every day until his son came home. Initially, there was hope that Chuck might have been a prisoner of war and could still return, but as the years passed, that possibility seemed less and less likely. As an MIA, Chuck was promoted to the rank of chief master sergeant in 1976. In 1978 the military changed Chuck's status to killed in action. This would allow his widow, Vivian Fellenz, to remarry, but she never did. "She never wanted to," Sue says.

Herbert continued to raise his flag. "When Chuck would have come back he'd have been stationed in Hawaii," he said in 1987.[8] "And I told him when you come back here, I'll still have the flag out there. And it's been there ever since. If there's ever no flag flying in Marshfield, there'll be one here, always."

> The movies I went to at Naha are appearing here now on base. So there isn't too much to do but read books. Next Tuesday I can start seeing new movies.

Unknown to the Fellenz family, in 1990 the Joint Casualty Resolution Center (JCRC) met with Lao representatives and put forward several crash sites that they wished to study, including that of Chuck's crew. The site was approved and was excavated from October 21 to November 8, 1993. Despite having been scavenged for scrap metal by locals in the late 1980s, there remained a great deal of material from the crash. Among the wreckage was found much of the engine and propeller, three survival knives, three belt buckles, three .38 caliber revolvers, one combat boot, and Chuck Fellenz's wedding ring.

Four dog tags were found. One read: Fellenz, Charles R. Among the hundreds of bone fragments found at the site, only one tooth could be used for identification purposes. And it was identified as Chuck's.

The Fellenz family didn't learn of Chuck's identification until 1995. The news was bittersweet. "It's an awful long time to wait for the news," said Richard Fellenz, a cousin.[9] At the same time, Sue acknowledged that "[It was] kind of a relief to know he had gone that way instead of being a prisoner of war."[10]

> Well I guess I'll close this letter off. I just got another call from work. Next week at this time I hope my troops will know enough so I can enjoy my day off. Remember me and Terry in your prayers.

A group ceremony for all the men aboard the C130-A was held at Arlington National Cemetery on November 29, 1995, twenty-six years and five days after the aircraft went down. A monument bears the names of all eight crewmembers.

Chief Master Sergeant Charles Fellenz served more than ten years in the Air Force before his aircraft disappeared in 1969. Courtesy the Vietnam Veterans Memorial Fund.

Because he was definitively identified, Chief Master Sergeant Charles R. Fellenz was given a private burial at Arlington National Cemetery with full military honors. On a rainy April 9, 1996, at 10:45 a.m., a funeral mass was held at Arlington Cemetery's Ft. Meyer Chapel. Following the service, six honor guards placed the flag-covered casket, containing CMS Fellenz's recovered tooth and dog tags, on a horse-drawn caisson. The caisson made its way to the burial site, preceded by members of the U.S. Air Force Honor Guard and Band, and followed by a procession of thirty family members from California, New York, Florida, Illinois, and Wisconsin. CMS Fellenz's memorial marker, previously placed in the section of the cemetery for bodies not recovered, was removed and laid beneath the casket. The Air Force played *Taps* and performed a twenty-one-gun salute. A United States flag was presented in his honor to his wife and sister. The ceremony gave the family the closure they needed as he was laid to rest.

In Washington, D.C., Panel #16W, Line #116 of the Vietnam Veterans Memorial Wall bears Chuck's name. For years a plus sign had been engraved beside it, indicating his MIA status. This was changed to a diamond to show that Charles Fellenz had been found.

> Don't worry about me. I'm safe. Even if I wasn't, don't worry because only God knows when you're leaving this world.
> See you.
> Love,
> Chuck
>
> P. S. Happy Birthday, dad, from all the Fellenz—Calif. and Thailand.

Major Dale Wayne Richardson
United States Army,
disappeared May 2, 1970

"Dale was kind of on the shy side and very studious. He was always smiling and well spoken."—Linda Gibbins

"He was a nice, nice man.... His demeanor was, 'Do your doggone job. Just sit down and do your job, please.'"—David Counts

During their senior year the White Hall High School Class of 1959 boarded a train and visited Washington, D.C. They saw the White House and the Washington Monument. They toured the Treasury Department and the Supreme Court. They walked through Arlington National Cemetery. For country kids from a small Illinois town, it was the trip of a lifetime. "I'm sure many of our young people in that class have never been back to Washington," says Bill Price, a 1959 White Hall graduate.

In October 2015 Dale Richardson returned to Arlington, more than fifty years after his class trip and forty-five years after his death.

Dale Wayne Richardson was born May 5, 1941, in Stone County, Arkansas. He grew up in Arkansas, Missouri, and Illinois, where he attended White Hall High School. White Hall, Illinois, had a population of roughly thirty-two hundred. On Friday nights, most of the city turned out to watch the White Hall high school sports teams compete with the Roodhouse teams from three miles to the south.[1]

Dale's father was the principal of White Hall High School, and Dale was an active member of the small school community. His senior year he worked on the yearbook, participated in the Christmas play, and was a member of Thespian Society. As an undergraduate, he was involved in a radio club, an industrial club, band, journalism, and the junior play. "He was a pretty quiet fella," remembers Bill, while also noting that Dale retained a slight accent from his time in the South.[2]

Outside of school Dale was a musician and amateur chemist. He attended Western Illinois University, then, in 1961, enlisted in the United States Army. Dale spent six months at the Field Artillery Officer Candidate School (OCS) at Fort Sill, Oklahoma, before deploying overseas with the 2nd Armored Cavalry Regiment, then stationed in Germany. In 1965 he was selected to attend the 7th Army Noncommissioned Officer Academy in Grafenwöhr.

Dale returned to Fort Sill in 1966 for U.S. Army Artillery and Missile Officer Candidate School, followed by further training at the U.S. Army Armor School. In September he joined the 2nd Battalion, 34th Armor in the Tây Ninh Province of Vietnam. Dale served as leader of the mortar platoon. The platoon's job was to aid infantry units in the field if they were pinned down by enemy fire. Dale was with the 2/34 when the unit partook in Operation Junction City, the only airborne operation of the Vietnam War. The operation took place in February 1967, but Dale's unit joined the battle on March 21. They fought near the abandoned village of Suoi Tre, where an American force of 450 was attacked by an enemy force of roughly 2,500. The 2/34 arrived with machine guns and tanks, providing desperately needed relief to the surrounded American infantry and forcing the enemy to retreat. The 634 casualties inflicted on the opposing forces nearly decimated an entire North Vietnamese division.

In August 1967 Dale reenlisted for another two years of service. Between tours, Dale married. He lived with his family in Cashton and Sparta, Wisconsin. Stationed overseas again, he kept a picture of his wife and two daughters with him in his office in Vietnam.

Dale was a respected officer, and one who stood out from many of the others. "He didn't act like he was gung-ho military," remembers David Counts of the 2/34.

First Lieutenant Brian McCarthy agrees:

> Most of the [captains] ... were tough guys who *wanted* to come back to Vietnam. I never received that impression from Dale. He [seemed] like a very decent man with a young wife and young family back home. I always felt he didn't belong in Vietnam with the rest of the captains.

Dale Richardson was serving his second tour in Vietnam when the helicopter in which he was a passenger crashed during the invasion of Cambodia. Courtesy Vietnam Veterans Memorial Fund.

In 1970, Dale was assigned again to Tây Ninh, where he served as one of the leading officers on the base. Shortly thereafter, the 2/34 was transferred to a location near Bearcat Base, in southern Vietnam. According to David, the base was more like an outpost, and a miserable one at that. "There was not a blade of grass in sight," he says. "And it was like 115° most days."

At Bearcat, Dale attended logistical meetings each morning with Thais and Australians operating from the base. When they first arrived, a sergeant was assigned to drive Dale to the daily meetings. One morning, when the sergeant failed to report, Dale asked David if he could drive instead. The duo discovered that they worked well together—David was directly responsible for the tanks on base. "It was my job," he explains, "to keep track of all the tanks, the missions they were on, the deadlines, when they would need back-up, what was needed, and also where our platoons were operating."

For Dale, it was convenient to have David fill

him in on the status of the tank platoons while they drove, so he asked for David to be his driver again the next day. It was an unusual situation because David ranked lower than the sergeant, and the sergeant was not pleased. The sergeant verbally harassed David so much that David planned to transfer to the field until Dale stopped him.

Dale didn't care who was ranked higher; he cared who got the job done. That, he felt, was David. "He should have backed [the sergeant]," David remembers. "Because he was over me, but [Dale] told him to stand down and never speak to me again." David drove Dale to his meetings every morning until they left Bearcat.

One evening in late April the 2/34 was informed that it was pulling out of Bearcat the next day and returning to Tây Ninh. They packed an entire tank battalion in one night and departed the following morning. They traveled about one hundred miles back to Tây Ninh and were moving out again within days. "You're not told a whole lot," David explains. "You're just told what you're doing, not why you're doing it."

They learned the cause of the sudden departure soon enough. On April 30, 1970, President Richard Nixon appeared on television sets across America and announced the invasion of Cambodia, stating, "This is *not* an invasion of Cambodia."[3] The 2/34, meanwhile, was already there.

Nixon explained that for years the North Vietnamese had ignored Cambodia's declared neutrality and hidden within its borders. The United States, frustrated but respectful of Cambodia's decision, could not pursue them. Nixon said South Vietnamese soldiers would primarily be responsible for carrying out the operation except in "one area … immediately above Parrot's Beak," where a joint United States–South Vietnamese coalition would force the enemy out. He ended the address, beseeching the American people:

> I ask for your support for our brave men fighting tonight halfway around the world—not for territory—not for glory—but so that their younger brothers and their sons and your sons can have a chance to grow up in a world of peace and freedom and justice.

Nixon's heartfelt plea for support was genuine; much of what preceded it, though, was not. By April 1970 the American military presence had been felt in Cambodia for over a year; the U.S. diplomatic presence had been there even longer.

While Cambodia had officially declared neutrality in the early 1950s, their Prince (later King) Norodom Sihanouk had always maintained a pro–Communist stance. Knowing this, the North Vietnamese built bases along the Cambodian border. In 1963, only days before John F. Kennedy's assassination, Sihanouk cut off all military and economic relations with the United States. After several Cambodians were killed in American bombing raids in 1965, Sihanouk ended all diplomatic ties with the United States as well. Cambodia began taking military steps against American planes flying over its territory and held captive all pilots who ejected from their planes or were shot down.

In 1968 Sihanouk opened the major port of Sihanoukville, along the Ho Chi Minh Trail, to the North Vietnamese and Vietcong. In July of that same year General Creighton Abrams, head of the Military Assistance Command in Vietnam, requested an air campaign to destroy enemy bases within three to ten miles inside the Cambodian border. The mission was approved and put into action on March 18, 1969.

"Operation Menu," with air raids missions titled "Breakfast," "Lunch," Supper," "Dinner," and "Dessert," succeeded in both destroying designated Communist bases in Cambodia yet remaining entirely secret to the American public. When *The New York Times* published an article about the covert raids on May 2, 1970, an excess of one hundred tons of bombs had already been dropped inside Cambodia.

For those American soldiers who had already crossed the border when the *Times* article was published, "it was awful," David recalls. "It was supposed to be a surprise attack. The surprise was they were waiting for us." The battalion was soon in need of supplies, namely, the .50 caliber machine gun barrels attached to the top of each tank, which tended to overheat and warp when used too often. And they were being used often in the opening days of the Cambodian incursion.

Captain Marvin Tieman sent 1st Lieutenant Brian McCarthy back from the field to Tây Ninh to collect as many .50 caliber machine gun barrels as possible for the unit's tanks. Dale Richardson was already on base, commanding D Company and responsible for the unit's supply-and-support functions.

That afternoon nine men boarded a Bell UH-1H Iroquois helicopter back to Cambodia: Captain Dale Richardson,[4] Warrant Officer Michael Varnado, Warrant Officer Daniel Maslowski, Staff Sergeant Bunyan Price, Sergeant Rodney Griffin, Specialist Frederick Crowson, Captain Robert Young, Private First Class Tony Karreci, and 1st Lieutenant McCarthy.

Also on board were four wooden crates, each containing eight 25-pound machine gun barrels, laundry, and mail being forwarded to the front. With these supplies and the passengers, it became apparent almost immediately that the helicopter was too heavy to fly. "The obvious solution," writes Brian, "was to off-load the barrels, laundry (and me), which lightened the load by about 1000 pounds." Approximately fifteen minutes later the Huey and its eight passengers took off.

Several hours later Captain Tieman, on the ground with the 2/34 in Cambodia, radioed Tây Ninh to say the helicopter was overdue.

Official documents say the helicopter encountered a rain squall. In the confusion the helicopter flew deeper into Cambodia than planned. "In the days before GPS, helicopters had a compass for navigation, an altimeter—which measures the distance from the ground—map coordinates, an azimuth,[5] and that was about it," says Brian. He explains:

> They could tell what direction they were flying, and their altitude, but could not be sure of where they were in relation to the ground.... They relied heavily on landmarks on the ground, rivers, intersections, roads, etc. Over rural areas, where all that could be seen was green jungle and rice paddies, navigation became very difficult. During inclement weather, impossible.

The helicopter was hit with antiaircraft artillery soon after crossing into Cambodia, and the back end caught fire. The pilot, Warrant Officer Michael Varnado, was injured so the copilot, Warrant Officer Daniel Maslowski, landed the Huey in a rice paddy about two miles inside the border, thirty miles from Tây Ninh. All eight men survived the crash, but within minutes of landing the enemy opened fire on the helicopter from all sides.

Of those aboard the Huey, only Tony Karreci returned to friendly territory. Four men were captured. Frederick Crowson and Daniel Maslowski remained prisoners of war until their release in 1973. Michael Varnado succumbed to his injuries, and Robert

Young died of illness while being held in captivity. Bunyan Price, Rodney Griffin, and Dale Richardson were last seen returning fire in the Cambodian jungle.

President Nixon's rationale for keeping the Cambodian invasion a secret for as long as he did proved justified. Despite his pleas for support of the troops, demonstrations erupted across the country. On May 4, two days after Dale Richardson's disappearance, any reports of the crashed Huey and her eight passengers were overshadowed by the deaths of four Kent State University students at the hands of the Ohio National Guard during an antiwar protest.

The next day, May 5, was Dale's birthday. He would have been 29 years old.[6]

Beginning in 1992 a joint team of American and Cambodian researchers began excavating the Huey crash site as well as a possible burial site nearby. Their initial searches proved unsuccessful, but in 2014 the remains of Dale Richardson, Bunyan Price, and Rodney Griffin were discovered in a shallow grave not far from the crash site. Their remains were returned to the United States on April 3, 2014, and positively identified on January 27, 2015. On October 20, 2015, all three men were interred at Arlington National Cemetery. Brian McCarthy gave the eulogy as the three soldiers were finally welcomed home.

Specialist Fourth Class
Peter Alden Schmidt

United States Army,
disappeared August 15, 1970

"He was a really, really super guy.... He was a very, very compassionate person. He was a loving person. He didn't have a mean bone in his body."—Paul DeNicola

"Pete was someone you could always depend on."—Steve Breese

"He was such a wonderful, loving, loyal friend."—Mary Carter

"Semper Paratus" is the official motto of the 16th Infantry Regiment of the United States Army. Translated, the phrase is Latin for always prepared. The words neatly summarize the mentality of both the regiment and the individuals who serve in it. Peter Schmidt would demonstrate this time and again during his service with the unit. Splitting his tour in Vietnam between the jungle and the sky, Pete's willingness to tackle any challenge, regardless of risk, was a common theme wherever he served.

Peter Schmidt was born November 7, 1949. He attended Solomon Juneau High School[1] in Milwaukee, where many of his classmates remember him for his great smile and sense of humor. In Tony Sciurba's yearbook, Pete wrote: "To a good kid that I had bad times in Chemistry with. Best of luck, Pete." Pete played on the Solomon Juneau football team as a sophomore, when the team practiced directly across from Fairview Mausoleum.

Growing up, Pete had one brother, three sisters, and a lot of pets. "He loved animals, and animals loved him," says his older brother, Mike. "He had every animal in the world as a pet." Pete owned raccoons, pigeons, parakeets, rabbits. He even had a skunk for a while. "It wasn't deodorized," Mike adds. "He didn't have that one for long. It got loose and disappeared."

Pete graduated from Solomon Juneau[2] in June 1968 and remained in Milwaukee, living downtown on State Street. He owned a '58 white Chevy, which he liked to drive up and down Bluemound Road. "We just hung out. We had a core group of eight guys and gals in the Milwaukee area," says Paul DeNicola, who met Pete at this time. "He was just a regular guy.... He had this heart and soul in him. A very, very peaceful guy."

At the peak of the Vietnam War, Pete was drafted in 1969. Following basic training, he was assigned to the 1st Battalion of the 16th Mechanized Infantry in the 1st Infantry Division. The battalion, known as the "Iron Rangers," operated in the jungles north of Lai Khe.[3]

Pete was part of a 1/16 mortar unit. His squad leader, Steve Breese, explains:

> We traveled in a group of about twenty armored personnel carriers and, basically, we would go into the jungle and set up kind of a lift, like wagon trains. We would set up our mortars there and then there were four infantry companies that kind of operated like spokes out around us. We would fire our mortars in support of them when we had contact. Most of our fire missions were through the night. When we suspected activity somewhere, then we would fire so many rounds into the area.... We were constantly chasing the enemy. Our days kind of consisted of that.

Pete Schmidt's graduation photo from Solomon Juneau High School, circa 1968. Courtesy the Schmidt family.

The men rarely had free time; the Iron Rangers conducted 690 ambush patrols in January 1970 and 803 in February.[4] In a way, it was almost better to be busy. Theirs was a dangerous job, and free time allowed them to dwell on its downside. "We were all just soldiers and trying to make the best of things," Steve says. Pete's "great sense of humor" helped with that. "We were able to keep things light, considering the situation we found ourselves in."

In early 1970 the Iron Rangers were pulled out of the jungle and moved to Fire Support Base Dakota, just off a main road in Saigon. "We worked that area just the same [as we worked the jungles], but we were stationed close to the road so we could go up at a moment's notice and head back to Saigon if anything happened," says Steve.

While there, the unit encountered a Vietcong basecamp of about three hundred enemy soldiers. The VC soldiers disappeared before the infantry units attached to 1/16 were able to attack. Steve was instructed to put together a six- to eight-man squad to look for the vanished enemy. It was a necessary assignment, but dangerous. Pete was one of two soldiers to volunteer for the job. The team found the Vietcong, but the unit never engaged them; they were vastly outnumbered. The courage of Pete and the other volunteer, Terry, impressed Steve. It cemented a close friendship between them for the remainder of their tours.[5]

The 1/16 Mechanized Infantry ceased combat operations on March 3, 1970, and the unit withdrew from Vietnam in April. Its members were either sent home or reassigned. Pete was among the latter group. His records show that he spent some time with the 3rd Battalion of the 21st Infantry before joining the 71st Assault Helicopter Company (AHC) of the 14th Aviation Battalion, a part of the 16th Combat Aviation

Group. The company operated out of Marble Mountain, Danang,[6] and Pete served as a helicopter door gunner.

Despite the risks attached to the job, Pete had actively sought this role. His friend Mary Carter, to whom he wrote frequently, recalls:

> In one of his letters he had written of his desire to become a helicopter gunman. He was very tall and I remember he had stated several times in his letter that the army and all of its marching was affecting his knees. I remember asking him not to do that because of the danger of the position of the helicopter gunman.

Using an M60 machine gun, door gunners provided fire support for infantry on the ground. They often disconnected the M60s from the helicopter's fixed mounts and attached them to bungee cords to improve their range of motion. Seated in the helicopter entryway, they were fully exposed to enemy fire. A morbid saying among soldiers at the time was that the life expectancy of a Huey door gunner in a hot landing zone was ten seconds.

Stationed in Chu Lai, the 71st Aviation Company flew a variety of missions, including combat assaults, resupply, observation, and special operations. The Bell UH-1 Iroquois, or Huey, used in these operations was nicknamed a "slick" to distinguish it from the more heavily armed gunships. The helicopter was identified by its radio call sign; gunship pilots in the 71st were referred to as "Firebird," while slick pilots were given the call sign "Rattler."[7]

"The Huey became synonymous with the Vietnam War," writes Chuck Gross, a Rattler pilot, "and would become the greatest military helicopter of all time."[8]

Peter Schmidt served with the 1st Battalion, 16th Mechanized Infantry and the 71st Assault Helicopter Company during his tour in Vietnam. Courtesy the Schmidt family.

In July 1970 the 71st AHC began assisting MACV-SOG, CCN[9] in performing covert operations in Laos. The missions were classified: Anyone caught revealing information about the assignments could receive up to ten years in jail and a $10,000 fine. Accompanying U.S. Special Forces on these missions were Special Forces from the Army of the Republic of Vietnam (ARVN.)

Participation in special operations was voluntary, and Specialist Fourth Class Peter Schmidt was among the volunteers. His mission on August 15, 1970, was a special ops mission. Operations were staged out of Kham Duc, near the Laotian border. Earlier that morning the base was notified that a CCN team in Laos had to be withdrawn. Five Hueys were sent into Laos to make the extraction. Pete was the door gunner on "Chalk Two," the second aircraft in the formation. Also on board were the pilot, Warrant Officer Andy Anderson; the copilot, Lieutenant James Becker; and the crew chief, Specialist Fourth Class Michael Crist.

Everyone was aware they were flying into a hostile environment. This was made unmistakably clear when, within a mile of the extraction site, the first aircraft in the formation was shot down.[10]

With Chalk One down, Chalk Two took over the extraction. The helicopter descended, released a rappelling ladder, and the five team members awaiting them on the ground climbed on. The helicopter readied for its ascent, when it suddenly pitched, crashed, and rolled onto its side.[11]

The crash knocked Lt. Becker unconscious, strapped in his seat. When the aircraft rolled, it pinned Pete beneath it. Spc4 Crist and WO Anderson tried unsuccessfully to free both trapped men. Due to the intense enemy fire surrounding them, they had no choice but to scramble up the nearby hillside.

Three of the five Hueys that began the mission were still airborne. One had rescued the downed crew of Chalk One and returned to base. The remaining two descended to pick up the CCN team members—the original extraction targets—and the two crew members of Chalk Two who had escaped the crash. Both helicopters returned to Kham Duc with every intention of refueling and returning to the site to retrieve Pete and Lt. Becker, both of whom were alive when last seen. It was only when they landed at Kham Duc that the CCN commanders told them in no uncertain terms that they were not to fly out again.

"We could not believe it," Chuck Gross writes in his book. "The thought of Becker and Schmidt out there and possibly alive terrorized us."[12]

Lieutenant James Becker was 26 years old. He was married and had a baby son.

Specialist Fourth Class Peter Schmidt was 20 years old. Although there were no remains to bury, a memorial service was held in his honor at Wisconsin Memorial Park in Milwaukee.[13]

"I had also lost a friend by the name of Joe Peterlich and I cried when I found out," recounts Mary Carter. "Peter was with me at the time and he asked me if he was killed in Vietnam, would I cry at his funeral also, and I said I would. Sadly, that's what happened.

"He is a hero in my eyes and always will be."

Specialist Fifth Class
Randolph Leroy Johnson
United States Army,
disappeared February 20, 1971

"He was a wonderful guy, and everybody—and I mean everybody—loved him. He was the epitome of cool—Fonzie cool."—Bud Dunlap

"Randy was kind of a quiet guy…. Really a laid-back guy, really a nice guy."—Curtis Haws

"Wisconsin should be very proud of Randy."—Richard Hickman

"The poor guys," Richard Nixon said to Henry Kissinger on May 10, 1971.[1] It was over a month since Operation Lam Son 719 had ended, the invasion of Laos that marked the first attempt at a land invasion led exclusively by the Army of the Republic of South Vietnam (ARVN). President Nixon wasn't speaking about the ARVN soldiers, though. He was speaking of the American helicopter crews that had been working tirelessly for months, providing air support and depositing and extracting troops from Laos. He was speaking about the 197 helicopters that were lost—and the crewmen lost with them—and although he didn't know it, he was speaking of Specialist Fifth Class Randolph Johnson.

Bud Dunlap knew Randy longer than anyone else in the service. They met at Helicopter Repairman School in Fort Eustis, Virginia. Bud and Randy hit it off right away; it was hard not to like Randy. "He never rubbed anybody the wrong way," Bud remembers. "He could have run for governor."

At Fort Eustis, men could follow two routes: either as repairmen working ground maintenance or as crew chiefs responsible for helicopter maintenance during aerial operations. Married men often leaned toward the former for the security remaining on base provided. Randy came from a big family in Milwaukee, Wisconsin, but wasn't married. He elected to go the crew chief route.

Although the men spent six months training at Fort Eustis, much of their true training occurred once they were in Vietnam. "We had some classroom stuff [at Fort Eustis], explaining basic stuff about turbine engines and systems, but it seemed like everything was at the height of the Vietnam War," says Bud. "So when we were there, there weren't enough helicopters to go around. Most were in Vietnam." Because of that shortage, it was common for the men to hear the instructors say, "We're going to simulate." The men hardly ever touched a helicopter before they headed overseas, and what they did learn barely prepared them for what they dealt with in the war.

Both Bud and Randy were assigned to the 48th Aviation Company in the 223rd Aviation Battalion, stationed in Ninh Hòa, near South Vietnam's coast. Neither knew the other had received the same assignment until they bumped into each other one day on base. "It caught me off guard," Bud remembers with a laugh. "I walked around the corner, and there was Randy. I yelled, 'Hey, man!'"

The motto of the 48th Aviation Company was "Skill, Not Luck." The company was composed of two companies of flight ships, called the "Snoopys" and the "Wild Deuces," and one company of gunships, called the "Jokers." For his first few months in Vietnam, Randy flew with the Snoopys. The flight ships had no external weaponry and were most often used for troop airlifts. Bud estimates that about 85 percent of their missions involved resupply and troop delivery.[2] "Randy didn't talk a lot ... when we were flying," remembers Richard Hickman, a member of Randy's flight platoon. "He was very professional."

On the base, there was an outdoor movie screen as well as an enlisted men's club where members of the unit could drink and play poker. So much of their time was spent in their aircraft that Randy and other members of the flight platoon often brought cards and played between missions in the helicopter. Randy's crew tended to play Hearts or Spades, quite often for money. Overall, though, helicopter crews did not have a lot of free time. "If we weren't flying, we were working on the ships," says Bud. Often, they were out so much during the day that they reached the base post office late and found it closed; many men asked someone else to pick up their mail for them.

The days were long already, but then the 48th moved close to the Demilitarized Zone (DMZ) between North and South Vietnam, where some of the worst fighting in the war was taking place. The invasion of Laos was about to begin, and the helicopter companies, shorthanded to begin with, were about to find themselves busier than ever.

The United States had been unofficially involved in Laos for over a decade. The country, officially neutral since the Geneva Conference of 1962, was home to an armed communist group called the Pathet Lao and served as a safe haven to North Vietnamese troops, whom Americans could not pursue over the border. Roadways through Laos soon became instrumental parts of the Ho Chi Minh Trail. The United States, unwilling to cross the border on the ground, instead conducted a bombing campaign over Laos to stem the flow of tens of thousands of North Vietnamese men and matériel along the trail. In May 1965, it was estimated that the U.S. was flying an average of fifteen hundred combat air sorties over Laos monthly.

Military plans were made to invade Laos and cut off the Ho Chi Minh Trail as early as 1966, but were continually disapproved or set aside by the Johnson administration. When Richard Nixon took office, he adopted his plan of Vietnamization. The plan called for the responsibility of fighting the war to be transferred to the South Vietnamese troops, allowing the American forces to gradually withdraw. Nixon wanted to leave the war without abandoning South Vietnam. He believed a successful South Vietnamese invasion of Laos was a perfect opportunity to demonstrate the South's military capabilities. On May 30, 1969, he ordered General Creighton Abrams to prepare such a plan.

The goal of the invasion was for the South Vietnamese troops to destroy three major North Vietnamese bases in Laos. The plan resembled a 1967 proposal[3] that had called for an attack from Khe Sanh into Tchepone, Laos. However, the new (1969) operation plan did not take into account two major changes that had occurred since the 1967 proposal. First, the number of North Vietnamese troops in Tchepone had increased significantly. Second, in the original proposal, U.S. troops, then numbering more than five hundred forty thousand, would have conducted the main ground assault. When implemented in 1971, the attack would instead be led by approximately seventeen thousand ARVN.

It was hoped that Operation Lam Son 719, as it was called, would validate Nixon's Vietnamization policy and give the United States the opportunity to withdraw from Southeast Asia. Nixon wanted the South Vietnamese to achieve a decisive victory that would prevent a North Vietnamese attack during the dry season—a second Tet Offensive—and discourage future attacks. He also wanted minimal casualties. So while ARVN troops crossed into Laos, the U.S. was to provide heavy artillery along the Laotian border. Helicopter and air support would be employed as well. What followed was the largest helicopter assault of the Vietnam War.[4]

The operation began January 30, 1971. In the first week U.S. troops cleared a path to the Laotian border and reopened the combat base and airfield at Khe Sanh, abandoned since the siege of 1968.[5] This initial troop movement gave ample warning to the North Vietnamese as to where the invasion would take place. Hence, Lam Son 719 faced some of the most intense antiaircraft defenses of the Vietnam War.

Helicopter crews flew resupply missions, delivered troops, and extracted them. Flight crews often required support from multiple gunships, but that became increasingly difficult as the operation continued. Helicopters were going down fast, and those that made it back to base were often heavily damaged. In addition, platoons and crews were shifting constantly. "Crew members were being bounced all over the place," remembers Curtis Haws, "It was so fast, you couldn't hardly keep up with it."[6]

Randy had switched from a flight platoon to a gunship partway through his tour. "Only the best of the best switched," says Richard. "It was not an easy task to take on." As a crew chief, Randy was responsible for much of what

Randy Johnson flew as a crew chief with the 48th Aviation Company during a critical invasion: Lam Son 719. Courtesy Richard Hickman.

happened in the helicopter while the pilot flew. "Rookies did not get this job," Richard adds.

Randy had been with the company longer than many others on base. He had extended his tour, and his year was almost up. Bud says it was hard to believe Randy was still flying at all. A week before a man was due to return home, he was taken off flight status, meaning he was grounded and no longer had to fly. Randy was, Bud believes, maybe a day or two away from being taken off flight status. "Just as it was his time to come home," says Bud, "he got killed."

On February 20, 1971, Sergeant Randolph Johnson was a member of a gunship crew providing cover for an emergency supply mission twenty miles southeast of Tchepone, Laos. Captain David May, Chief Warrant Officer Jon Reid, and Staff Sergeant Bob Acalotto made up the rest of the crew. After crossing the Laotian border, the helicopter was hit by hostile fire and crashed.

A second gunship from the 48th Aviation Company soon located the downed helicopter. Official records report that two men were spotted outside the helicopter, running toward a wooded area. The airborne helicopter made several unsuccessful attempts to reach the crew, but was forced to return to base as night fell. A second rescue attempt was made in the morning, but the helicopter was again turned away by enemy fire. They did not see the crew members during the second attempt.

When the crash site was excavated in 2000, David May's dog tags, the remnants of a flight suit, and the remains of Bob Reid and David May were located. The evidence suggests that the two crew members seen running toward the woods on February 20, 1971, were Randy Johnson and Bob Acalotto.

The 48th Aviation Company lost 12 men during Operation Lam Son 719.[7] The U.S. Army's Center for Military History states that 215 American men were killed in action in the invasion of Laos from January to April 1971, and 1,149 were wounded. The Center further notes that 38 men were missing. One of these men was a tall, skinny blond from Milwaukee, Wisconsin. He was born May 22, 1949, and was 21 years old when he was declared MIA. He was quiet in demeanor, fun to be with, and a consummate professional on the job. Bud Dunlap speaks for many who knew Randy Johnson when he calls him "a genuine American hero."

Specialist Fifth Class
Richard Jay Hentz

United States Army,
disappeared March 4, 1971

"Rick was always easygoing. Not much of anything got him upset. He was task efficient and, overall, more athletic than me."—Ron Hentz

"I remember him as a very nice, nice guy. Friendly. Quiet. Intelligent."
—Richard Sundell

A seventeen-month age difference meant little to Ron and Rick Hentz. The boys grew up like twins in Oshkosh, Wisconsin. They played sports together, worked together, and when the Vietnam War came around, they both served as linguists in military security agencies. It was the little things they did together, however, the conversations and companionship they offered each other, that Ron misses most about his brother.

Richard Jay Hentz was born to Francis and Dorothy Hentz on November 7, 1947. Rick was the second of the four Hentz children, older than Kate and Randy, younger than Ron. One academic grade behind his brother, Rick found himself compared to Ron often at St. Vincent School, the Catholic elementary and middle school all four children attended. Learning came more naturally to Ron than it did Rick. Rick was smart, but following just behind his brother, the nuns held him to high standards. It didn't bother him. According to Ron, not much did.

He was also efficient and hard working. "Chores that took me an hour and a half he could do in an hour," Ron says. The boys worked several jobs growing up, the longest of which, newspaper boys for the *Oshkosh Daily Northwestern*, lasting from age 10 through high school. Rick delivered on the street where they lived, and Ron delivered on the next street over.

Outside of work, the boys played sports. Their favorite by far was baseball. "We excelled at it," Ron says. A headline from the June 21, 1958, *Daily Oshkosh Northwestern* backs Ron up. It reads, "Hentz Allows No Hits in Winning, 11–0." Rick's pitching in that game moved his south side Minor League team, the Junior Indians, into first place in their league. The boys took advantage of a nearby practice field. In the summer they

180

wore their swimming trunks beneath their jeans while they played, then crossed the street and went to the beach to cool off.

If they weren't playing baseball, they were bowling. They worked as pin boys at the bowling alley and bowled for free when the lanes were clear, setting the pins up for each other. Frequent games built their skills, and in high school both boys bowled close to a 200 average. Ron remembers one Sunday afternoon when he, Rick, and the two sons of the bowling alley owner bowled a game in which nearly every person in the building stopped to watch. When it was over, the combined score exceeded 1,000, and the lowest individual score was 254.

Ron thinks he was the better baseball player and bowler, and believes Rick would agree, but says that Rick "could whip me hands down in golf!" He golfed in high school, and was known to break 70 every now and again. He could play with the best of them. Ron remembers:

> [Rick] once went to a JC tournament for high schoolers and came home to tell me of someone he'd played golf with that day. He said that I should remember that kid's name because some day I would see him on the pro golf circuit. Coming from Rick, who was already the best high school golfer I'd seen, this had to be high praise. He said the kid's name was Andy North. I never forgot that name, and Andy North went on to win the U.S. Open twice, one of the four major golf tournaments held each year throughout the world. Andy is now a golf commentator on TV and still plays from time to time on the Pro Senior Tour.

Like baseball and bowling, the boys had plenty of opportunities to practice. They both caddied at the Oshkosh Country Club, and Rick worked in the pro shop, helping customers and assigning other caddies to the golfers. His senior year of high school, Ron wore the #1 badge as the best caddy in the club; the year after he left, the badge went to Rick.

Had he decided to take up another sport, Rick might have tried racecar driving. He had the nickname for it, and one incident at the club proved that he had the speed. Ron tells it best:

> A [club] member went to Milwaukee to play in a tournament and forgot his golf clubs. In a panic he called the pro shop and asked if his clubs could be delivered to him at the course in Milwaukee. He said that his Cadillac was parked in the club lot with the keys in the ignition and that Rick could use it to bring him his clubs. The only problem was that the member was due to tee off in an hour and a half and the course was 100 miles away. Rick made it to the course in just under an hour by speeding that Cadillac as fast as he could make it go.

The member, Ron says, was shocked and happy, and Rick earned the nickname A.J. after the racecar driver A. J. Foyt.

Ron joined the Air Force after graduating from Oshkosh High School.[1] After Rick graduated the following year, 1965, he attended Wisconsin State University–Oshkosh, then completed two years at Oshkosh Technical Institute, where he earned an Associate degree in accounting. By then Rick was of draft age, and rather than wait to have his future decided for him, he enlisted in the United States Army. The Army offered him a choice: He could find work in the field of his degree or he could go to language school, for which his test scores qualified him. Ron was already a Russian linguist. When Rick asked his brother his thoughts on the work, Ron said it "was very important and exciting." Perhaps not surprising, Rick chose this path.

In December 1968 Rick married Debbie Harris, with her parents' permission because she was still in high school at the time. Ron was already away on active duty, but came home from Alaska to serve as Rick's best men. All the men in the wedding party were in the military and all wore their uniforms for the service.

When Rick and Debbie left for their honeymoon the next day, they noticed an odd smell coming from under the car. Unknown to them, Rick's father, "a notorious prankster," says Ron, had put a piece of smelly Limburger cheese on the manifold of the car's engine during the wedding reception. Rick thought it was funny, but spent part of that day scraping melted cheese off the engine.

Rick then spent 47 weeks learning Vietnamese from native speakers at the Defense Language Institute Support Command at Biggs Field, Fort Bliss, Texas, graduating in early 1970. He received further training at the Defense Language Institute in Monterey, California, before being assigned to active duty in South Vietnam on October 10, 1970. When he left, his son Bradley was not quite six months old.

Rick was assigned to the 138th Aviation Company, 224th Aviation Battalion, 509th Radio Research Group. The 509th was part of the Army Security Agency (ASA), an Army intelligence unit that listened to and deciphered enemy radio transmissions. Ron, who flew as a member of the USAF

Richard Hentz joined the Army in 1968 and trained as a Vietnamese linguist. Courtesy the Vietnam Veterans Memorial Fund.

Security Service, explains that "security" was a euphemism to maintain the agency's secrecy:

> I like to think we used that word in the same way that the Soviet KGB, their answer to our CIA, used the word. Everyone knows what the KGB was about, but the translation into English of the three words that make up the initials KGB is Committee for State Security, an innocuous sounding title meant to disguise [the agency's intent].

The ASA had been in Vietnam since before the war "officially" began, performing reconnaissance and intelligence gathering on the ground. This proved fatal on December 22, 1961, when Specialist Fourth Class James Davis of the ASA was ambushed on a road outside Saigon. He became the first acknowledged American fatality of the Vietnam War. Changes to the way missions were conducted were necessary. The solution, it was believed, was in the air.

For most of the Vietnam War, the ASA conducted missions via the Special Electronic Mission Aircraft (SEMA). This kind of aircraft was designed for intelligence work, equipped with such tools as Doppler navigational systems and blade antennas in the wings that enabled them to home in on transmitters. The 138th flew several types of modified aircraft, but they were the only organization to fly the JU-21. Lee Hendley of the 138th explains the plane's unique role:

> The JU-21A looked different. The antenna system was contained in a large, elongated, egg-shaped dome, which dropped down from the center of the aircraft. The antenna[2] itself was inside the dome and rotated around and around. This antenna, along with a Litton Corporation Inertial Navigation System (INS) allowed the crew to pick up communication signals and locate the position of those signals. The JU-21A was not in olive drab colors like other SEMA aircraft. It was painted in gloss Army green and white. That information was then transmitted back to the 8th Radio Research Field Station at Phu Bai, for further action.

The unit was stationed in Phu Bai when Rick arrived. The men lived in hooches across from an ASA compound, which housed the mess hall, an officer's club, an enlisted club, and an NCO club. The compound was enclosed; only members of the ASA could enter or exit. They often took advantage of the compounds amenities when not on missions. If it was raining (as it often was in Phu Bai during the monsoon season), they simply hung around their hooches. Rick could often be found playing volleyball outside a friend's hooch, in an area they called the "Swamp."

Some members of the 138th, including Rick, were part of a special project called "Left Jab." These project members were selected following a rigorous background check and granted a security clearance. Most of the members trained at Fort Huachuca, Arizona, and arrived in Vietnam together.

Information about the operation and its mission remain classified in 2017. The unit conducted "radio research," a euphemism for monitoring radio transmissions. Flying the JU-21A, the men intercepted enemy communications, deciphered them, and passed the intelligence onto other agencies that used them to launch missions. As a Vietnamese linguist, Rick was charged with screening and translating the intercepted communications in real time and sending the report to those who could process and analyze it in more depth.

On March 4, 1971, Specialist Fifth Class Richard Hentz was a crewmember on JU-21A, tail number 18065, performing an intelligence-gathering mission near the DMZ. The rest of the crew included Captain Michael Marker, Warrant Officer Harold Algaard, Specialist Sixth Class John Strawn, and Specialist Fifth Class Rodney Osborne.[3] The base lost contact with the aircraft, and it failed to return to Phu Bai.

"Very few people in the ASA died," says Richard Sundell, who lived with Rick in Phu Bai. "I was devastated when I heard they had been shot down, and, of course, we tried to gather what information we could on the event."

Because of its classified nature, few details can be revealed about the mission or the aircraft's loss. What can be said is that on the day of the crash, a PAVN unit near the DMZ radioed that it had launched a surface-to-air missile and struck an aircraft it had been tracking. United States intelligence later confirmed this to be Rick's plane.

The aircraft was the last of only three ASA crews lost during the entire Cold War, and it was the only fixed-wing ASA plane shot down from the 138th Aviation Company.

Word of the crash soon reached Oshkosh, where Rick was due home in a month for a ten-day leave. By May, though, Rick's status had gone from missing in action to killed in action. He was 23 years old.

A bench at Menasha's Isle of Valor stands as tribute to Rick and all POW/MIAs. Funds for the memorial that bears Rick's name were raised by the Appleton VVA, Chapter 351. Photograph by the author.

Today, Rick's name is inscribed on a bench at the Isle of Valor, in Menasha, Wisconsin. Chapter 351 of the Vietnam Veterans of American, Appleton chapter, raised the funds for a memorial to stand tribute to all POW/MIAs lost in the Vietnam War, and for Rick, the only unaccounted-for serviceman in the area. He has a son, Brad, who is a deacon at a parish in Illinois, and two granddaughters who are both "smart as a whip," says Ron. Rick has a wife who raised their son as a Roman Catholic, even though she was not, to honor a promise she made to him. Rick also has Bob Dvorak, his wife's second husband, who raised Brad as his own. Rick's father is deceased, but he has a mother who is always an honored guest at local veteran remembrance ceremonies. He has a younger sister and younger brother, who live near enough to visit his memorial often. And he has an older brother, his best friend, who remembers him well and misses him still.

Warrant Officer
Albert Raymond Trudeau

*United States Army,
disappeared October 26, 1971*

"He was intelligent and he liked to follow the rules, which is good in the Army. And he was very generous. He always watched out for other people."—Bobbie (Trudeau) Connolly

"He did not portray himself to be anything other than what he was.... Dedicated. Honest. Trustworthy."—Mike Trudeau

Albert Trudeau lived his life on the move and he liked it that way. His was a military family, who were accustomed to moving every two to three years across the country or across the globe. Born in New Jersey, Al would live in Maine, France, Louisiana, Wisconsin, and Germany, all before graduating from high school. For some, it could be disorienting; for Al, who loved to travel, it was exciting. He couldn't get enough. Al took a cross-country road trip to California in a blue Corvette, joined the Army, trained in two more states, and then left for a new place, one last time—South Vietnam.

Born September 18, 1949, Al was the fourth of Francis and Ruth Trudeau's nine children, all of whom were known almost exclusively by their nicknames. There was Bobbie (Barbara), Cissie (Frances), Mike (Robert), Alby (Albert), Taffi (Catherine), Connie (Constance), Gene (Eugene), Jet (John), and Jimmy (James).[1]

Their frequent moves were made to accommodate Francis Trudeau's career as an Army officer. The family rarely had excessive furniture; it wasn't worth the trouble to pack and ship it with each move. Their houses were occasionally sparsely furnished. Their large house in Milwaukee, with two living rooms side by side, was spacious enough to play soccer indoors.

"The hardest part was the friends," says Mike Trudeau, Al's older brother. "You'd make friends. You'd leave. Leave them behind. You'd go someplace else, make new friends, and then leave them behind. And you just can't stay in touch with them all."

As a result, the Trudeau kids were close to one another. With little more than a year between them, Al and Mike spent much of their childhood together. As Cub Scouts they went camping with their father, a local Boy Scout troop leader. As they grew, both played Little League, though not always on the same team. Mike recalls a time when their teams faced off, Mike as the pitcher and Al up to bat. Al crushed Mike's pitch. "Maybe my heart wasn't in striking him out," he jokes.

Of the two of them, Mike was the one more likely to concoct a plan, and Al was the one more likely to say, "Maybe we shouldn't do that."

"He had a big heart," Mike says. "Smart brain."

Al had a trusting nature, a good conscience, and an honest streak and he expected the same of others. Not everyone lived up to his expectations. Mike remembers an incident at the end of the school year. One student had been bothering Al all year, trying to pick a fight, but Al had resisted. Finally, Al had had enough. He told Mike that he planned to fight the other student. Mike tells what followed:

> I said, "Who are you bringing with [you]?" And he says, "Nobody, it's just me and him." I go, "You think that, huh? ... So you think this guy's going to show up by himself?" He says, "Yeah, why wouldn't he?"

Al didn't cheat people. He played by the rules. That someone else wouldn't was unfathomable to him. In this instance, though, Mike was right, because the boy showed up with four or five other guys. But there was no fight. Mike also showed up with four or five guys of his own.

"From the time they were little, Mikey was always protecting Alby," their sister, Bobbie, says. "Always sticking up for Alby."

The non-fight took place at West Division High School, in Milwaukee. The Trudeaus had been in Milwaukee several years at that point, longer than they usually stayed in any one place. Al finished middle school there and completed his first two years of high school before their father was reassigned and they were, again, on the move.

The family's destination was Pattonsville, West Germany, an American housing area just outside of Ludwigsburg, Baden-Württemberg. There, Al and Mike attended Ludwigsburg American High School with dozens of other children of American servicemen. Perhaps the biggest difference between an American high school and German high school took place at lunchtime, when students wandered off campus to the nearby *gasthaus*, or restaurant, for lunch and beer. There was no minimum drinking age, and the boys learned to order one drink by holding up their thumb. Holding up one's forefinger in Germany got them two.

Al ran on the cross country team as a senior before graduating from high school in 1967. Then he and Mike returned to the United States via an Air Force standby flight arranged by their father and moved in with Bobbie, her husband Fran, and their family in Milwaukee. Living with Bobbie came with two conditions: (1) They had to decorate the tree on Christmas Eve and (2) they had to help watch her kids. Al was her son's first babysitter.

Al got a job at a Big Boy restaurant food preparation center, making the food that would be shipped out to the Milwaukee area Big Boy restaurants. He worked the night shift and slept most days. "I remember one time needing a ride," Mike recalls. "And he was like dead on his feet, but he offered to drive me anyway."

When he wasn't working at Big Boy, Al loved to work on his cars. He had a '55

Al in Milwaukee in 1969 about to do one of his favorite pastimes: driving a car. Courtesy Mike Trudeau.

Chevy, all primer gray, a Ford coupe, and a blue Corvette, among others, that he would fix up. He also frequented the local Washington Park, a popular spot, especially during the winter, when the lagoon froze and was used for skating.

There were several kids the same age within a few blocks who spent time together. Six or seven of the boys entered the military during that time, joining the fight overseas against North Vietnam. Mike's draft letter came in December 1968, and he left for training two months later. Al enlisted in the United States Army in the summer of 1969. He completed Basic Training at Fort Polk, north of Leesville, Louisiana, before continuing to Fort Wolters, in Texas, to train at the U.S. Army's Primary Helicopter Center. He graduated as a warrant officer in the Class 70–33.[2]

During training Al discovered something he hadn't known: He was colorblind. To his family, some of his more questionable wardrobe choices suddenly made sense.[3] He worried that it would prevent him from becoming a helicopter pilot, but it turned out to work in his favor. Colorblindness is a benefit when wearing night vision goggles.

Both Al and Mike would soon depart for deployments overseas, but they were headed for different destinations. "I was a grease monkey.... Track vehicle machines. So I figured my chances were a lot better [than Al's]," Mike explains. "And, besides, like I said, only the good die young, and that was him. That wasn't me. So I put in for Vietnam so that he wouldn't have to go, but they sent me to Korea instead."

Al's tour in South Vietnam began on February 25, 1971. He was a helicopter pilot in the 68th Assault Support Helicopter Company,[4] 52nd Aviation Battalion, 17th Aviation Group, in the 1st Aviation Battalion. Al flew the Boeing CH-47 Chinook, a troop and cargo transport helicopter. The unit was stationed at Camp Holloway, near Pleiku, in Vietnam's central highlands.

For the most part, Al liked the military. His primary complaint was a little unusual, Bobbie remembers, quoting some of the letters he sent home: "I don't know what's wrong with this military. Some people don't abide by the rules the way they should." And, "They should have more stringent rules."

The family also got letters in which he talked about how beautiful Vietnam was. "It's terrible that there is a war," he wrote. "This would be a beautiful place." He included pictures of the ocean and exotic landscapes.

Al called home frequently. Bobbie arranged it so all his phone calls came collect through her phone number so he didn't have to spend his military pay on phone calls. He'd tell them when and whom he was going to call, adding that they let him know the cost so he could pay them back.

Al came home once on leave about halfway through his tour. Mike managed to get his leave from Korea at the same time, and the boys stayed with Bobbie again. One night during their stay, Al started out of the room, saying he was going to take a shower. Mike told him, no, *he* was going to shower first. Al protested until Mike finally said, "I'm older."

The Trudeaus' last family photo, taken during Al's leave in October 1971. Back row: Francis and Ruth; middle row left to right: Cissie, Mike, Connie, Gene, Al, Bobbie, Jet, and Taffi; front row: Jimmy. Courtesy Mike Trudeau.

Al replied, "I outrank you."

It was, Bobbie says, the one time she remembers Al getting the better of Mike, and it's one of her favorite memories of that visit.

There was another significant moment from that visit that Bobbie won't forget— the end of it. She says:

> We had to take him to the airport…. You know, with our family, we used to take people to the airport and stuff like this all the time. And so we took him to the airport and we're standing there, and the weather wasn't that great. And so he says goodbye and gets on the plane, and the plane taxis out and it sits out there at the end of this runway. And it sits there, and it sits there. It must have been out there almost an hour or more. And the longer it sat out there, the more tense and stressed out I got. And I said to [Fran], "We've got to go out there. Somehow we've got to get him off that plane." And he said, "You can't go get him." And I said, "Something's telling me he needs to be off that plane." And it turned out to be real.

Al returned to Vietnam and continued his tour. One night, roughly three months before he was due home for good, he called Bobbie in Milwaukee. He was going to be flying the next day, he told her, and he'd have a chance to pick up Christmas presents for everyone. What did they want?

He wasn't originally scheduled to fly that next day, October 26, 1971. Someone was sick, and 22-year-old Warrant Officer Albert Trudeau was chosen to replace him. The rest of the crew included Chief Warrant Officer Leonard Maquiling, Specialist Fifth Class Michael Lautzenheiser, Specialist Fourth Class Mickey Eveland, and Private First Class Thomas Green. They were scheduled to depart Camp Holloway at 7:50 a.m. They took off with three passengers, plus cargo, to be delivered in the Cha Rang Valley. Before takeoff, Spc5 Lautzenheiser was seen taking a picture of Al Trudeau in front of their CH-47 helicopter.

From Cha Rang Valley the crew proceeded to Lane Army Heliport in An Son, where they picked up more cargo and eight more passengers, four destined for Tuy Hòa and four for Cam Ranh Bay. The latter group consisted of Staff Sergeant Rufus Falkner, Jr., Staff Sergeant Sanford Finger, Sergeant Edward Himes, and Specialist Fifth Class Robert Nickol.

The crew landed at Tuy Hòa at 11:15 a.m., and delivered four of their passengers. The crew ate lunch, refueled, unloaded their cargo, and picked up one new passenger destined for Cam Ranh Bay, 1st Sergeant James Skinner. There were ten people aboard the helicopter when it took off at 1:50 p.m.—five crewmembers and five passengers.[5] It was expected to arrive at Cam Ranh Bay thirty minutes later.

It never did. That day a devastating storm raged up and down Vietnam's coastline, directly in the helicopter's path. At 2:50 p.m., the Chinook was reported as overdue. The severe weather that afternoon and evening made it impossible for search-and-rescue operations to look very long for the missing helicopter.

Over the next two weeks, debris found off the coast indicated that the helicopter had crashed into the water at high speed. The bodies of three passengers were recovered: Sgt. Skinner, SSgt. Falkner, and Sgt. Himes. Of the crew, the only body found was that of CWO Maquiling. All ten aboard the helicopter were killed; six, including Al, were missing.

Bobbie was the first to find out. "I told them…. 'You must have the wrong people because, you know, he's not missing,'" she remembers. "I said, 'I just talked to him.' And they said, 'When?' And I said, 'Last night.'"

"This happened today," the Army officers told her.

That he was missing was what hit them the hardest. There was the initial fear that Al may have been taken prisoner, but as time passed and it became clear that was not the case, it was the lack of closure the family felt most deeply, with Al so far from home.

Searches are ongoing. There are time and weather constraints, but excavations on nearby islands, where bodies may have been found and buried, were conducted as recently as 2013. There are talks of reactivating the search. It's been more than forty years since Albert Trudeau died, but it's not too late to bring him back.

Speaking of the possibility, the family would like to have him home, buried on American soil. But if the searches don't meet with success, that's okay, too.

"He's in Heaven. He can go anywhere he wants," Bobbie says.

"Without a helicopter," Mike agrees. "He can fly."

Captain David Leverett Leet

United States Marine Corps, disappeared April 13, 1972

"Dave was one of those kinds of persons who you instantly like. He was calm and always pleasant.... Dave Leet was a good husband, a good pilot, and a good Marine officer. He was one of the nicest guys I ever met in Marine Corps or civilian life, and I have wondered many times why the good ones have to die."—John Hall

"For me, there's nobody better: as a friend, as a dad, as a husband. You couldn't wish for anybody better."—Bill Steinberg

"He was a really good person. He was smart, he was capable, and it was a terrible loss to our family. And our family was never quite the same because it was never quite as happy as it was before."—Donna Leet

Theirs was a family of deep American and Wisconsin lineage. William Leete arrived in the American colonies from England in 1639. He served first as the Governor of the New Haven Colony from 1661 to 1664, then as the Governor of the Colony of Connecticut from 1676 to 1683. Over time, *Leete* became *Leet*, and the named lived on. Charles Leet, a veteran of the War of 1812, brought the family to Wisconsin. There, the family name would endure through his great-great-grandson David.

"I can remember when he was born," says his sister, Donna. "My father was so excited, and it didn't register with me that it was because he was a boy. It was because we had a baby, and that was exciting! But in hindsight, I realize that that is what it was about." The date was December 21, 1946. Donna was 5, and her sister, Janet, 3. Their parents, Leverett and Virginia, owned 160 acres of farmland and rented another 150 seven miles outside the city of Kenosha, Wisconsin. The kids grew up accustomed to hard work. There were tomatoes and potatoes, sugar beets and corn, oats, barley, wheat, and cabbage, about eighty-five head of beef cattle, and plenty of chores to go around.

Donna, Janet, and David had nearly an hour of chores to do each day after school, no matter the season; at certain times of the year, that workload increased. Donna remembers cabbage harvesting at the end of the summer to be some of the most exhausting work they did on the farm, which always led to a good night's sleep. The farm, she says, "was a place where you learned to be resilient and thoughtful and creative." It was also a lot of fun, and a little dangerous.

David learned that the hard way, when he was 9 years old and herding horses. The Leet children were taught never to herd horses while riding a horse, but that afternoon, David rode his pony, Goldie, as he tried to herd a full-sized American Saddlebred named Miss Grasslands Gezabe. The horse reacted to the pony's presence by rearing and kicking her hind legs so hard that she left David with a compound fracture in one leg. "He was lucky he didn't have two broken legs because he said he could feel the end of her kick on his pants on the other side," Donna remembers. "So her legs just went right on either side of the horse."

All the kids had pets. Besides Goldie, David had a pig named Ruby, who acted more like a dog than a farm animal. David had only to yell, and she would come running to him to have her ears scratched. All three Leet children participated in 4H Club, and Ruby was David's project. The purpose of 4H is to educate children in a variety of areas: farming, cattle raising, cooking, photography, and more. In addition to Ruby, David competed with his cattle. In 1961 he won a blue ribbon for both his Hereford senior steer and his Hereford summer yearling steer at the Kenosha County Fair.

Donna competed in 4-H as well, and in 1961 participated in the Senior Dress Revue. Her green corduroy suit was modeled by her brother. David had asked his parents for a suit, but they said he didn't need one. He turned to Donna to make him one instead. She agreed, on the condition that he wore it on stage. "He was the only male model," she remembers. "I thought it would be novel. And it would be a way to 'get' him a little bit."

David's high school graduation photo, circa 1965. "You can see how cheeky he was," his sister, Donna, says. Courtesy Donna Leet.

It was a small role reversal—someone in the family getting the better of David. He was the comedian, undoing his mother's aprons strings when he walked past her in the kitchen and performing memorized skits to make the children at church laugh. At only 2 years old, he made Donna laugh so hard after she had surgery that she begged their mother to take him away. "David did not take himself too seriously," she says.

He was a hard worker, though, and while Leverett had an "equal opportunity" policy on the farm—if something needed to be done, someone better do it—David handled certain aspects of the farm more than the girls. "My dad never taught my sister and [me] how to back-up a four-wheeled wagon," Donna says, but he taught David. David was involved in the decision-making processes on the farm and did much of the heavy lifting. "My father had the hope that he would farm with my brother, so he was intent on teaching him to be a farmer," she explains.

It's possible that David had the same idea because after two years at the University of Wisconsin–Parkside, he transferred to the University of Wisconsin–Madison to pursue a degree in turf management, incorporating his knowledge of soil and his love for playing games. On campus David played intramural softball with his friend, Bill Steinberg, who credits David as one of the best pitchers he's ever seen. Bill was catcher and padded his glove when catching for David, but still ended every game with a swollen hand. David's sisters liked to claim that they taught him to play as well as he did (Donna still has a scar on her lip from where her brother hit her with the bat), but much of David's drive came from Leverett. Their father had dreamed of playing baseball professionally, but put those dreams aside to provide for his family. He passed those dreams to his son instead.

Halfway through college David became interested in the Marine Corps flight program. The inspiration for this career move was likely his Uncle Elwin, who was also a Marine. Their uncle couldn't have been prouder of David's decision to enlist.

David was accepted into the Marine Corps Platoon Leaders Class Aviation program, which he completed in the summers of 1965 and 1967. The program, based in Quantico, Virginia, served as boot camp for the officer candidates. The course was rigorous, but once completed there were no further requirements on campus. That David did not have to wear a uniform around Madison, an unpopular thing to do at that time, was an added benefit.

David's experience on the farm paid off at Quantico. According to the family, when David arrived in Virginia, the military staff had just designed a new physical fitness program. David scored a record high. He was later summoned to the general's office without explanation, where the general informed him of his success, saying something along the lines of "Congratulations, you exceeded our expectations. You are dismissed."

"He got the message that he was supposed to go see the general and he was absolutely petrified," Donna laughs. "He thought he was in some kind of big trouble."

After graduating from the UW, David married Kathy Goodwin, a cheerleader he'd dated since high school in Kenosha, then proceeded to Pensacola, Florida, for flight training. The first stage of training was pre-flight instruction, during which David and Bill (who followed the same track for most of their military careers) were introduced to the technical aspects of flying such as navigation, meteorology, leadership, communications, engines, and aerodynamics. Next came flight training at Saufley Field, also in Pensacola. Along with their mutual friend John Hall, they "learned how to take off, land, and perform some basic acrobatics in a T-34 Mentor," says Bill. Following initial flight training, the trio departed for basic jet training in Meridian, Mississippi, before David and Bill returned to Pensacola for carrier qualification and air-to-air gunnery.

After Pensacola David went to Naval Air Station Kingsville, Texas, for advanced jet training. The curricula involved a lot of review of earlier programs such as instrument flying, weapons systems, air-to-air tactics, and aerodynamic understanding, but with increased intensity. There was also a final carrier qualification before David, Bill, and John received their Wings of Gold in March of 1970.

"It was a real accomplishment," explains Bill, but "it was a foregone conclusion" that their ultimate destination would be a combat tour in Vietnam. For David, as was common with the men who came out of flight training, enlisting in the Marine Corps had been about flying; the war came with it.

On being designated naval aviators, David, Bill, and John were all assigned to Marine Composite Reconnaissance Squadron 2 at MCAS Cherry Point, North Carolina. David and John flew the Grumman EA-6A Intruder, an electronic warfare aircraft, while Bill flew a McDonnell Douglas RF-4B Phantom, a fighter aircraft. They spent a year becoming acquainted with their planes in the United States.

While at Cherry Point, the men underwent a survival training exercise called SERE school, or Survival, Evasion, Resistance, and Escape. The men had completed their first SERE exercise in 1968, just before leaving Pensacola the first time, but the training became progressively more difficult. Part sea, part land survival, it was "a hell of a hard lesson," Bill explains:

> So you actually dropped off the back of a Landing Craft doing twenty or thirty miles an hour with your parachute harness on. So you jumped off a platform into the water with this harness attached and it was to simulate getting dragged through the water if you bailed out of an airplane and the chute was still inflated and pulled along by the wind so you had to get out of your fittings and then, for the next hour or so, mess around with all the things in your survival kit. Because if you ejected, there's a seat pan, which is part of the ejection seat with all your survival gear, like signal mirrors, fishing line, hooks, and whistles. And then you get picked up by a helicopter and dropped off on shore and then the survival exercise started. So you were out there the next two or three days, pretty much on your own; sometimes in groups.

During SERE school, the survival experience was harsher and included a faux prisoner

David and his son, Jason, age 2. The photo was taken a few months before David went missing. Courtesy Donna Leet.

of war camp. The men were given a half-day's head start once they were dropped off on shore, before "aggressors" were sent after them. For two or three days the men traveled through an evasion course made up of a series of safe houses; if they were caught, they were taken to the mock POW camp.

An unusual occurrence took place when the men were given their first overseas assignment—unusual for the Marine Corps, at least, but not out of character for David Leet. David was scheduled to leave for his overseas tour with First Marine Air Wing one month before John Hall, but John's wife was pregnant at the time and waiting to return to their home in South Carolina after he left. Waiting another month would have made the move difficult for her. John asked David to switch orders with him so John could get his orders and she could return home a month earlier. David agreed without hesitation. He understood. He had a baby too—a son named Jason.

David was assigned to Marine Composite

Reconnaissance Squadron 1 (VMCJ-1), then stationed at Iwakuni, Japan. He arrived in August 1971. After North Vietnamese forces invaded South Vietnam in 1972, David and the squadron moved to Cubi Point in the Philippines. There were several reasons for this move. First, it was still out of the active war zone, but closer to Vietnam. It also gave the appearance of not re-escalating the war. Stateside, the politics of de-escalation called for stationing service personnel some distance from Vietnam, and there was a cap on the number of Marines who could be in South Vietnam at the time. Placing troops in the Philippines technically kept them beneath the cap, while keeping them involved in the war effort. Perhaps most important, the Da Nang Air Base in South Vietnam was periodically under attack by rockets, and the EA-6A David flew was too valuable an aircraft to risk exposure to enemy fire. The pilots flew to Da Nang AB early in the morning, engaged in their missions, then returned to the Philippines at night.

The North Vietnamese used SAMs to fire on U.S. aircraft. The SAMs became increasingly accurate and powerful as the war ground on. SAM 1 became SAM 2, which could travel at speeds of Mach 3 or 3.5.[1] American airplanes flying over North Vietnam would have been easy targets for this missile system, if not for several established electronic countermeasures. Inside the aircraft, devices tracked SAM radars and triggered a "warble" alarm in the pilot's headset to alert him to incoming missile acquisition-and-tracking radars. There were also combat air patrols that, when available, provided backup for the pilots should complications arise during a mission. And there were men like David, who flew aircraft specifically designed to jam the enemy's radar and protect American planes from North Vietnamese SAMs.

On April 13, 1972, Captain David Leet and his electronic countermeasures officer, Captain John Christensen, flew one aircraft in a two-flight mission to provide electronic countermeasures for operations taking place in Hanoi and Haiphong as part of "Operation Linebacker." The two aircrafts followed an orbit pattern approximately twenty miles off the coast, while monitoring and jamming SAM sites ashore.

There was rarely communication during missions such as these, either between pilots or with the air traffic control on a Navy ship below them. They did not want to give the enemy any indication of where they were or what was going to happen. Captain Leet checked in via radio at 3:50 a.m. to report that he was on station. He radioed again at 4:47 a.m. to say he was checking out upon completion of his mission.

The aircraft was scheduled to return to base at 5:35 a.m. It didn't return.

Although search-and-rescue operations were launched immediately, no wreckage could be found in the water, nor was there any sign of David Leet or John Christensen. Theirs was the only EA-6A lost during the war.[2]

In Wisconsin, Donna's newborn daughter was five days old. The joy in her arrival counterbalanced the grief that overtook the family when an officer arrived at their house with the news. David was listed as missing in action, but the family knew he was gone. "There were lots of people who didn't know what to say to my parents," Donna remembers. "There were these barriers with people we knew well."

Five years later, the family held a celebration of David's life to remember the brother, the son, the father, and the friend they had lost and to share the wonderful memories he'd left them. "He really loved flying," Donna says. "He was happy doing that."

And he was proud. Nothing shows the type of man David Leet was better than the words he wrote the very morning of his last mission in a letter to the family he loved so much[3]:

> Please don't worry about me.... It's too bad this had to happen, especially with Kathy and Jace here, but believe me I'm extremely fortunate. I really don't believe in [the politics of] what we're doing here, but as long as other pilots, Navy, Air Force and Marine, are flying missions well in the range of SAM's and anti-aircraft fire, I'm more than willing to put up with a little inconvenience on my part to try and protect them from the possibility of being shot down and not seeing their families. They have so much more risk involved in their jobs....
>
> All I can say is that in my position, a side must be chosen and I've chosen the side of the U.S. The U.S. might be wrong with its foreign policy, shaky in its leadership and destined to fail eventually, but being a part of this same U.S. has given me immeasurable joy and happiness in my short 25 years of life....
>
> I'm sure there are pilots and crewmen who have families, and love their families, like I do mine. So, for that reason too, I'll continue to put up with small inconveniences in order that I can protect them all I can by simply flying and utilizing my training to the fullest.

Staff Sergeant
Todd Michael Melton

United States Air Force,
disappeared February 5, 1973

"I admired Todd and his fellow linguists. They were a good group."—Phil Pratt

"Todd was an intelligent individual who knew what he wanted to do and how to achieve his goals. He had a baby face, and I can't recall ever seeing him irritated. He was younger than us that hung out together, but fit right in. He was a hard-working individual who could be relied upon to do a good job."—John Pitzeruse

"He was a great guy."—Jim Bolton

What happened to Baron 52? And what happened to her crew? Officially, the aircraft was shot down in hostile territory on February 5, 1973, and all aboard were killed in the crash. When a rescue team investigated the crash site two days later, they found the bodies of four of the eight crewmen. But questions persisted about the four missing crew members, including a Vietnamese linguist out of Milwaukee, a staff sergeant named Todd Michael Melton.

Todd was born on April 11, 1949, and was adopted by his parents, John and Lili Melton, three months later. Because he was so small when they first met him, Todd's father nicknamed him Mouse. He grew up in Milwaukee alongside two older siblings.

In September 1963 Todd joined roughly one hundred ninety students at St. Francis de Sales Seminary, a religious high school in St. Francis, a Milwaukee suburb. He was a residential student, boarding at the school during the week and spending weekends at home with his family. "Todd was very intelligent and very mischievous and always smiling," remembers Father Jim Kimla, a classmate. "He tended to associate with the more intelligent guys in the class."

The class schedule was rigorous and, as expected in a Catholic school, heavily emphasized religion: The students attended church three times a day, and regularly performed the Stations of the Cross in the nearby woods. Underclassmen took Latin classes; upperclassmen studied Greek.

A Danang crew enjoying some downtime at Nakhon Phanom Royal Thai Navy Air Base in Thailand. Todd sits on the bench, wearing a hat. Courtesy the 6994th Squadron Association.

Todd was on the school's honor roll, but kept busy with more than academics. He sang in the choir, performed in the school talent show, worked as a lifeguard, served on the Fine Arts Committee and the Student Council Executive Board, where he was the head of the Public Service Committee, and was president of the school's Mission Society. "He was outgoing and a good organizer," recalls David Agnew, who succeeded Todd as the Mission Society's president. "He had a good sense of humor and could give it as well as take it."

Todd worked several summers at the Maynard Steel Casting Company in Milwaukee, then, on March 28, 1969, he enlisted in the United States Air Force. His initial training took place at Lackland Air Force Base. He then completed technical school at Chanute AFB in Illinois before enrolling in a forty-seven-week course at the Vietnamese Language School in Fort Bliss, Texas. There, he spent six to seven hours a day learning the Vietnamese Hanoi dialect. The process was taught through immersion and constant repetition. According to Jim Bolton, who completed the course alongside Todd, it was a fairly enjoyable training experience.

The men trained for the more physical aspects of life in the Air Force, too. They attended survival school at Fairchild Air Force Base, Washington. At Goodfellow Air Force Base, San Angelo, Texas, they learned to operate radios and other technical equipment in an airborne simulator.[1] Jim recalls trips to Mexico and evenings at the bars, and that Todd was smart, young, and very good at a dangerous job. "It was a fun and crazy time," remembers Jim Bolton, "but it was also pretty serious, too."

Todd was assigned to Detachment 2 of the 6994th Security Squadron; he would later transfer to Detachment 3. In 1970 the squadron, composed of about one hundred fifty Morse operators and thirty linguists, including Todd, was stationed at Da Nang Air Base. Paired with pilots, copilots, and navigators from the 362nd Tactical Electronic Warfare Squadron, the 6994th flew about ten missions a day. The missions were classified. Although lower in rank than the crewmembers who operated the aircraft, the men of the 6994th Security Squadron were in charge on missions. "Everything we did was top secret, and everyone who was a member of our squadron had a top-secret clearance," remembers Vern Holm, a member of the 6994th. They referred to their pilots as their bus drivers.

Missions were flown in modified versions of the Douglas C-47 Skytrain. "Our planes had been modified for electronic warfare and came in three models," explains Vern, "the EC-47N, the EC-47P, and the EC-47Q." Typical flights consisted of three Morse Intercept operators and a Vietnamese linguist from the 6994th in the back of the plane (often referred to as the "back end crew"), with a pilot, a copilot, and a navigator of the 362nd operating the aircraft. The men located and listened to enemy radio transmitters. The transmitters only used one or two watts of power, which meant that the crew had to be within one or two miles of the radio to pick up a signal. Once they located the transmitter, what happened next depended on where they were flying. If they were in Vietnam, they reported the location to the nearest Marine Corps fire support base, which decided whether to shell the area. If they were in Laos or Cambodia, the crew called for fire support to hit the target. Missions typically lasted 5½–8 hours, after which the men had two days off before their next flight.

In their downtime the men of the squadron played a lot of cards. Todd played bridge; others played pinochle. There were outdoor movies and volleyball games and drinks at the NCO club, but life in the barracks was otherwise quiet. Local Vietnamese were hired to clean the living facilities on base, and Todd and the other linguists were often called to translate conversations. "It was sometimes like having someone from New York State conversing with someone from the Deep South," recalls Phil Pratt, a member of the 6994th Security Squadron. These interactions helped improve community relations on base.

Todd was younger than many other squadron members, only in his early twenties during his time at Da Nang AB. He had "a baby face," remembers fellow squadron member John Pitzeruse. Vern adds, "He was a little like the Pillsbury doughboy."

As Todd neared the end of his tour in Vietnam, he approached some of the other members of the squadron, asking for their opinions. He planned to attend college and contemplated extending his tour to save money for school. After discussing the situation, the men agreed this was a smart plan, so Todd extended his tour of duty.

Todd spent the holidays of 1972 with his family (and ran into Jim Bolton in the Bangkok airport). In a 1983 interview Lili Melton remembered the last time she saw Todd.[2] It was mid–January 1973, and he was boarding the plane that would take him back to the war. He turned, caught sight of his parents, smiled, and saluted. Shortly thereafter, the plane departed for Thailand, where his unit had been transferred.

The opening months of 1973 represented a crucial time for everyone in the United States Armed Forces. On January 27, 1973, President Richard Nixon signed a peace

Members of the 6994th Security Squadron and the 362nd Tactical Electronic Warfare Squadron celebrate the final combat mission of Roger Eddleman (center). Todd stands on the far left. Courtesy the 6994th Squadron Association.

treaty with the leaders of North Vietnam, the leaders of South Vietnam, and the Vietcong, formally titled "Agreement on Ending the War and Restoring the Peace in Vietnam," usually referred to as the Paris Peace Accords. All parties agreed to a ceasefire, with a pullout of United States troops and advisors within sixty days. It also called for the withdrawal of foreign troops from Laos and Cambodia and prohibited troop movement in either countries. For America the 1973 Paris Peace Accords meant the war was over—in Vietnam.

On February 4, 1973, as America celebrated the end of a long, drawn-out war, Staff Sergeant Todd Melton was assigned a mission over Laos.

The night's mission was no different from any other: locating armored units of the People's Army of Vietnam (PAVN) traveling south along the Ho Chi Minh Trail. Todd's aircraft, call sign Baron 52, took off at 11 p.m. Over the next two hours Baron 52 had frequent contact with other planes in the region. At 1:25 a.m. on February 5 the crew radioed that it had received several rounds of antiaircraft artillery, but reported no damage to the aircraft. The aircraft was in radio contact twice more over the next thirty-five minutes before missing its scheduled radio call at 2:00 a.m. Aerial searches for Baron 52 began within twenty minutes. The plane wasn't found for another two days.

"The thing that really bothers me to this day," says John Pitzeruse, "is the aircraft Todd was flying on was shot down in Laos. It was a sticky situation."

On February 7 a radioman from the 6994th and three pararescue specialists inspected the crash site, roughly eight to ten minutes north of Baron 52's last reported location. The plane was burned, but much of Baron 52's structure was intact. The search team located and identified the remains of the pilot, 1st Lieutenant Robert Bernhardt, the copilot, Captain George Spitz, and 2nd Lieutenant Severo Primm III. One body was found near the engineer's compartment, but could not be identified. Four of the eight crewmembers were unaccounted for.[3]

The search team extracted 1st Lieutenant Bernhardt's body, but judged the other three men to be too difficult to extract in the limited time they had at the crash site. After fifteen or twenty minutes on the ground, at a site that was still actively hostile, the search team left.

In an after-action report the Commander of the 8th Tactical Fighter Wing reported that, given the extensive training of Baron 52's crewmembers, he believed

> that in the case of an emergency at least one crew member would have instinctively used one of the many pieces of communication equipment that were available to transmit a distress call or to lead rescue forces to his location; unless the aircraft crashed as a result of some catastrophic incident that immediately and completely incapacitated the crew members.

The search team found shrapnel holes in the plane's exterior, but found no sign of any attempt at a controlled landing. When it crashed, the Baron 52 still had five hours of fuel left in its tank, and no one appeared to have attempted to bail out. The plane's fate is likely what the commander described; however, years later, questions remain, not only regarding what caused the crash, but what happened to half the crew.

Speculation on the fate of the four missing crewmen began the day of the crash, February 5, 1973, when an element of the PAVN was reported to have taken four pilots captive. A second report followed, stating "Presently Group 210 has four pirates[4]; they are going from 44 to 93, they are having difficulties moving along the road."

The U.S. military spent the next several days investigating these reports, unable to disregard the theory that four of Baron 52's eight crewmen had somehow escaped the fiery crash and been captured by the PAVN. The issue was further complicated on February 27, when the United States Air Force Security Service HQ released more information about the supposed hostages:

> According to a reliable source, the enemy was moving four prisoners on trucks northward along Route 914 in Laos on 5 Feb. 73. This source reported they may have been in [*sic*] route to a staging area in Laos just west of the DMZ. It is speculated by Hq USAFSS that these prisoners may have been crewmembers of the Baron 52.

No one could obtain concrete evidence to support these claims. A May 23 report summarizes the incident and concludes that "our position is that there is a possibility some of the EC-47 crew survived, but the evidence was sketchy and inconclusive."

For John and Lili Melton, one thing was certain: Their son was not coming home. They cleaned his bedroom, then sold their house. They contacted the Air Force and received a small, government-issue headstone with Todd's name and laid it in the Melton family plot. They visited it, even though Todd wasn't there. Neither the Meltons nor any of the crewmen's families were made aware of the possibility for another five years that four of the men may have been captured. John and Lili made peace with their son's death, continuing to visit his grave every month. They enshrined it with wreaths and flowers and flags for decades.

Members of Congress pressed for further investigation of the crash site, but none was ever conducted. In 1992 the Joint Task Force for Full Accounting excavated the Baron 52 crash site and recovered partial remains of the men who had been left in the aircraft on February 7, 1973. They could not be identified and were buried at Arlington National Cemetery in December 1995 in a communal grave: Section 34, Site Number 4402.

Todd's name is on that grave. He may have died in the crash. He may not have. According to the National Archives and Records Administration, of the 1,161 men from Wisconsin killed during the Vietnam War, Todd Melton was the last. He was the only Wisconsin man lost after the war was over.

Epilogue

Anyone walking the streets of Washington, D.C., on Memorial Day weekend 1995 was treated to an unusual sight: four motorcyclists standing watch at the center of the Vietnam Veterans Memorial Wall around the clock. The scene by itself may have been unusual, but what drew the eye had to be the motorcycle they were guarding, for it was anything but ordinary.

The handgrips, from Indiana, are colored the yellow, red, and green of the Vietnam Service Medal. The seat, handmade in Ohio, had never been used. The license plate, authorized by the governor of Wisconsin, reads simply, "Hero." Hand-painted gas tanks, designed by a 14-year-old girl, show a solider kneeling before a fading and forgotten Vietnam Wall. 37 names are painted on the Wall. The same 37 names hang on dog tags from the front of the bike. The motorcycle, a labor of love that took longer than a year to create, is known as the MIA/POW Bike. It is dedicated to Wisconsin's 37 MIA/POWs.

The idea for the bike came a year earlier, in 1994, during the annual Rolling Thunder Ride to the Wall in recognition of all MIA/POWs. A group of Wisconsin bikers observed the objects left behind at the Vietnam Wall and wondered what they could place there to remind the nation of a group of people whom so many seemed ready to forget. Traditional "Wisconsin" items—beer or cheese—were too unmemorable, too small. A motorcycle, however, would not go unnoticed.

The bike was built lovingly, piece by piece, an assemblage of parts donated by people across Wisconsin and across the nation, by a determined group of Wiscon-

The MIA/POW Bike, left at the Wall in May 1995. Courtesy the Vietnam Veterans Memorial Fund.

sin bikers. Joined by more than one hundred other riders, they brought the bike to Washington, D.C., in May 1995. They guarded it, and left it there, the largest memento ever to be left at the Wall.

Thirty-seven men from Wisconsin were missing when the bike was left at the Wall that spring. Chief Master Sergeant Charles Fellenz would be buried in Arlington the following November. Staff Sergeant Todd Melton was returned one month later. Major Norman Billipp and Petty Officer John Hartzheim would be recovered before the turn of the century.

The first decade of the 2000s saw the homecomings of Lieutenant Michael Allard, Private Thomas Blackman, Lance Corporal Raymond Heyne, Sergeant James Tycz, and Gunnery Sergeant Richard Fischer. Lance Corporal Merlin Allen, Staff Sergeant James VanBendegom, and Major Dale Richardson were welcomed back in the first seven years of the next decade, nearly fifty years after the start of the war that had claimed their lives.

Twenty-five men whose names are painted on the bike remain missing in 2018. Some, lost over the sea, may never be recovered. But they have not been forgotten. Their names are memorialized in Washington, D.C., on the Vietnam Veterans Memorial Wall and on the MIA/POW Bike. More than just names, though, they are remembered by so many, their losses felt acutely by the people who knew them and loved them in life, and their sacrifices recognized by those for whom they were made.

Appendix
Awards and Commendations

No database exists to document all awards and commendations. The most complete list of awards given to each serviceman can be found within military records. The author filed requests through the Freedom of Information Act to acquire complete award and commendation history for each man. In some cases, no records were found. The following appendix has been compiled to the best of my ability from records obtained through FOIA requests, family sources, and reliable online resources and I apologize if any awards have been omitted. Unit awards and service medals are not included.

Michael Allard
Purple Heart
Air Medal

Merlin Allen
Purple Heart
Good Conduct Medal

William Arnold
Purple Heart
Air Medal
Navy Commendation Medal with
 combat "V"

Norman Billipp
Bronze Star (Valor)
Distinguished Flying Cross (2)
Purple Heart
Air Medal
Republic of Vietnam Gallantry Cross
 with Palm

Thomas Blackman
Silver Star Medal
Purple Heart

Richard Bowers
Bronze Star Medal
Purple Heart
Prisoner of War Medal
Good Conduct Medal

Robert Bush
Air Force Commendation Medal
Silver Star Medal
Distinguished Flying Cross
Purple Heart
Good Conduct Medal

Paul Derby
Purple Heart
Air Medal
Navy Commendation Medal with "V"
Republic of Vietnam Gallantry Cross

Donald Downing
Distinguished Flying Cross
Bronze Star Medal
Purple Heart
Air Medal
Good Conduct Medal

Walter Draeger, Jr.
Air Force Cross
Purple Heart
Air Medal

William Evans
Bronze Star
Purple Heart
Air Medal
Army Commendation Medal (Valor)

Charles Fellenz
Purple Heart
Good Conduct Medal

Edwin Fickler
Purple Heart
Air Medal
Navy Commendation Medal

Richard Fischer
Purple Heart

Paul Frazier
Distinguished Flying Cross
Bronze Star (Merit)
Purple Heart
Air Medal

Donald Gallagher
Good Conduct Medal

Paul Gee
Purple Heart
Air Medal

John Hartzheim
Purple Heart
Air Medal
Navy Commendation Medal with
    "V" Device

Richard Hentz
Purple Heart
Air Medal

Raymond Heyne
Purple Heart

Roy Huss
Air Medal

Randolph Johnson
Purple Heart
Air Medal

James Ketterer
Distinguished Flying Cross with
    2 Oak Leaf Clusters
Purple Heart
Air Medal
Air Force Commendation Medal

Roy Kubley
Silver Star Medal with 1 Oak Leaf
    Cluster
Distinguished Flying Cross with
    3 Oak Leaf Clusters
Bronze Star Medal
Purple Heart
Air Medal

James La Haye
Distinguished Flying Cross
Purple Heart
Air Medal
Navy/Marine Corps Commendation
    Medal with Combat "V" and Star
Republic of Vietnam Gallantry Cross
    with Palm
Republic of Vietnam Military Merit
    Medal
National Order of Vietnam Medal—
    5th Class

David Leet
Purple Heart

Todd Melton
Distinguished Flying Cross
Purple Heart
Air Medal

Harold Moe
Purple Heart
Air Medal
Good Conduct Medal

William Pierson III
Purple Heart
Air Medal

Dale Richardson
Purple Heart
Army Commendation Medal 2nd Oak
    Leaf Cluster
Good Conduct Medal

Peter Schmidt
Purple Heart
Air Medal

Albert Trudeau
Bronze Star (Merit)
Air Medal

James Tycz
Navy Cross
Purple Heart
Good Conduct Medal

James VanBendegom
Purple Heart
Prisoner of War Medal
Good Conduct Medal
Republic of Vietnam Gallantry Cross
    with Palm Device

Robert Wilke
Air Force Cross
Distinguished Flying Cross with
    1 Oak Leaf Cluster
Bronze Star Medal
Purple Heart
Air Medal
Good Conduct Medal
Republic of Vietnam Gallantry Cross

Glossary

Air Force Cross—The second-highest decoration for valor awarded in the Air Force.

Air Medal—Awarded for meritorious achievement during an aerial flight mission.

AO—Aerial Observer.

Bronze Star Medal—Awarded to anyone in the U.S. Armed Forces who distinguishes him- or herself through heroic or meritorious service or achievement.

CAP—Combined Action Platoon.

Charlie—A shorthand reference by the American servicemen to the Vietcong. In the phonetic alphabet, "VC" is "Victor Charlie."

Da Nang Air Base—Former French air base in the city of Danang. Various U.S. Army, Air Force, and Marine units were stationed there throughout the war.

Danang—The second largest city in South Vietnam after Saigon. Home to the large Da Nang Air Base.

Demilitarized Zone (DMZ)—The dividing line between North and South Vietnam, established at the Geneva Convention of 1954.

Distinguished Flying Cross—Awarded to members of the Armed Forces who show extraordinary heroism or outstanding achievement during an aerial flight mission.

DOD—Department of Defense

FAC—Forward Air Control.

Flak—Antiaircraft artillery.

H&M—Headquarters and Maintenance Squadron.

Hanoi—The capital of North Vietnam and the current capital of Vietnam. During the war, Hanoi's Hỏa Lò Prison housed American prisoners of war and was sarcastically referred to as the "Hanoi Hilton."

Ho Chi Minh Trail—A network of roads running from North Vietnam through Laos and Cambodia into South Vietnam that was used by the North Vietnamese and Vietcong for troop and material transport throughout the war.

Hooch—The term used for almost all living quarters for servicemen in Vietnam.

JPAC—Joint POW/MIA Accounting Command. The agency merged with several others to form the Defense POW/MIA Accounting Agency (DPAA) in 2015.

Khe Sanh—The capital of Hướng Hoá District, Quảng Trị Province, and the site of two major battles during the Vietnam War: The Hill Fights of 1967 and the Siege of Khe Sanh Combat Base in 1968.

KIA—Killed in Action.

KIA-BNR—Killed in Action, Body Not Recovered.

MACV—Military Assistance Command, Vietnam.

MAG—Marine Air Group.

MCAS—Marine Corps Air Station.

Medevac—Medical evacuation, generally by helicopter.

MIA—Missing in Action.

MOS—Military Occupational Specialty.

NAS—Naval Air Station.

Navy Cross—The second-highest decoration for valor awarded in the Navy and the Marines.

NCO—Non-commissioned officer

NFO—Naval Flight Officer.

NVA—North Vietnamese Army. The American term for trained troops from North Vietnam.

OCS—Officer Candidate School.

Ordnance—Weapons, ammunition, and artillery.

PAVN—People's Army of Vietnam. Synonymous with NVA.

POW—Prisoner of War.

Purple Heart—A military decoration awarded to those wounded or killed while serving with the U.S. military.

R&R—Rest and relaxation, either in-country or out of country

Recon—Reconnaissance.

RIO—Radar Intercept Officer.

Quantico—Headquarters the Marine Corps OCS and TBS in Virginia.

ROTC—Reserve Officers' Training Corps.

RVN—Republic of Vietnam.

SAC—Strategic Air Command.

SAM—Surface-to-Air Missile.

SERE—Survival, Evasion, Resistance, Escape—a survival training course for members of the Marine Corps and Air Force.

Silver Star—The third-highest medal for valor in the United States Armed Forces.

Slick—An Army nickname for the Huey helicopter.

TBS—The Basic School.

Tet Offensive—A coordinated series of surprise attacks launched by the North Vietnamese and Viet Cong across over one hundred cities and towns in South Vietnam. The attacks began January 30, 1968, on the Vietnamese New Year (Tet). Although it was a tactical victory for the U.S. and South Vietnamese, it was considered a political victory for the North Vietnamese.

USA—United States Army.

USAF—United States Air Force.

USMC—United States Marine Corps.

USN—United States Navy.

UW—University of Wisconsin–Madison

Vietcong (VC)—South Vietnamese Communists supported by North Vietnam.

VMA—Marine Attack Squadron.

VMCJ—Marine Composite Reconnaissance Squadron.

VMF—Marine Fighter Squadron.

VMFA—Marine Fighter Attack Squadron.

VMO—Marine Observation Squadron.

The Wall—Officially the Vietnam Veterans Memorial, the Wall is a national memorial in Washington, D.C., bearing the names of every American killed in the Vietnam War. It is customary for visitors to place a piece of paper over the name of a loved one and rub crayon or pencil as a personal memorial called a "rubbing."

Chapter Notes

Introduction

1. Their names appear in the Acknowledgments section.

2. This number does not include American civilians, agency personnel or contractors who died.

3. Until January 2015 these activities were coordinated by its predecessor agency, the Joint POW/MIA Accounting Command.

4. Lt. Col Armstrong, a West Point graduate, remains listed as MIA.

Captain Walter Frank Draeger, Jr.

1. Mach is a ratio that represents the speed of an aircraft compared to the speed of sound. Flying at Mach 1 is matching the speed of sound in air.

2. A trainer jet.

3. She remained in contact with the Draeger family for a time after Junior's death. Beth and Diana, both children at the time, do not remember her name.

4. Other models, like the A-1G Skyraider, were two-seaters.

5. It would be used by the U.S. Air Force, as well as international air forces, at different times during its lengthy career. The A-1 was a piston-powered, propeller-driven combat aircraft that saw service well into the jet age.

6. Although five were selected, only four eventually went to Da Nang AB. Of those four, two returned home. Lieutenant Colonel William "Score" Hail was shot down on August 2, 1965. After Junior was lost, Lt. Col. Hail planned to meet with the Draeger family upon his return to the United States. Both men had written letters to be opened in case they were killed, Junior to his parents, Lt. Col. Hail to his sister.

7. In addition to Da Nang and Tan Son Nhut, Bien Hoa was the third main operating base. Many more would be added over the course of the war.

8. The city of Danang is one word; the air base Da Nang is two.

9. Junior's letters were donated by the family to the Madison Veterans Museum and can be found in their archives.

10. Ray Jones describes the mission in detail in his book *Memoir: Dynamite, Check Six.*

11. The aircrafts' call signs.

12. The family held a memorial on May 8, 1965. One week later Beverly's son was born. She named him Walter William.

Commander James David La Haye

1. Naval Academy annual registers can be accessed online.

2. During this time, the Naval Academy advanced classes to get officers into action earlier so the smartest students were pushed forward.

3. Indicating surrender.

4. Although he's not sure when it happened, Don La Haye remembers one dive bombing mission during which his father had to abandon his A-1 aircraft in the sea and climb out. Jim was over land when the transmission failed, but maneuvered the aircraft over water to prevent any civilian casualties.

5. Flak suppression is a mission to destroy, suppress, or reduce enemy ground attack from the air.

6. Recollections of Jim La Haye's final mission were provided to Don La Haye in 2003 by squadron members, including Tom Howard, Bob Pearl, and George Schulstad. Don provided these recollections to the author in 2015. General Schulstad was assigned to VF-111 with CDR La Haye as a U.S. Air Force officer on exchange duty.

7. The association paid the USS Midway Museum $10,000 to sponsor the names on the F-8.

Captain Robert Ira Bush

1. This would later be replaced by a "primary-basic" program, with all three stages merged into a single training regimen.

2. This organization, still in existence today, was later renamed the North American Aerospace Defense Command (NORAD).

3. The training classes would eventually adopt a more recognized naming structure in which the classes were referred to by the year and the class number. For example, the tenth graduating class of 1965 would be Class 65–10.

4. The citation states that Robert "was approached by armed tribesmen, but rather than fire on them and attempt to evade, Captain Bush took the great risk to determine if they were actually friendly. The natives immediately took up defensive positions to protect Captain Bush and greatly assisted his rescue." Ten days before this incident, Robert earned a Silver Star Medal on a different mission.

Commander William Tamm Arnold

1. Cdr. William T. Arnold, LCdr. John S. Lyman, Maj. Norman K. Billipp, Maj. Dennis A. Dogs, Lt. Walter G. Updike, Lt. Steven Plotz, Lt. Lawrence P. Beam, Capt. John T. Chapman, Capt. John M. Pagel, Capt. David J. Lueder, Lt(jg) Michael A. Fox, Lt(jg) D.N. "Nick" Norris, Lt(jg) Charles D. Collins Jr., Ens. Michael Strole, Ens. Duane J. Hofhine II.

2. A typical first solo flight involves a new pilot taking off, conducting a short flight, and landing independently. It is a landmark achievement for pilots.

3. Women Accepted for Volunteer Emergency Service.

4. The desired altitude for avoiding radar detection in low-level nuclear mission simulations.

5. The harbor was bombed from 1965 to 1968, when President Johnson halted the bombing during negotiations with the North Vietnamese. President Nixon resumed the mining and bombing of Haiphong Harbor and the city of Hanoi in 1972. Ironically, when the mining resumed in 1972, the first mines were laid by pilots flying off Bill's aircraft carrier, the USS *Coral Sea*.

6. Surface-to-air missiles.

Captain Roy Robert Kubley

1. These statistics was compiled by Bill Abbott in an article, "Names on the Wall: A Closer Look at Those Who Died in Vietnam." The article was originally published in *Vietnam* magazine in June 1993. It was updated in November 2004.

2. At about 6′ 3″, Roy towered over most people.

3. France pulled out of NATO in 1966, and all American Air Force bases were closed by 1967.

4. Now called Rickenbacker Air National Guard Base.

5. After the unit was deactivated in 1972, American intelligence estimated that up to seventy thousand lives were saved through the work of Ranch Hand. The program, however, remains controversial.

6. All the targets were in free-fire zones under direct control of an airborne forward air controller (FAC). The FAC was familiar with the target area and which troops were nearby and prevented friendly troops from entering the area.

7. The modified planes were called UC-123Bs.

8. Once the program began to expand in 1967, the personnel would reach as many as one hundred at a time.

9. If the planes encountered ground fire, the mechanics also had smoke grenades to throw to mark the enemy so escort fighter planes knew where to fire.

10. The article was printed under different names in different newspapers. Among them, "Defoliation of Vietnam Is Big Job for Pilots" in the *Kingsport Times* and "Defoliation Becomes Weapon in Vietnam" in the *Anderson Herald*.

11. Also lost were Captain Howard Barden, Captain Harvey Mulhauser, and Airman 1st Class Ronald Miyazaki.

Private First Class Duwayne Marshall Soulier

1. These statistics were compiled by Tom Holm and presented in his article, "Forgotten Warriors—American Indian Servicemen in Vietnam," originally printed in *Vietnam Generation I*. As he notes in the article, it is impossible to pinpoint the exact number because "Native American" was not an option on the list of races on enlistment papers or casualty reports at the time.

2. Merl and Marshall enlisted in the Marines at nearly the same time. Merl served with the 3rd Reconnaissance Battalion and would be MIA barely one month after Marshall. Cynthia attended Merl's memorial. His story is found later in this book.

3. Three young men from Bayfield were killed in the Vietnam War: Marshall, Merl, and Corporal James Hessing, who served in the Army and was killed in 1970 at age 21.

4. MOS stands for military occupational specialty. The number is the code that identifies the specific job within his military branch.

5. Operation Napa (September 4–7), Operation Monterey (September 29–30), Operation Dover (October 19–30), and Operation Sutter (November 30–December 7). Marshall also took part in Operation Clay (February 1–3, 1967) with 3/5.

6. Because CAP India was administered by the 7th Communication Battalion, Marshall's records show him as assigned to HQ Co., 7th Bn.

7. Cynthia still has the sweatshirt.

8. Kevin Kelly believes it is also possible that

the helicopter was damaged when they were shot at over land, leading to the crash.

9. Staff Sergeant Stan L. Corfield (crewman), Lance Corporal Earl Dillworth, Jr., Sergeant John Bailey, Corporal Roger Gaughan, Lance Corporal Carl Smith, Lance Corporal Joseph Lipton, Private Hilario Guarjardo, Private Duwayne Soulier.

Sergeant James Neil Tycz

1. Statistics were found in Lawrence C. Vetter Jr.'s book, *Never Without Heroes: Marine Third Reconnaissance Battalion in Vietnam*.

2. Pronounced "Tice."

3. Quote from "U.S. Brings Home Remains of Missing Vietnam Troops," an article by Frederic J. Frommer of the Associated Press, May 9, 2005.

4. His article, "'Whitey, You Scrounge,' Dies with Jim," appeared on March 22, 2005 in The *Green Bay Press-Gazette*.

5. Both Neil and Ted helped train the 5th Marine Reconnaissance Battalion before they were sent to Vietnam.

6. The Second Battle of Khe Sanh began in January 1968. The People's Army of Vietnam put the Khe Sanh Combat Base under siege for seventy-seven days. The Marines held the base with the help of the U.S. 1st Cavalry Division and several South Vietnamese units, but were unable to provide support against the Tet Offensive, which began shortly after the siege. Per the request of III MAF, all Marine units were pulled out and the Khe Sanh Combat Base disassembled by early July 1968.

7. Within the company, the Marines were organized into individual teams for patrols.

8. The following information on the battle comes from Chapter 11 of Lawrence C. Vetter, Jr.'s, book, *Never without Heroes: Marine Third Reconnaissance Battalion in Vietnam, 1965–70*, as well as a personal interview with Ted Biszko. The book covers the patrol in detail.

9. Neil originally served with 3rd Platoon. Consistent with Marine philosophy, Neil was transferred to 1st Platoon after his promotion so he wouldn't command those he had previously served alongside.

10. The letter was published online by the *Wisconsin State Journal* in May 2005.

Lance Corporal Merlin Raye Allen

1. Alden Allen bought the land in the 1930s and was forced to sell to the government when it created the Apostle Islands National Lakeshore out of twenty-one islands and several beaches of Lake Superior.

2. As quoted by David Kennedy in a *Daily Press* article titled "Remembering a Brother Comrade," published June 30, 2013.

3. F***ing new guy.

4. Including Sergeant James Neil Tycz, another Wisconsin MIA

5. One was the 3rd Division G-2 Forward, and one was the 26th Marines.

6. Captain John House attempted to fly the helicopter to safety over a ridge but died along the way, and the helicopter fell into an uncontrollable crash. Only Jeff, Mariano Acosta, Eugene Castanada, and Dennis Perry survived. Lance Corporal Perry died in a hospital in Japan on August 2. Sergeant Castanada was killed on a mission on August 12. Of the men in the helicopter, only Jeff and Mariano Acosta left Vietnam alive.

7. Remains of John Killen, Glyn Runnels, and John House II were identified in early 2017.

Staff Sergeant James Lee VanBendegom

1. The NVA operated out of Cambodia. Because the country was officially neutral, American troops were unable to follow the North Vietnamese fighters once they crossed the border.

2. The Red Warrior Association website has a comprehensive battle report and synopsis of the events that occurred on July 12, 1967.

3. PFC Stanley Newell, PFC Richard Perricone, Sergeant Cordine McMurray, and Spc4 Martin Frank were the only survivors from 3rd Platoon. All four were taken prisoner and survived to be released. From headquarters platoon, PFC Nathan Henry also survived his imprisonment. Spc4 James Schiele of 2nd Platoon died on the way to the field hospital. Counting his death and Jim's, thirty-one Americans died as a result of the July 12th battle.

Lieutenant Michael John Allard

1. Several accounts of Mike's childhood were collected by Mancer Cyr for Mike's memorial in 2001 and were shared with permission with the author.

2. Brockmeyer coached the legendary Elroy "Crazylegs" Hirsch during his time at Wausau High School. Hirsch played in the NFL during the 1950s. Mike was also a Crazylegs fan.

3. Of the three, only Dick would survive. On September 31, 1965 Lieutenant Donald Watson became the first United States Air Force Academy graduate killed in the war.

4. The term for a non-aviator Naval officer. Naval aviators wore brown shoes.

Lieutenant Colonel Donald William Downing

1. During this time it went through a series of names: Aeronautical Section, Signal Corps (1909),

Aviation Section, Signal Corps (1914), United States Army Air Service (1918), United States Army Air Corps (1926), and United States Army Air Forces (1941).

2. Major and Specified Commands refer to levels of organization within the USAF and DoD. Major Command in the USAF is the second-highest level of command within the branch, while Specified Command refers to a command with a broad mission composed largely of members from one branch, but with representatives from other units or organizations.

3. The nuclear triad refers to the U.S. nuclear weapons arsenal. The third leg of the triad was submarine-launched ballistic missiles operated by the Navy.

4. Portions of Don's last letter were printed in *The Janesville Gazette* in Carla McCann's article, "Vietnam: Facing up to our Past—Fourth in a Series" on July 19, 1984.

5. During their time as MIA, Captain Donald Downing was promoted to the rank of Lieutenant Colonel and 1st Lieutenant Paul Raymond to the rank of Captain.

Captain Harold John Moe

1. Now called Eau Claire High School.

2. Two other promoted officers in the squadron, Edward Keglovits and Fred MacGeary, were also killed in Vietnam.

3. Richard Alvarez was interviewed by Tom Giffey for an article that appeared in the Eau Claire *Leader-Telegram* on November 11, 2012. All subsequent information provided by Alvarez comes from the 2012 article "Honor Bound: Memories of Fellow Soldier Run Deep."

4. According to KIA records, Harold switched squadrons and flew in VMFA 542, the "Tigers."

5. Most new crew members were assigned to a flying squadron. It is likely that Harold first flew with another squadron and was then assigned to H&MS.

6. From Tom Griffey's November 11, 2012 article in the Eau Claire *Leader-Telegram.*

7. Described in the "summary of action" portion of Harold's award recommendation and signed by Colonel Edward Le Faivre, USMC, on January 20, 1968.

8. Per an after-action witness statement.

9. Nancy Moe told Mary Black that she'd spoken with Major Cole, who felt sure the reason the parachute did not open was because they'd been shot. Major Cole suffered wounds to his back and thought Harold's parachute had been hit before it opened.

Gunnery Sergeant Richard William Fischer

1. The letter, along with other military records, was donated by the family to the Madison Veterans Museum and can be found in the archives.

2. Known by local Vietnamese as La Huan.

3. In accord with military regulations, Dick continued to be promoted while in MIA status. By the time of the presumptive finding of death, he had been promoted to gunnery sergeant.

4. Ann adds that the women at JPAC involved in the case and the Marine officers they worked with later were wonderfully helpful throughout the process. "They were our guardian angels."

Captain Paul Stuart Gee

1. Information provided by the Forest Park Presbyterian Church website.

2. The drama club, "dramatics" spelled backward.

3. Carroll University as of 2009.

4. Paul enlisted out of Manitowish Waters.

5. After completing OCC, new officers either went onto The Basic School (TBS) in Quantico for platoon commander training or to Pensacola if they were selected for the flight program. Some Marines, following Basic School, chose to enter the flight program and went onto Pensacola from there. Terry Cox surmised that, based on the dates Paul was in Pensacola and Glynco, he seems to have gone directly to Pensacola following OCC. Terry offers this explanation: "At the time Paul graduated from OCC the Marine Corps was desperate for naval flight officers (NFOs) and sent those interested in flying directly to Pensacola instead of sending them to Basic School."

6. This would be replaced by the RF-4B in October 1966. The unit would also fly the Grumman EA-6A Intruder.

7. Surface-to-air missiles. Missiles launched from the ground at approaching aircraft. As the Vietnam War continued, the North Vietnamese SAM systems grew increasingly advanced.

8. Also lost on the 1967–68 cruise from VMCJ-1 were 1st Lieutenant Tom Grud, 1st Lieutenant Ariel Cross (MIA), and Captain Lionel Parra (MIA).

Colonel Robert Frederick Wilke

1. The Air Force became an independent branch of the military in 1947.

2. The UW registrar provided the dates of Bob's enrollment. It has a Robert Frederick Wilke listed, born on September 14, 1923, two years earlier than Bob's birthdate. These dates concur with family recollections, though, and are believed to be correct.

3. The KC-97, however, was eventually replaced by a more efficient KC-135.

4. The Air Force's aviation cadet schools were all stationed in San Antonio so Bob could have attended any of the following Air Force bases: Lackland, Kelly, Randolph, or Brooks.

5. Swept-wing aircraft have wings that angle

forward or backward. Most jets today employ this design because it prevents air drag, making the planes faster and easier to maneuver.

6. Renamed Chennault Air Force Base.

7. Through the U2 program, it was determined that Soviet claims about their nuclear capacity were greatly exaggerated.

8. Both the 6250th and 505th were assigned to Tan Son Nhut Air Base, while the 19th was at Bien Hoa Air Base.

9. The term apparently came from one specific rescue of a pilot with the call sign Sandy.

10. Originally Karman HH-43 Huskies, Sikorsky H-3 "Jolly Green Giants" became the preferred helicopter starting in November 1965.

11. In the 1970s the Air Force switched to the Fairchild Republic A-10 Thunderbolt, which could fly higher and faster than the A-1.

12. The jets were carrying large bombs, which, unknown to the Air Force at the time, had faulty fuses that caused them to explode prematurely. They caused the two Phantoms to crash.

Major James Alan Ketterer

1. Now Joint Forces Training Base Los Alamitos.

2. Numbers provided by the Office of the Secretary of Defense, *Southeast Asia Summary*, November 21, 1973.

3. Both men were posthumously promoted. Their final ranks were Lt. Colonel Tilden Holley and Major James Ketterer.

Chief Petty Officer Donald Louis Gallagher

1. In 1973 an additional stage was introduced. The candidates also had to stand before a CPO selection board for a peer evaluation.

2. Lynn, the youngest, was never in high school with the boys.

3. Records show Don's place of entry as Treasure Island, San Francisco.

4. At the time, the squadron was known as "Bombing Squadron" VB114. It went through several designations before settling on "VP-26" in September 1948.

5. The aircraft was based in West Germany and intercepted by Soviet aircraft over Latvia.

6. In reports Don's rating was referred to as either chief petty officer (CPO) or aviation ordinance chief (AOC). The latter specifies that he had achieved the rating of CPO in the field of aviation ordinance.

7. This is considered the old creed. The updated version is similar, but leaves out much of the talk of brotherhood and fraternity.

8. CPO Donald Gallagher, LCdr. Robert Meglio, Lt.(jg) Thomas Jones, Lt.(jg) Lynn Travis, Lt.(jg)

Roy Huss, AXCS Donald Burnett, AE1 Melvin Thompson, ADR1 James Newman, AXI Billy McGhee, AMH2 Homer McKay, AX3 William Farris, AX3 Armando Chapa, Jr.

9. MIA bracelets were produced in the 1970s with the name, rank, and casualty date of missing in action servicemen during the Vietnam War to raise awareness of POWs and MIAs. If a serviceman returned home, it was not uncommon for them to receive dozens of bracelets in the mail welcoming them back.

Lieutenant (Junior Grade) Roy Arthur Huss

1. It should be noted that Naval flight officers can use their training as a path toward becoming Naval flight officer astronauts.

2. The bodies of LCdr Robert Meglio and AX1 Billy McGhee were recovered. Lt. Thomas Jones, Lt.(jg) Roy Huss, Lt.(jg) Lynn Travis, AXCS Donald Burnett, CPO Donald Gallagher, ADR1 James Newman, AE1 Melvin Thompson, AMH2 Homer McKay, AX3 Armando Chapa, and AX3 William Farris were not.

3. Crew 1: LTJG Frank Hand, LTJG Brian Mathison, LTJG Stuart Mclellan, LTJG Michael Purcell, AME2 Donald Burnside, AT1 Kenneth Crist, AO2 William Cutting, AXC Donald Kulacz, AX3 Delmar Lawrence, AE1 Donald Wood, ADJ2 Edward Wynder, AX1 Alvin Yoximer.

4. In August VP-26 was awarded the "Battle E," the Battle Effectiveness Award, for its readiness and overall performance in the Southeast Asian theatre of war.

Petty Officer Second Class John Francis Hartzheim

1. Although John and Bob never encountered one another in the service, they ran into each other in Appleton when both were on leave, resulting in the intersection incident mentioned earlier. Bob Woldt died in 2013. Steve Conto, who shared this story, comments that the friends are probably "doing handstands in heaven."

2. VO-67 also dropped air delivered seismic intrusion detectors (ADSIDS), which required flying at a higher altitude. High-altitude flights, where aircraft could be hit with larger antiaircraft weapons, were often more dangerous than low-altitude flights, where flak typically came in the form of machine gun fire.

3. VO-67 was the last military air squadron to use Norden bombsights in combat.

4. John Driver was told that one crewmember put a parachute on John before bailing out.

5. For his heroism that day Commander Milius was awarded the Navy Cross. His remains weren't found. On October 28, 1995 an Arleigh Burke–

class guided missile destroyer was christened the USS *Milius* in his honor.

6. Crew 2, lost on January 11, 1968: Cdr. Delbert Olson, LT(jg) Denis Anderson, Lt.(jg) Phillip Stevens, Lt.(jg) Arthur Buck, ADJ2 Donald Thoresen, AO2 Michael Roberts, PH2 Kenneth Widon, AE2 Richard Mancini, ATN3 Gale Siow. Remains were repatriated in 2003.

Crew 5, lost on February 17, 1968: CDR Glenn Hayden, Lt. Curtis Thurman, ENS James Wonn, Lt.(jg) James Kravits, ADJ2 Chester Coons, ATN1 Paul Donato, AO3 Clayton Ashby, ADJAN Frank Dawson, AEAN James Martin. Remains were repatriated in 1993.

Private First Class Thomas Joseph Blackman

1. Private Kenneth Haakenson graduated the year before Tom and was killed in Vietnam on March 13, 1968.

2. Peter Jackel's "Team spirit—Racinian Killed in Vietnam Always Gave of Himself" was published in *The Journal Times* on August 11, 2005.

3. Tet is the most important holiday in Vietnam, the celebration of the Lunar New Year. Until 1968 the holiday was used as an informal truce between the two sides.

4. South Vietnam was divided into four corps tactical zones (later called military regions) for military purposes: I Corps, II Corps, III Corps, and IV Corps. I Corps was the northernmost region and under the control of the Marine Corps.

5. Seven kilometers.

6. Chinese/Vietnamese mercenaries. Because of their mixed heritage the Vietnamese would not grant them citizenship, which enabled them to fight for either side in the war.

7. The exact number at the outpost from May 4–10 varied. Some of the Marines at the base were evacuated to resupply or for health purposes during that time. Bruce Davies, author of *Battle at Ngok Tavak*, states that forty-six Marines were at one time at the outpost, and forty-one remained by May 10.

8. This knowledge led to the dispatch of Captain White's team to Ngok Tavak to perform regular reconnaissance along Route 14 and the Marines of X-ray Detachment to provide artillery support to the patrols in the field.

9. A detailed account of the attack can be found in Bruce Davies's book, *Battle at Ngok Tavak*, which many of the survivors regard as the best source of information available about the battle.

10. Marines: PFC Thomas Blackman, LCpl Raymond Heyne, LCpl James Sargent, Corporal Gerald King, PFC Robert Lopez, PFC William McGonigle, LCpl Donald Mitchell, LCpl Thomas Fritsch, LCpl Paul Czerwonka, LCpl Joseph Cook, PFC Barry Hempel.

Army Special Forces: Sgt. Glenn Miller was killed

in the battle. Spc4 Thomas Perry, lost during the escape, remains missing.

11. More information about the recovery is included in the following chapter on Lance Corporal Raymond Heyne.

Lance Corporal Raymond Thomas Heyne

1. LSD stands for landing ship, docks, a type of ship designed to transport troops, equipment, and landing craft to an enemy beachhead to conduct an assault from the sea.

2. Likely as a member of an artillery battery from the 10th Marine Regiment, 2nd Marine Division at Camp Lejeune attached to an infantry battalion.

3. Due to the Tet Offensive, the entire 27th Regiment with the entire 2/13 Battalion was loaned to the 1st Marine Division. D/2/13 went with 1/27.

4. Captain White was the commander of the men at Ngok Tavak, but he had not requested the Marines. He was concerned that the helicopters delivering the Marines would bring unwanted attention to the post.

5. Chinese-Vietnamese mercenaries.

6. Kham Duc was attacked May 10–12. Army and Marine rescue helicopters performed a largely successful airlift and evacuation to save the trapped Special Forces, but the battle ended with the North Vietnamese in command of Kham Duc.

7. The Marines, true to their training, rendered the two howitzers inoperable by placing thermite grenades in the barrels and breeches.

8. Marines: LCpl Raymond Heyne, PFC Thomas Blackman, LCpl James Sargent, Corporal Gerald King, PFC Robert Lopez, PFC William McGonigle, LCpl Donald Mitchell, LCpl Thomas Fritsch, LCpl Paul Czerwonka, LCpl Joseph Cook, PFC Barry Hempel. Two Marines died of their wounds after the evacuation: SSgt. Thomas Schriver and LCpl Verle Skidmore.

Army Special Forces: Sgt. Glenn Miller, Spc4 Thomas Perry.

9. The medic, Thomas Perry, lost during the escape, was not found.

10. The remains that were positively identified by DNA were incomplete.

Sergeant Paul Reid Frazier

1. This information was provided by Jeff Dentice and recorded in Tom Mueller's book, *Duty, Honor, Country, and Wisconsin*. The author spoke to Mr. Dentice as well.

2. "He was a salt of the earth-type commander. His nickname was Little John because he was a big guy. We all loved him. He was a great leader," says Victor Milford.

3. "Cederlund was brand new. He'd been in

country one or two months. He was one of these happy guys. Everything was happy. There was a bright side to everything," says Victor.

4. Ed Davis survived his wounds. He died in 1997.

Captain Paul David Derby

1. The content of this chapter was provided by Dorothy Franczyk in a personal interview with the author on July 29, 2015.

2. Now the University of Wisconsin–Stout.

3. Dorothy's family has history of military service as well. Her maternal uncle, William Avery, served as a sergeant in the 22nd Infantry Regiment during World War II. His division landed on Utah Beach and fought in the Battle of the Hürtgen Forest, during which he was killed. He was buried in Belgium.

4. Chuck Derby died in a car crash in Germany in 1983 at age 37.

5. A close air support mission took place when a ground commander requested air strikes against an enemy target. The missions were coordinated with artillery as well as with the unit on the ground that requested the airstrike. It could be extremely difficult, flying low and firing at targets.

6. Commissioned by the American Battle Monuments Commission at the Grand Staircase of the Punchbowl National Cemetery on Oahu, Hawaii.

Captain Edwin James Fickler

1. Arnold and Jim ran into each other once in Vietnam. Jim related a story to him about a takeoff at Da Nang during which one flap on his aircraft stayed down, as it was supposed to, but another came up, causing the aircraft to roll and Jim to eject.

2. Those who didn't qualify as officers went into the ranks as enlisted men.

3. The Beechcraft T-34 Mentor was used in flight school.

4. The first of its kind, the aircraft was designated a "medium-attack" plane.

Sergeant William Anthony Evans

1. At the request of the Evans family, no personal information has been included.

2. Pages 275 through 280 explain the mission in detail.

Major Richard Lee Bowers

1. The 14th OCS class expected to graduate in 1967.

2. The Black and Blue phases referred to additions made to the candidates' uniforms to distinguish them from others behind them in the program. Candidates "turned black" by adding black felt backings to their military brass; they "turned blue" by adding felt infantry-blue epaulet shoulder boards to their uniforms. They also wore white gloves with their dress uniforms, white scarves called ascots with their OCS insignia on them when in fatigues, and helmet liners with their insignia emblazoned in infantry blue.

3. Ten more were "recycled back" and joined the class, bringing the number of candidates in the class to around two hundred fifty.

4. Including Richard, twelve members, or tactical officers, of Class 14–67 were killed during their service in Vietnam. The others were 2nd Lt. William Bray, 2nd Lt. Howard Coles, Jr., Cpt. Robert Gallagher, 1st Lt. Omar Jones, 2nd Lt. Robert Lazaro, 1st Lt. Harold Martin, 1st Lt. Clyde Moore (Tac Officer), 2nd Lt. William Ordway, Cpt. William Phillips, 1st Lt. Peter Zanca (Tac Officer), 1st Lt. William Zimmerman, Jr. The class purchased a plaque at Fort Benning in remembrance of their fallen comrades.

5. With the collapse of the ARVN government, Ba Xuyên Province was renamed Sóc Trăng Province, also the name of the provincial capital.

6. David was in Texas for his Green Beret training.

7. John was from nearby Johnson Creek.

Chief Warrant Officer William Cooper Pierson III

1. A Republican Congressman from Indiana, Zion was an alum of the University of Wisconsin–Madison.

2. This was almost certainly a staged situation used for propaganda by the North Vietnamese, as many POWs attested after their release. North Vietnamese prisoner of war camps were notoriously brutal.

3. The school changed its name to Lourdes Academy for a brief period in the 1980s, changing it permanently in 2012.

4. Named after Blessed Brother Benildus of France.

5. His father, William Pierson, Jr., was also in the military and would retire as a major.

6. Today, there is a plaque dedicated to Biff at the school.

7. Fort Jackson had both basic and advanced individual training. As William's later military career required AIT, it's likely that he completed both at Fort Jackson. He would then have gone to flight school at either Fort Rucker, Alabama or Fort Wolthers, Texas.

8. The actual B Troop of 2/17th Cavalry had been deployed in 1967 before the Tet Offensive. The Army could not have two units with the same

designation so the Fort Hood unit was called "B Packet."

9. A light-observation helicopter (LOH).

Major Norman Karl Billipp

1. "Unlike *The Great Santini* as portrayed in the movie, however, Norm had only deep love and caring for his family, friends, and comrades in arms," says Norm's brother, Andy.

2. Others, called contract students, took part in the program for two years and graduated with a status in the Reserves.

3. The most infamous protest at the university, the Sterling Hall Bombing, came on August 24, 1970 and resulted in the death of postdoctoral researcher Robert Fassnacht.

4. Now the Chazen Museum of Art.

5. This was the process in theory. Oftentimes, even those at the top of their class received their third choice, based on the Marine Corps's needs at the time.

6. Pilots only served with VMO-6 for a period of six months.

7. Often, artillery fire missions were employed to attack enemy units when air resources were unavailable.

Aviation Boatswain Mate Third Class William Dale Gorsuch

1. Now Cambria-Friesland High School.

2. Cecil Field was deactivated as a military base in 1999, but remains a joint civil-military airfield.

3. Crewmen of the USS *Constellation*: AME3 Terry Beck, ATR3 Richard Bell, ASE3 Michael Bowman, HM2 Donald Dean, AMH2 Carl Ellerd, MMI Paul Gore, AMS3 Delvin Kohler, AN Howard Koslosky, FTM2 Robert Leonard, AE2 James Fowler, HM3 Roy Fowler, ABH3 William Gorsuch, AQB2 Ronald Montgomery, ADJ2 Kenneth Prentice, SD2 Fidel Salazar, DS3 Kevin Terrell.

Crewmen of the USS *Walker:* PN1 Rolando Dayao and YNC Leonardo Gan.

Crewmen of the USS *Long Beach:* MM2 William Moore.

Crewmen of the USS *Hamner:* TN Reynald Viado.

Members of VFC-50: Lt. Herbert Dilger, Lt. Richard Livingston, AMS3 Rayford Hill, ADJ3 Paul Moser, ADJ3 Michael Tye.

Civilian technical representative: Frank Bytheway.

Chief Master Sergeant Charles Richard Fellenz

1. All excerpts from Chuck's letters are copied as written in letters provided by Sue Adler.

2. Renamed Lucius D. Clay Kaserne in 2012.

3. Renamed Grissom Air Reserve Base in 1994.

4. Today, the teddy bear belongs to Cheryl's daughter. "It's been through a lot," she says.

5. An early version of military night vision technology.

6. Maj. Michael Balamoti, Capt. Earl Brown, CMS Charles Fellenz, SMS Rexford DeWispelaere, Lt.Col. Richard Ganley, CMS Larry Grewell, Maj. Peter Matthes, CMS Donald Wright.

7. Permanent change of station.

8. Carla David's article, "Chuckie's Flag," was published in the *Milwaukee Journal* magazine.

9. Quoted in Joe Williams's article, "Identified MIA Remains Include Marshfield Man," printed in the *Milwaukee Journal* magazine.

10. Quoted in "Remains of Viet MIA from City Discovered," printed in the *Marshfield News-Herald.*

Major Dale Wayne Richardson

1. Although smaller than White Hall, Roodhouse lost three young men during the war: Jesse Hawk III, George Peters, Teddy Steelman. Official records list Bobby Tunison as the only White Hall citizen killed in the war.

2. Since graduation, the Class of 1959 has held a reunion every five years. At each reunion the class takes time to remember everyone who has passed away. Bill remembers the reunion after Dale's disappearance, when very little was known, and has retained information about the incident in the decades since. Dale is remembered at every reunion.

3. Emphasis those of the author.

4. Dale Richardson likely had a security clearance and was on board the helicopter that day to deliver classified documents about the invasion to men at the front.

5. "A direction [bearing] based on a compass, from where the helicopter is located, to where it needs to go," explains Brian.

6. Dale was posthumously promoted to the rank of major.

Specialist Fourth Class Peter Alden Schmidt

1. Solomon Juneau High School closed in 2006, and the building now houses MacDowell Montessori School.

2. Ten Juneau Solomon High School students died during the Vietnam War. They were Peter Schmidt, Stephen Dibb, Richard Carter, Mark Chmiel, Randall Woolcott, Vincent Mager, Jayson Ulrich, Russell Schwartz, Randy Molkentine, John Carroll. The school maintains a War Memorial with the names of all their school casualties from Vietnam as well as the Korean War and World War II.

3. Until October 1968, 1/16 was solely an in-

fantry battalion. By the time Pete joined, it was operating as mechanized infantry.

4. Statistics and unit history found at the 16th Infantry Association website, compiled by regimental historian Steven Clay.

5. In the mid–1990s Steve looked for both Pete and Terry, also from Wisconsin. It was then that he learned that Pete had not returned home.

6. The CAG was also attached to the 23rd Infantry Division as a support company.

7. Pilots were also assigned numbers. Chuck Gross's call sign, for example, was "Rattler One-Seven."

8. More information about the incident on August 15, 1970 as well as about the 71st AHC and the Hueys can be found in Chuck Gross's book, *Rattler One-Seven.* Information in this chapter comes from the book and the author's interview with Chuck Gross.

9. Military Assistance Command Vietnam-Studies and Operations Group, Command and Control North.

10. The Huey landed safely.

11. Chuck Gross notes that although they were under heavy fire at the time, it was unclear if the Huey was hit, if the ladder had gotten caught and pulled the ship down, or if the engine died.

12. The crash site has been investigated three times, but no remains have been found.

13. The grave marker for Peter Schmidt is in Milwaukee's Forest Home Cemetery.

Specialist Fifth Class Randolph Leroy Johnson

1. "Conversation between President Nixon and his Assistant for National Security Affairs (Kissinger)." *Foreign Relations of the United States, 1969–1970, Volume VII, Vietnam, July 1970—January 1972.*

2. The 48th worked closely with the White Horse Division, South Koreans who aided in the war.

3. Operation El Paso 1 and El Paso 2.

4. More information about Lam Son 719 can be found in *Invasion of Laos, 1971* by Robert D. Sander.

5. Two helicopter pilots were lost the first week of the operation: Warrant Officer James Paul and Warrant Officer Carl Wood.

6. Curtis Haws's roommate was Bob Acalotto, who was shot down on the same aircraft as Randy Johnson. Haws went on leave early in the operation. "When I got back thirty days later," he says, "half my platoon was killed or missing in action."

7. In addition to the four men lost on February 20 and the two pilots lost the first week of the operation, Capt. Edmond Bilbrey, Spc5 John Lockhart, and Lt. Joseph Marshall were lost March 11, and CW3 Frederick Christman, SFC Ricardo Garcia, and CW2 Jon Sparks were lost March 20.

Specialist Fifth Class Richard Jay Hentz

1. Now Oshkosh West.

2. Called a "Phase Loop Antenna."

3. Rick and Rodney "Ozie" Osborne were close friends and flew most of their missions together.

Warrant Officer Albert Raymond Trudeau

1. Ruth and Francis let the children choose John's name. Nicknames were so ingrained in their family that the children chose John Edward Trudeau solely so he could be called Jet. With jet airplanes seemingly the aircraft of the future, they wanted him to have a nickname that would endure.

2. The 33rd class in 1970.

3. "I would ask him, 'Are you sure you want to wear that?'" Mike remembers. "And he'd go, 'Well, yeah, why? What's wrong with it?' ... I'd go, 'If you don't know, I'm not telling you, man.'"

4. Until April 1971 the 68th ASHC was C Company of the 228th Assault Support Helicopter Battalion (ASHB), a part of the 1st Cavalry Division. The unit was renamed when 1st Division left Vietnam.

5. Because of the change of passengers, multiple witnesses were interviewed following the crash to determine exactly who was on the helicopter. Witness reports provided the details in this chapter.

Captain David Leverett Leet

1. One Mach equals 761.2 mph.

2. A report dated April 27, 1972 stated there was no evidence to suggest the aircraft had failed or malfunctioned or that weather had played a role in the aircraft's loss. It was believed that the cause of crash was due to direct enemy action.

3. The letter was reprinted in the *Kenosha News* in an article by Don Jensen title, "The Story of a Missing Somers Airman" shortly after David's disappearance.

Staff Sergeant Todd Michael Melton

1. In 1976 a hall at Goodfellow AFB was renamed Melton Hall in Todd's honor.

2. "Their Son's Grave Marks More than a Resting Spot," by Dean Jensen, was published in *The Milwaukee Sentinel* on May 30, 1983.

3. The missing men were: SSgt. Todd Melton, Sgt. Joseph Matejov, Sgt. Peter Cressman, Sgt. Dale Brandenburg, Capt. Arthur Bollinger. One of these crewmembers was killed in the crash, but his remains were unidentifiable.

4. An assumed reference to American pilots.

Bibliography

Interviews

The following individuals, either by phone, email, or personal interviews, provided information for this book:

Lieutenant Michael John Allard

Brockmeyer, Michael, email, 18 June 2015.
Brockmeyer, Michael, email to Mancer Cyr, 2001.
Christenson, Dick, email, 30 Apr. 2015.
Corsini, Gene, email, 3 Sept. 2016.
Cyr, Mancer, email, 17 Mar. 2015.
Healy, John, email, 23 Sept. 2017.
Higgins, Denny, email, 22 Oct. 2017.
Libman, Barry, email, 29 Apr. 2015.
Marquardt, Jud, email, 29 Apr. 2015.
McCarten, Mary Lou, email to Mancer Cyr, 14 Feb. 2001.
Tumpak, John, telephone interview, 7 Sept. 2016.
Wilson, Frank, email, 19 Aug. 2016.

Lance Corporal Merlin Raye Allen

Allen, Sean, and Jeff Savelkoul, telephone interview, 6 Nov. 2015.
Hawkins, Cindy, email, 24 Mar. 2017.
Savelkoul, Jeff, email, 3 Nov. 2015.

Commander William Tamm Arnold

Ashmore, Jack, telephone interview, 28 Aug. 2015.
Brandes, Stuart, email, 1 Sept. 2015.
Kirkpatrick, Jane, email, 17 Jan. 2017.
Miefert, Mickey, telephone interview, 22 Oct. 2015.
Murdoch, Christopher, email to John Sharpless, 22 July 2016.
Redenius, Suzanne, email, 30 Sept. 2015.
Saucier, Tom, email, 11 Sept. 2015.
Wold, Norm, telephone interview, 2 Sept. 2015.

Major Norman Karl Billipp

Annable, Ross, email, 26 May 2016.
Arnold, Kevin, email, 26 May 2016.
Beers, Steve, telephone interview, 27 May 2016.
Billipp, Andy, email, 14 July 2016.
Bruss, James, telephone interview, 28 May 2016.
Freckman, Jack, telephone interview, 27 May 2016.

Hoffman, Duncan, telephone interview, 9 June 2016.
Hurst, Ken, telephone interview, 26 May 2016.
Ketterer, George, telephone interview, 28 May 2016.
Lawrence, Jim, telephone interview, 4 June 2016.
Losee, Ron, email, 27 May 2016.

Private First Class Thomas Joseph Blackman

Adams, Bob, telephone interview, 9 Jan. 2016.
Brown, Tim, telephone interview, 2 Jan. 2016.
Campbell, Terry, email, 16 Dec. 2015.
Jackson, Joe, email, 30 Dec. 2015.
Konkol, Nancy, email, 20 Dec. 2015.
O'Brien, Mike, telephone interview, Aug. 2015.
Scheller, Tom, email, 21 Dec. 2015.
Smith, Randall, email, 18 Feb. 2015.

Major Richard Lee Bowers

Baum, John, email, 30 Oct. 2015.
Baum, John, telephone interview, 30 Aug. 2015.
Funkhouser, Pres, telephone interview, 11 Aug. 2015.
Schmitz, Cindy, personal interview, 24 Aug. 2015.
Smith, Brian, email, 29 Aug. 2015.

Captain Robert Ira Bush

Bush, Greg, email, 23 Jan. 2016.
Nelson, Elmer, telephone interview, 19 Dec. 2015.
Urbanic, Frank, telephone interview, 21 Dec. 2015.

Captain Paul David Derby

Franczyk, Dorothy, personal interview, 29 June 2015.

Lieutenant Colonel Donald William Downing

Downing, Darryl, telephone interview, 4 Oct. 2015.
Greve, Nancy, telephone interview, 23 Oct. 2015.
Malayney, Norman, email, 15 Dec. 2015.
Sherwood, E. J., telephone interview, 15 Sept. 2015.

220

Captain Walter Frank Draeger, Jr.

Annen, Beth, and Diana Imhoff, personal interview, 14 July 2016.

Jones, Ray, telephone interview, 25 July 2016.

Schaaf, James, telephone interview, 18 July 2016.

Warner, Sam, telephone interview, 18 July 2016.

Chief Master Sergeant Charles Richard Fellenz

Adler, Sue, email, 3 Nov. 2015.

Adler, Sue, and Tom Adler, personal interview, 27 Aug. 2015.

Adler, Sue, Vivian Fellenz, and Cheryl Clancy, telephone interview, 15 July 2015.

Bembry, Shelton, telephone interview, 19 June 2015.

Captain Edwin James Fickler

Admire, John, telephone interview, 6 May 2016.

Baxter, Richard, telephone interview, 14 May 2017.

Forney, Mike, email, 3 May 2016.

Garvey, Jim, email, 8 May 2016.

Husser, Arnold, email, 3 May 2016.

Mellon, Dave, email, 6 May 2016.

Nelson, Bob, telephone interview, 4 May 2016.

Schoenbeck, Frank, email, 9 Aug. 2015.

Gunnery Sergeant Richard William Fischer

Blankenheim, Jim, telephone interview, 17 Feb. 2016.

Fischer, Ann, personal interview, 26 Feb. 2016.

Sergeant Paul Reid Frazier

Falcon, John, telephone interview, 7 Dec. 2015.

Frazier, Myron, email, 22 July 2016.

Kraemer, August, telephone interview, 21 Nov. 2015.

Kahn, Jerry, telephone interview, 28 Dec. 2015.

Milford, Victor, telephone interview, 3 July 2016.

Walker, Robert, email, 21 Nov. 2015.

Walker, Robert, telephone interview, 22 Nov. 2015.

Chief Petty Officer Donald Louis Gallagher

Bray, Ron, telephone interview, 25 Feb. 2016.

Roehre, Nancy, and Lynn Schmitt, personal interview, 12 Dec. 2015.

Captain Paul Stuart Gee

Dresdow, Jack, email, 5 June 2016.

Driscoll, Tom, telephone interview, 7 June 2016.

Heidner, Chuck, telephone interview, 15 June 2016.

Kohls, Chuck, telephone interview, 6 June 2016.

Gee, Jody, email, 19 Mar. 2017.

Griffin, Rhonda, email, 28 June 2016.

Lohuis, Art, telephone interview, 15 June 2016.

Mellon, Dave, email, 15 May 2016.

Ottman, Dick, telephone interview, 8 June 2016.

Aviation Boatswain Mate Third Class William Dale Gorsuch

Davis, Ken, email, 30 Jan. 2017.

Gorsuch, Duane, personal interview, 14 Nov. 2015.

Petty Officer Second Class John Francis Hartzheim

Conto, Steve, email, 18 Feb. 2015.

Driver, John, telephone interview, 29 July 2015.

Maubach, Edward, telephone interview, 3 Sept. 2015.

Weber, David, email, 10 July 2015.

Specialist Fifth Class Richard Jay Hentz

Dean, Jon Gary, email, 24 Apr. 2017.

Hendley, Lee, telephone interview, 24 Apr. 2017.

Hentz, Ron, email, 30 June 2015.

Methvin, James, email, 1 May 2017.

Sundell, Richard, telephone interview, 24 Apr. 2017.

Lance Corporal Raymond Thomas Heyne

Adams, Bob, telephone interview, 9 Jan. 2016.

Brown, Tim, telephone interview, 2 Jan. 2016.

Jackson, Joe, email, 30 Dec. 2015.

Kostello, Janice, telephone interview, 7 Jan. 2016.

Lieutenant (Junior Grade) Roy Arthur Huss

Ahlmeyer, John, email, 12 July 2016.

Brown, Bob, telephone interview, 5 Aug. 2016.

Bunkelman, Richard, telephone interview, 1 Aug. 2016.

Karstens, Jack, personal interview, 11 Oct. 2016.

Moore, Larry, email, 4 July 2016.

Teidt, Donald, email, 11 July 2016.

Verlhurst, Verl, telephone interview, 15 July 2016.

Voelker, Richard, telephone interview, 1 Aug. 2016.

Weideman, Jerry, telephone interview, 8 Aug. 2016.

Specialist Fifth Class Randolph Leroy Johnson

Dunlap, Bud, telephone interview, 31 Aug. 2015.

Haws, Curtis, telephone interview, 30 Aug. 2015.

Hickman, Richard, telephone interview, 31 Aug. 2015.

Meadows, Al, email, 31 Aug. 2015.

Major James Alan Ketterer

Bretsch, Karel, telephone interview, 3 Nov. 2015.

High, Chip, telephone interview, 28 Oct. 2015.

Wallrath, Jeanne, telephone interview, 14 Nov. 2015.

Captain Roy Robert Kubley

Dresser, Ralph, email, 24 Feb. 2016.

Logeman, Don, email, 8 Feb. 2016.

Logeman, Don, telephone interview, 13 Feb. 2016.
Marshaleck, Walter, email, 24 Feb. 2016.
Morgan, James, telephone interview, 11 Feb. 2016.
Peshkin, Dick, telephone interview, 6 Mar. 2016.

Commander James David La Haye

Howard, Tom, email to Don La Haye, 20 Nov. 2003.
La Haye, Don, email, 15 Sept. 2015.
La Haye, Don, telephone interview, 15 Sept. 2015.
Pearl, Bob, email, 20 Jan. 2017.
Pearl, Bob, email to Don La Haye, 12 Nov. 2003.
Schulstad, George, email to Don La Haye, 11 May 2014.

Captain David Leverett Leet

Hall, John, email, 1 Apr. 2015.
Leet, Donna, personal interview, 3, Apr. 2015.
Steinberg, Bill, personal interview, 29 May 2015.

Staff Sergeant Todd Michael Melton

Agnew, David, email, 29 May 2015.
Bolton, Jim, telephone interview, 18 Feb. 2015.
Dudek, Duane, email, 24 May 2015.
Holm, Vern, email, 18 Feb. 2015.
Kimla, James, email, 29 May 2015.
Pitzeruse, John, email, 13 Apr. 2015.
Pratt, Phil, email, 20 Mar. 2015.

Captain Harold John Moe

Black, Mary, telephone interview, 4 Dec. 2015.
Rodosky, George, telephone interview, 2 Jan. 2016.
Wittren, Donald, telephone interview, 29 Nov. 2015.

Chief Warrant Officer
William Cooper Pierson III

Boehm, Karen, email, 8 Sept. 2015.
Matthews, James, email, 24 Sept. 2015.
Phipps, Dave, telephone interview, 13 Sept. 2015.
Schumerth, Steve, phone message, 15 Sept. 2015.
Van Treese, Phil, email, 18 Sept. 2015.

Major Dale Wayne Richardson

Counts, David, telephone interview, 27 May 2015.
Forster, Pat, email, 25 May 2015.
Gibbins, Linda, email, 25 May 2015.

McCarthy, Brian, email, 25 May 2015.
Price, Bill, telephone interview, 3 June 2015.

Private First Class
Duwayne Marshall Soulier

Hiekel, Rodney, telephone interview, 28 July 2016.
Jackson, Joe, email, 13 Aug. 2016.
Kelly, Kevin, telephone interview, 22 June 2016.
Manning, Cynthia, telephone interview, 26 June 2016.
Norwell, John, telephone interview, 14 June 2016.

Specialist Fourth Class
Peter Alden Schmidt

Arndt, Peter, email, 14 Sept. 2015.
Breese, Steve, telephone interview, 1 Sept. 2015.
Carter, Mary, email, 22 Aug. 2015.
Davis, Ken, email, 5 Feb. 2017.
DeNicola, Paul, telephone interview, 13 Aug. 2015.
Gross, Chuck, telephone interview, 24 Sept. 2015.
Koeberl, Donovan, email, 15 Aug. 2015.
Schmidt, Mike, telephone interview, 4 Jan. 2016.
Sciurba, Tony, email, 19 Jan. 2017.

Warrant Officer
Albert Raymond Trudeau

Connolly, Barb, and Mike Trudeau, personal interview, 30 Sept. 2016.

Sergeant James Neil Tycz

Biszko, Ted, telephone interview, 14 July 2016.
Wines, Roger, telephone interview, 16 June 2016.

Staff Sergeant James Lee VanBendegom

VanBendegom, Mike and Darlene VanBendegom, personal interview, 1 Apr. 2015.

Colonel Robert Frederick Wilke

Ambrose, Susan, email, 13 Jan. 2016.
Moe, Thomas, email, 20 June 2015.
Wilke, Mary, email, 15 Dec. 2015.
Wilke, Susan, email, 21 Dec. 2015.

Epilogue

Thompson, Robert, phone interview, 30 May 2017.

Library of Congress Documents

The Library of Congress's Vietnam-ERA POW/MIA Database proved an invaluable resource in writing this book. The database can be found at: http://lcweb2.loc.gov/pow/. The records used for this book are listed below.

Lieutenant Michael John Allard

"Biographic/Site Report as of 18 December 1991." 18 Dec. 1991.
Trowbridge, Charles F., Jr. "Reporting in the Case of Lieutenant Michael John Allard." 1 July 1992.
"Transmittal of Documents/Transmittal of Source Report." 26 Nov. 2001.
Wold, James W. "Letter to Dr. Mark M. Allard." 11 Dec. 1995.

Commander William Tamm Arnold

"Photographs and Biographic/Incident Information." Undated.

Major Norman Karl Billipp

Evans, Daniel R. "Detailed Report Sent to Subject's Parents on his Status." 2 July 1969.
Greisen, Bruce. "Photo of PW Said to Resemble Subject." 30 Sept. 1970.
Mason, S. T. "Alleged MIA Correspondence/Sighting." 6 Jan. 1985.
Thomas, H. R. "Subject Remains MIA." 26 May 1969.

Private First Class Thomas Joseph Blackman

Rose, Kenneth. "Witness Statement." 13 May 1968.
Sebens, M. L. "KIA—Battle." 20 May 1968.

Major Richard Lee Bowers

Allen, W. E. "South Vietnam, pre–1975: Bright Light." Oct. 28 1971.
"Bowers, R./Biographical Data, Summary of Incident." 4 Apr. 1969.
England, W. L. "Post-1975 Vietnam: Transmittal of Awards." 31 Oct. 1978.
"Post-1975 Vietnam: JCRC Rpt. T87–526B; Dog Tag Data and Account of Death of Richard Bowers (REFNO 1414–0–01); Dog Tag List with Related Source Information Report." 1988.
South Vietnam, pre–1975: JCRC Rpt T87–526B, Dog Tag Data and Account of Death of Richard Bowers." Apr. 1988.

Captain Robert Ira Bush

"Multiple ACFT Mishap Report; Casualty Reports." 12 June 1966.
North, R. S. "Statement of Service." 10 Aug. 1966.
"Updated Biographic/Site Reports—November 1994." 9 Nov. 1994.

Captain Paul David Derby

Haley, C. K. "KIA—Battle." 18 Nov. 1966.

Lieutenant Colonel Donald William Downing

Goodman, Ellen. "Their Pilot-Husbands Are 'Missing in Action' Over Vietnam." 20 July 1969.
"JTF-FA Biographic/Site Report Update on REFNO 0829." 13 Oct. 1993.
White, Floyd, "Review of Missing Status (Captain Donald W. Downing, FV3040347)." 7 June 1981.

Captain Walter Frank Draeger, Jr.

Smith, Douglas T. "Statement of Service." 12 Apr. 1965.

Chief Master Sergeant Charles Richard Fellenz

"Detailed Report of Investigation/Survey of JCRC REFNO Case 1530; Crash Site Evaluation with Analysis of Material Evidence Associated with REFNO 1530." 11 Feb. 1993.
"Laos: Status Review: Chief Master Sgt Charles R. Fellenz; Summary of Facts and Circumstances; Report of Casualty 728—Final." 26 May 1978.
Maples, William R. "CILHI 0208–93A Case Review." Letter. 8 May 1994. MS. The C.A. POUND Human Identification Laboratory, Gainesville, Florida.
Murphy, Dean. "Status Review: Chief Master Sgt Charles R. Fellenz; Summary of Facts and Circumstances; Report of Casualty 728—Final." 30 June 1978.
"Summary of Incident Involving REFNO 1530." Undated.

Captain Edwin James Fickler

"Laos: Source Reports Finding an 'F5' with Remains in the A Shau-A Luoi Area of the A Shau Valley." Undated.

Gunnery Sergeant Richard William Fischer

Blacksmith, Edward L. "US Personnel Missing/Captured in Southeast Asia." 14 Jan. 1968.
Keller, Bruce. "Possible Grave Site of an Unidentified US Soldier; Evaluation." 1 Feb. 1977.
"RVN: Biographic Site Report for REFNO: 0977." 4 Aug. 1993.

Sergeant Paul Reid Frazier

Wickham, Kenneth G. "Narrative." 5 Sept. 1968.
"Reports of Casualty, September–November 1968." 25 Nov. 1968.

Chief Petty Officer Donald Louis Gallagher

"Biographic Site Report for REFNO 2022." 22 Dec. 1993.

Captain Paul Stuart Gee

Belle, Roy L. "KIA—Battle." 28 Aug. 1974.
Jaskilka, S. "Accession Number 0435—Forwarding of Pilot's Helmet Bag." 15 Jul. 1974.
Lewis, R. W. "Missing in Action—Fifteen Day Report." 30 Jan. 1968.

Aviation Boatswain Mate Third Class William Dale Gorsuch

"Final; Certificate of Death." 6 Oct. 1969.
"Biographic Site Report for REFNO 2004." 30 Dec. 1993.

Petty Officer Second Class John Francis Hartzheim

"Biographic/Site Report on Case 1062." 9 Feb. 1994.

Specialist Fifth Class Richard Jay Hentz

"JTF-FA Biographic/Site Report Update on REFNO 1715." 9 Nov. 1993.
Hibbs, K. K. "Release of Information—Board of Inquiry." 25 May 1971.

Lieutenant (Junior Grade) Roy Arthur Huss

"Biographic Site Report for REFNO 2022." 22 Dec. 1993.

Specialist Fifth Class Randolph Leroy Johnson

JCRC Liaison Officer, "Hearsay Information About an American Helicopter Containing Remains; Refugee Report and Evaluation." 9 Dec. 1981.

Major James Alan Ketterer

"Case: 0998—Circumstances of Loss." 17 Apr. 1975.
Gratch, A. W. "Proposed Changed of Status of Captain James A. Ketterer; Summary of Facts and Circumstances; Casualty Reports." 11 June 1976.
"Updated Biographic/Site Report—16 November 1994; Case 0998." 16 Nov. 1994.

Captain Roy Robert Kubley

Smith, Douglas T. "Statement of Service." 10 Feb. 1967.

Staff Sergeant Todd Michael Melton

"Analyst Notes, Subject: Loss of BARON 52 and Crew, 5 February 1973." 10 Feb 1987.
"Assessment of captive status at homecoming of individuals on the Senate Select Committee lists." 10 July 1992.
Berbrich, John T. "Report of Casualty." 23 May 1973.
"Biographic/Site Report as of 3oct90." 3 Oct. 1990.
Ferguson, Lyn. "Laos: Newspaper Article—'Airman's Fates Kept Secret." 4 Aug. 1978.
Gaines, Kimball M. "Transmittal of DIA Analysis." 23 Feb. 1987.
"Information regarding pararescue activities at crash site." Undated.
Mills, Alice M. "Casualty message to NOK; MIA changed to KIA." 23 Feb. 1973.
Moore, Powell A. "Response to Congressional inquiry concerning joint investigations of crash sites with the Lao govt." Undated.
Scott, L. "C-47 Crash 5 Feb 73 Laos with eight USAF personnel on board; investigation of crash site." 26 Feb. 1973.
Tallman, K. L. "Casualty message to NOK; MIA changed to KIA." 22 Feb. 1973.

Captain Harold John Moe

Le Faivre, Edward N. "Award Recommendation for Harold J. Moe, USMC—(4th Through 6th Award—Air Medal)." 12 Feb. 1968.
Serens, M. L. "Death Report." 4 Nov. 1967.
Simpson, M. M. "Witness Statement." Undated.

Chief Warrant Officer William Cooper Pierson III

"Biographic Site Report for REFNO: 1425." 17 Feb. 1994.

Caruana, A. F. "Photo identification, 1969 POW Christmas film." 18 Nov. 1970.

Clarke, Ellsworth S. "Review of missing person's status: Pierson, William C., III." 26 Oct. 1978.

"Correspondence between army and NOK." Undated.

"Photo Results: ICO Pierson, W." 9 Feb. 1971.

"Summary of POW Returnee Report Regarding Pierson." Undated.

Wicham, Kenneth G. "Letters to NOK, location of site where serviceman was reported missing." 26 May 1970.

Private First Class Duwayne Marshall Soulier

Clelland, W. M. "South Vietnam, pre–1975: Letter to Mother of PFC Duwayne Soulier." 5 May 1967.

"Combat History—Expeditions—Awards Record." Undated.

Holbrook, J. R. "Report of Casualty—Casualty Status and List of Interested Persons." 10 May 1967.

R., L. "Corrected Copy of Archival Research Report (13–02) Concerning 0665 Conducted at the National Archives and Records Administration in College Park, Maryland, During September 2012." 3 Apr. 2013.

W., R. "Detailed Report of Investigation of Case 0665 (Site VM-00118) Conducted During Joint Field Activity 09–3VM (95th JFA) in the Socialist Republic of Vietnam." 6 Oct. 2009.

Weiler, Philip G., Jr., and Robert L. Daniels, "Certificate of Death." 3 May 1967.

Warrant Officer Albert Raymond Trudeau

R., L. "Excavation Summary Report of Case 1775." 3 June 2013.

"Witness Statements; Casualty Reports." Undated.

Sergeant James Neil Tycz

Holbrook, H. "KIA." 23 May 1967.

"JCRC RPT VN91–009, Two Vietnamese Provided Identification Media Allegedly Associated with Ten Unaccounted for Americans." 28 Oct. 1991.

Langley, H. F. "Report of Death—Hostile." 13 May 1967.

Spock, Raymond. "JCRC RPT VN91–020; Vietnamese Citizen Provides Identification Media and Remains Allegedly Associated with Unaccounted for Americans/Hearsay." 14 May 1992.

Towbridge, Charles F. "Dog Tag Information on 2Lt Heinz Ahlmeyer and Sgt James N. Tycz, Both U.S. Marine Corps." 13 June 1991.

Colonel Robert Frederick Wilke

Bauernfeind, Susan. "Chaplain's Insignia Tipped Wife of Pilot." *San Antonio Light.* 7 Dec. 1970: 3.

Clark, Bill. "26 Cadets at Reese Air Base Receive Wings at Graduation." *Lubbock Journal.* 23 June 1950: 32.

"Floral Gift from Hawaii." *Del Rio News-Herald.* 11 Nov. 1962, sec. C: 15.

Unit Histories

The Texas Tech Virtual Vietnam Archive provides physical and digital records of war for all branches of the Armed Forces. The following unit reports were used and can be accessed online at http://www.recordsofwar.com/vietnam/.

Commanding Officer, 2nd Battalion, 13th Marines, to Commanding General, 1st Marine Division. "Command Chronology, Period of 1–31 May 1968." 1 June 1968.

Commanding Officer, 3rd Battalion, 5th Marines, to Commanding General, First Marine Division. "Command Chronology for Period 01000Z May67 to 312A00Z May67." 1 June 1967.

Commanding Officer, 3rd Reconnaissance Battalion, to Commandant of the Marine Corps. "Command Chronology for Period 1 May 1967 to 31 May 1967." Undated.

Commanding Officer, Marine All Weather Attack Squadron 242, to Commanding Officer, Marine Aircraft Group 11. "Command Chronology Report (U)." 8 Feb. 1969.

Commander U.S. Naval Forces, Vietnam, to Commander in Chief U.S. Pacific Fleet. "U.S. Naval Forces, Vietnam Monthly Historical Summary, February 1968." 5 Mar. 1968.

Madison Veterans Museum Archives

The Madison Veterans Museum archives holds material on two of Wisconsin's MIAs that was donated by the men's families. Multiple documents from the following archives were used in their chapters.

Draeger, Walter F. *Papers and Photographs.* 1955–1996. Archival material.
Fischer, Richard W. *Papers and Photographs.* 1961. Archival material.

Newspaper Articles

Articles obtained through the Access Newspapers Archive are listed below.

Lance Corporal Merlin Raye Allen

"Funeral Rites to Be Set for Merlin Allen." *The Capital Times* [Madison]. 5 July 1967: 18.
"Merlin Allen, Former Resident, Killed in Vietnam." *The Capital Times* [Madison]. 4 July 1967: 1.

Major Norman Karl Billipp

Behnke, Clifford C. "Ban on Recruiting Asked at UW." *Wisconsin State Journal* 7 [Madison]. Dec. 1966: 1–2.
"MIA's Family Finally Learns His Fate." *The Indiana, PA Gazette.* 29 Sept. 1996: B-2.

Private First Class Thomas Joseph Blackman

"Angel Harriers in Easy Win." *The Journal Times* [Racine]. 20 Oct. 1965: 1C.
"Angel Harriers Remain Unbeaten." *The Journal Times* [Racine]. 13 Oct. 1965: 2C.
"Angels 7th in Relays." *The Journal Times* [Racine]. 10 May 1965: 3B.
Imrie, Robert. "From MIA to Home: Soldiers' Remains Returned." *The Capital Times* [Madison]. 11 Aug. 2005: 5A.
Trower, Ralph. "City Prep Notes." *The Journal Times* [Racine]. 9 Nov. 1965: 5A.

Major Richard Lee Bowers

"Bowers, R./Biographical Data, Summary of Incident," 4 Apr. 1969.
"JCRC Rpt T87–526B, Dog Tag Data and Account of Death of Richard Bowers," July 1988.

Captain Robert Ira Bush

"Bailed Out of Burning Jet, Ex-Racine Man in Fair Condition." *The Journal Times* [Racine]. 14 Sept. 1963: 3.
"Fliers Listed as Satisfactory, to Return Here." *Oxnard Press Courier.* 9 Sept. 1963: 1.
"If Air Force Life Were Only Like This—Officers' Wives Put on Skits for Husbands." *Oxnard Press Courier.* 12 July 1962: 25.
"Nine Enlist for 4 Years." *The Journal Times* [Racine]. 11 July 1959: 4.
"Officers' Wives Win Crazy Hat Awards, View Millinery Fashions at Luncheon." *Oxnard Press Courier.* 18 Apr. 1963: 19.
"Parties and Personals." *Oxnard Press Courier.* 4 May 1962: 19.
"Racine Pilot, 28, Killed in Vietnam Air Crash." *The Journal Times* [Racine]. 10 June 1966: 1–2.
"Robert I. Bush Wed in Nevada." *The Journal Times* [Racine]. 5 Nov 1961: sec. 2, pg. 2.
"Stars and Stripes." *The Journal Times* [Racine]. 16 Aug. 1956: 6.
"Stars and Stripes." *The Journal Times* [Racine]. 22 June 1957: 3.
"Stars and Stripes." *The Journal Times* [Racine]. 10 May 1959: 6.
"Stars and Stripes." *The Journal Times* [Racine]. 28 Dec. 1959: 4.
"Stayed in Flaming Aircraft, Racine Pilot Wins Medal." *The Journal Times* [Racine]. 19 Dec. 1964: 2.

Captain Walter Frank Draeger, Jr.

"Deerfield Air Force Pilot Killed in Viet." *Wisconsin State Journal* [Madison]. 7 Apr. 1965: 4.
"Deerfield to Be Host to Forensic Contest." *Wisconsin State Journal* [Madison]. 18 Mar. 1951: 2.
"Sun Prairie, Johnson Creek, Marshall Share Suburban Lead." *Wisconsin State Journal* [Madison]. 16 Dec. 1950: 6.

Lieutenant Colonel Donald William Downing

"Bedford Flying Lab Checks Missile Re-entry." *The Lowell Sun.* 3 Mar. 1963: 9.

Chief Master Sergeant Charles Richard Fellenz

"Marshfield Airman is missing in action." *The Daily Tribune* [Wisconsin Rapids]. 25 Nov. 1969: 2.

Captain Edwin James Fickler

Held, Ruth. "Uncertainty Almost Over." *Fond du Lac Reporter*. 18 Feb. 1974: 17.
"Missing Soldier's Parents Receive Proclamation Copy." *Fond du Lac* Reporter. 17 Feb. 1971: 17.
"Obituaries: Edwin J. Fickler." *The Sheboygan Press*. 8 Aug. 1955: 16.
"Random Lake Halfback All-Conference Choice." *The Sheboygan Press*. 29 Nov. 1960: 17.
"Services Scheduled for Soldiers." *Fond du Lac Reporter*. 26 Mar. 1976: 26.

Gunnery Sergeant Richard William Fischer

"Ends Training." *The Capital Times* [Madison]. 30 Nov. 1966: 13.
"Father, 2 Sons Die in Crash." *The Troy Record*. 28 July 1958: 16.
"Fischer to Receive Honor for JA Work." *Wisconsin State Journal* [Madison]. May 1964, sec. 2, pg. 4.
"Five Madison Marines End Combat Training." *The Capital Times* [Madison]. 18 Jan. 1967: 6.
Ziff, Deborah. "Road to Recovering Sergeant Fischer." *Wisconsin State Journal* [Madison]. 16 Nov. 2007: A1+.

Chief Petty Officer Donald Louis Gallagher

"Memorial." *The Sheboygan Press*. 31 Jan. 1969: 9.
"Nominations Made for SFHS Officers." *The Sheboygan Press*. 22 Sept. 1954: 29.
"Sheboygan Falls Personals." *The Sheboygan Press*. 9 Oct. 1957: 22.

Aviation Boatswain Mate Third Class William Dale Gorsuch

"Markesan, Rio Remain Pacemakers." *The Capital Times* [Madison]. 12 Feb. 1966: 13.

Petty Officer Second Class John Francis Hartzheim

"Marriage Licenses." *The Post-Crescent* [Appleton]. 30 Aug. 1967: C10.
"Medals Awarded Posthumously to Appleton Sailor." *The Post-Crescent* [Appleton]. 24 June 1968: B1.
"Memorial Mass Scheduled for War Victim." *The Post-Crescent* [Appleton]. 16 Mar. 1968: B1.

Specialist Fifth Class Richard Jay Hentz

"Has Language Course." *Oshkosh Daily Northwestern*. 14 Jan. 1970: 10.
"Hentz Allows No Hits in Winning, 11–0." *Oshkosh Daily Northwestern*. 21 June 1958: 12.
"High Junior Scores." *Oshkosh Daily Northwestern*. 4 Mar. 1963: 14.
"Missing Soldier Listed as Dead." *Oshkosh Daily Northwestern*. 24 May 1971: 28.
"Oshkoshian Is Missing." *Oshkosh Daily Northwestern*. 10 Mar. 1971: 60.

Lieutenant (Junior Grade) Roy Arthur Huss

"Abbotsford Officer on Crashed Plane." *The Eau Claire Leader*. 10 Feb. 1968: 3.
"Births—Luther." *The Eau Claire Leader*. 6 Nov. 1965: 3.

Major James Alan Ketterer

"314 Compete in Model Plane Meet Here." *The Kokomo Tribune*. 21 Aug. 1961: 9.

Captain Roy Robert Kubley

"49 Special Awards Given at ROTC's Annual Review." *Wisconsin State Journal* [Madison]. 14 May 1960: sec 2, pg. 1.
"Ceremony on U.W. Campus: 63 ROTC Cadets Honored at President's Review." *The Capital Times* [Madison]. 5 May 1961: 18.
"Nothing Left When Pilots Defoliate Vietnam Areas." *Defiance Crescent-News*. 15 Dec. 1966: 7.

Captain David Leverett Leet

"Junior Fair Poultry Foods and Crops." *Kenosha News*. 11 Aug. 1961: 9.
"Senior 4-H Girls Show Handiwork." *Kenosha News*. 28 July 1961: 16.
"Somers." *Kenosha News*. 16 Aug. 1956: 29.

Captain Harold John Moe

"Marine Officer Killed in Action in Vietnam." *The Eau Claire Leader-Telegram*. 3 Oct. 1967: 3A.

Specialist Fourth Class Peter Alden Schmidt

"Correspondence Between Sister, Congressman Clawson, Senator Murphy, and Army," 1970.
"Statement of Biographical Data of Missing or Captured Personnel, USARV Form 520-R," 4 Aug. 1969.
"Updated Biographical/Site Report as of 10 August 1994; Case 1657," 10 Aug. 1994.

Private First Class Duwayne Marshall Soulier

Olivio, Rick. "New Clubhouse Symbolizes VFW Post's Rebirth." *Wisconsin State Journal* [Madison]. 13 June 2010: D11.
"State GI Killed." *The Sheboygan Press.* 18 May 1967: 2.
"Veterans group emerges after almost closing." *The Daily Globe* [Ironwood]. 14 June 2010: 1A–2A.

Colonel Robert Frederick Wilke

Ballard, Bobby D. "Colonel Robert F. Wilke," 23 Apr. 1973.
"Proceedings of Status Review Hearing Re: Robert F. Wilke," 22 May 1978.
"Updated Biographic/Site Reports—November 1994," 9 Nov. 1994.

Additional newspaper articles from sources other than the Access Archives:

Lieutenant Michael John Allard

Hansen, Jessica. "Long-awaited Funeral, Bracelet Honor Fallen Pilot." *JSOnline.* Milwaukee Journal Sentinel, 26 May 2001.
Wasson, Peter J. "A Final Farewell." *Wausau Daily Herald.* 18 Mar. 2001.

Lance Corporal Merlin Raye Allen

Kennedy, David C. "Bayfield Community Honors Fallen Marine Merlin Allen: Final Goodbye Comes 46 Years After his death in Vietnam." *Ashland Daily Press.* APG Media of Wisconsin, 30 June 2013.
Jones, Meg. "46 Years After His Death in Vietnam, Marine Returns Home for Funeral." *JSOnline.* The Milwaukee Journal Sentinel, 29 June 2013.
Jones, Meg. "Vietnam War-era Veteran Keeps Solemn Vow to His Lost Brother in Arms." *JSOnline.* The Milwaukee Journal Sentinel, 30 Apr. 2013.
"Obituary for LCpl Merlin Raye 'Merl' Allen." *Bratley Family Funeral Homes.* Bratley Family Funeral Homes, June 2013.

Commander William Tamm Arnold

Nelson, Bill. "The Unending Ordeal." *The Milwaukee Journal.* 24 May 1987: 7–14. Print.

Private First Class Thomas Joseph Blackman

Jackel, Pete. "Team Spirit—Racinian Killed in Vietnam Always Gave of Himself." *Journal Times.* Journal Times, 11 Aug. 2005.

Captain Robert Ira Bush

Foley, Quentin. "Norton—Key to Defense." *The San Bernardino County Sun.* 6 Feb. 1964: 18. Newspapers.com.
Golub, Rob. "Who Will Weep for this Heroic Veteran?" *Journal Times* [Racine]. 11 Nov. 1999. Journaltimes.com.

Lieutenant Colonel Donald William Downing

Lux, Anna Marie. "MIA's Family Accepts Fate." *The Janesville Gazette.* 4 Dec. 1986: 1A+. Provided by Cathy Idzerda.
McCann, Carla. "Vietnam: Facing up to our Past—Fourth in a Series." *The Janesville Gazette.* 19 July 1984. Provided by Cathy Idzerda.
"Obituary." Undated. Provided by Cathy Idzerda.
"Stratofreighter, with Janesville Man as Co-Pilot, Ends a Colorful Career." Provided by Nancy Greve.

Chief Master Sergeant Charles Richard Fellenz

David, Carla. "Chuckie's Flag." *Milwaukee Journal Magazine.* 24 May 1987: 1–2. Print.
"Remains of Viet MIA from city discovered." *Marshfield News-Herald.* 24 Oct. 1995: 1–2.
Williams, Joe. "Identified MIA Remains Include Marshfield Man." *Milwaukee Journal Sentinel.* 24 Oct. 1995: 1+. Print.

Chief Petty Officer Donald Louis Gallagher

McAlpine, Linda. "Confusion Clouds Falls Mother's Grief for Son Who Died in Vietnam." *The Sheboygan Press*. 28 Sept. 1994: B1–B2. Print.
Trident Gram. 13 Feb. 1968. Print.

Captain Paul Stuart Gee

"Planner for Waukesha to Join Marines." *Waukesha Daily Freeman*. 10 Feb. 1966: 2. Newspapers.com.

Aviation Boatswain Mate Third Class William Dale Gorsuch

Kelly, Berneice. "A Memorial: Cambria Scoreboard Dedicated to Youth Who Died in Service." *Portage Daily Register*. 28 Oct. 1970. Print.
Uebelherr, Jan. "Hope Was All Family Had to Bury." *The Milwaukee Sentinel*. 25 July 1985: 15.

Lieutenant (Junior Grade) Roy Arthur Huss

"VP-26 to Return from War Duty." *Time Record* [Bath-Brunswick]. 4 May 1968: 1. Print.

Major James Alan Ketterer

"Youth to Seek National Model Airplane Title." *Milwaukee Sentinel*. 24 July 1959: 7. *Google News*.

Staff Sergeant Todd Michael Melton

Jensen, Dean. "Their Son's Grave Marks More Than a Resting Spot." *The Milwaukee Sentinel*. 30 May 1983: 1+. *Google News*.

Captain Harold John Moe

Giffey, Tom. "Honor Bound." *Eau Claire Leader-Telegram*. 11 Nov. 2012: 4C. Print.

Chief Warrant Officer William Cooper Pierson III

"Prisoners' Film Cheers Kin; Seen as Red Propaganda." *Watertown Daily News*. 1 Sept. 1970: 3. *Google News*.

Specialist Fourth Class Peter Alden Schmidt

Nelson, Bill. "The Unending Ordeal." *The Milwaukee Journal*. 24 May 1987: 7–14. Print.

Sergeant James Neil Tycz

Duke, Lynne. "The Last Goodbye." *The Washington Post*. The Washington Post Company, 10 May 2005.
Fromer, Frederic J. "Remains of three U.S. soldiers buried at Arlington." *Reno Gazette-Journal*. 11 May 2005: 18. Newspapers.com.
Frommer, Frederic J. "U.S. Brings Home Remains of Missing Vietnam Troops." *The Cincinnati Enquirer*. 9 May 2005: A3: Newspapers.com.
Gerds, Warren. "'Whitey, you scrounge,' Dies with Jim." *Green Bay Press-Gazette*. 22 Mar. 2005: A5. Newspapers.com.
Lerner, Jane. "Marines to Get Arlington Burial." *The Journal News* [White Plains]. 9 May 2005: 1A–2A. Newspapers.com.
Jones, Meg. "Marine Killed in 1967 Finally Coming Home." *Milwaukee Journal Sentinel*. 20 Mar. 2005: 17A+. *Google News*.
Meyer, Paul. "Marine Who Died a Hero Heads Home." *The Dallas Morning News*. 24 Feb. 2005. Arlington National Cemetery. Michael Patterson.
Nelson, Bill. "The Unending Ordeal." *The Milwaukee Journal*. 24 May 1987: 7–14.

Staff Sergeant James Lee VanBendegom

Brines, Jon. "A Fallen Son Is Laid to Rest." *Kenosha News*. 12 Nov. 2014: A1. Print.
Brines, Jon. "From Grisly Trove, a Long Awaited Answer." *Kenosha News*. 12 Nov. 2014: A13. Print.
Brines, Jon. "VanBendegom Remains Return to Kenosha Section." *Kenosha News*. 9 Nov. 2014. Web. 26 Apr. 2015.
"In Memory of James Lee 'Jim' VanBendegom." Proko Funeral Home, Nov. 2014. Web. 26 Apr. 2015.
"VanBendegom's Fate: Viet Vet Tells How Kenoshan Died in the War." *Kenosha News*. 7 June 1973. Print.

Colonel Robert Frederick Wilke

Anonymous. *News Release*. 1952/53. A fake press release by Bob Wilke's friends. Klau-Van Pietersom-Dunlap, Inc., Milwaukee.
"Janet Christie Wilke." *Porter Loring*. Memorial Networks, Apr. 2012.

Books

The following books, yearbooks, and Navy cruise books were used for this book.

Lieutenant Michael John Allard

Wausau High School. *Wahiscan 1958.*

Lance Corporal Merlin Raye Allen

Vetter, Lawrence C. *Never Without Heroes: Marine Third Reconnaissance Battalion in Vietnam, 1965–70.* New York: Ivy, 1996.

Commander William Tamm Arnold

Pape, Robert A. *Bombing to Win: Air Power and Coercion in War.* Ithaca: Cornell University Press, 1996. Print. Cornell Studies in Security Affairs.

University of Wisconsin–Madison. *1963 Badger.*

Major Norman Karl Billipp

Manheim Township High School. *Neff Vue, 1962.*

University of Wisconsin–Madison. *1966 Badger.*

Private First Class Thomas Joseph Blackman

Davies, Bruce. *The Battle at Ngoc Tavak: Allied Valor and Defeat in Vietnam.* Lubbock: Texas Tech University Press, 2009.

Captain Robert Ira Bush

Ashcroft, Bruce. *We Wanted Wings: A History of the Aviation Cadet Program.* Washington, D.C.: HQ AETC Office of History and Research, 2005. *Air Force Historical Studies Division.* United States Air Force, 2005.

Crosby, Francis. "McDonnell F-101 Voodoo." *A Handbook of Fighter Aircraft.* New York: Hermes House, 2002.

Grant, Larry A. "Radar." *Encyclopedia of Military Science.* Ed. G. Kurt Piehler and M. Houston Johnson V. Thousand Oaks: SAGE Publications, 2013. 1171–173.

Shaw, Frederick J., ed. *Locating Air Force Base Sites History's Legacy.* 2nd ed. Washington, D.C.: Library of Congress, 2004. *Air Force Historical Studies Division.* United States Air Force, 2014.

Captain Paul David Derby

Mueller, Tom. "The Lives of 5 Who Became MIAs in Vietnam." *Duty, Honor, Country, and Wisconsin: Honoring the Ultimate Sacrifice and Veterans From the Civil War to Afghanistan.* Indianapolis: Dog Ear, 2013. 228–48.

Stout State College. *The Tower.*

Lieutenant Colonel Donald William Downing

Ashcroft, Bruce. *We Wanted Wings: A History of the Aviation Cadet Program.* Washington, D.C.: HQ AETC Office of History and Research, 2005. *Air Force Historical Studies Division.* United States Air Force, 2005.

Captain Walter Frank Draeger, Jr.

Jones, Ray. *Memoir: Dynamite, Check Six.* Bloomington: AuthorHouse, 2013.

Loftin, Laurence K., Jr. "The Swept Wing Emerges." *Quest for Performance: The Evolution of Modern Aircraft.* Washington, D.C.: NASA Scientific and Technical Information Branch, 1985. *NASA History Program Office.* NASA, 6 Aug. 2004.

Sergeant William Anthony Evans

Cosmas, Graham A. *MACV: The Joint Command in the Years of Escalation, 1962–1967.* Washington, D.C.: Center of Military History, 2006. *The U.S. Army Center of Military History.* CMS.

Lindsey, Fred S. *Secret Green Beret Commandos in Cambodia: A Memorial History of MACV-SOG's Command and Control Detachment South (CCS) and Its Air Partners, Republic of Vietnam, 1967–1972.* Bloomington: AuthorHouse, 2012.

Captain Edwin James Fickler

Morgan, Rick. "Introduction." *A-6 Intruder Units of the Vietnam War.* Oxford: Osprey, 2012. 6–9.
Mueller, Tom. "The Lives of 5 Who Became MIAs in Vietnam." *Duty, Honor, Country, and Wisconsin: Honoring the Ultimate Sacrifice and Veterans From the Civil War to Afghanistan.* Indianapolis: Dog Ear. 228–47.
University of Wisconsin–Stevens Point. *Iris, 1965.*

Sergeant Paul Reid Frazier

Mueller, Tom. "The Lives of 5 Who Became MIAs in Vietnam." *Duty, Honor, Country, and Wisconsin: Honoring the Ultimate Sacrifice and Veterans From the Civil War to Afghanistan.* Indianapolis: Dog Ear. 228–47.

Chief Petty Officer Donald Louis Gallagher

MacDonald, Charles B. "A US Strategy to Stem Communist Tide." *The Vietnam War: A Comprehensive and Illustrated History of the Conflict in Southeast Asia.* Ed. Ray Bonds. London: Salamander, 1999. 96–105.

Captain Paul Stuart Gee

Cox, Terry. *Pride: A Journey That Changed My Life.* Raleigh: Lulu, 2013.

Aviation Boatswain Mate Third Class William Dale Gorsuch

USS *Constellation* (CVA 46). *Western Pacific Cruise 1969–1970.* 1970.

Petty Officer Second Class John Francis Hartzheim

Jacobsen, Annie. "The Electric Fence." *The Pentagon's Brain: An Uncensored History of DARPA, America's Top Secret Military Research Agency.* New York: Little, Brown, 2015. 197–212.
Jones, Gregg. "Muscle Shoals." *Last Stand at Khe Sanh: The U.S. Marines Finest Hour in Vietnam.* Cambridge: De Capo, 2014. 62–67.

Lance Corporal Raymond Thomas Heyne

Davies, Bruce. *The Battle at Ngoc Tavak: Allied Valor and Defeat in Vietnam.* Lubbock: Texas Tech University Press, 2009.

Specialist Fifth Class Randolph Leroy Johnson

"200. Conversation Between President Nixon and His Assistant for National Security Affairs (Kissinger)." *Foreign Relations of the United States.* Ed. David Goldman, Edward C. Keefer, and Erin Mahan. Vol. VII. Washington, D.C.: United States Government Printing Office, 2010. N. pag. *Office of the Historian.* United States Department of State. Web.
Hinh, Nguyen Duy. *Lam Son 719.* Washington, D.C.: U.S. Army Center of Military History, 1979. *Defense Technical Information Center.* Web.
Sander, Robert D. *Invasion of Laos, 1971: Lam Son 719.* Norman: University of Oklahoma Press, 2015. Print.

Captain Roy Robert Kubley

University of Wisconsin–Madison. *1960 Badger.*
University of Wisconsin–Madison. *The Badger 1961.*

Commander James David La Haye

Jenkins, Dennis R. "Navy Full-pressure Suits." *Dressing for Altitude: U.S. Aviation Pressure Suits, Wiley Post to Space Shuttle.* Houston: US National Aeronautics and Space Administration, 2012. 24.
United States Naval Academy. *Annual Register of the United States Naval Academy, 1946–1947.* Washington, D.C.: U.S. Government Printing Office.

Captain Harold John Moe

Sambito, Major William J. *A History of Marine Fighter Attack Squadron 312.* Washington, D.C.: US Government Printing Office, 1978. *Korean War Project Digital Initiative.*

Chief Warrant Officer William Cooper Pierson III

Mueller, Tom. "The Lives of 5 Who Became MIAs in Vietnam." *Duty, Honor, Country, and Wisconsin: Honoring the Ultimate Sacrifice and Veterans From the Civil War to Afghanistan.* Indianapolis: Dog Ear, 2013. 228–48.

Major Dale Wayne Richardson

Clymer, Kenton. "The War Outside Vietnam." *Rolling Thunder in a Gentle Land: The Vietnam War Revisited.* Ed. Andrew Wiest. Oxford: Osprey, 2006.

Frankum, Ronald B., Jr. "Swatting Flies With a Sledgehammer: The Air War." *Rolling Thunder in a Gentle Land: The Vietnam War Revisited.* Ed. Andrew Wiest. Oxford: Osprey, 2006. 191–207.

Tho, Tran Dinh. *The Cambodian Incursion.* Rep. no. 19970428 039. Washington, D.C.: U.S. Army Center of Military History, 1979. Defense Technical Information Center.

Tucker, Spencer. *Encyclopedia of the Vietnam War: A Political, Social, and Military History.* 2nd ed. Santa Barbara: ABC-CLIO, 1998.

Specialist Fourth Class Peter Alden Schmidt

Gross, Chuck. *Rattler One-Seven: A Vietnam Helicopter Pilot's War Story.* Denton: University of North Texas Press, 2004.

Sergeant James Neil Tycz

Murphy, Edward F. *The Hill Fights: The First Battle of Khe Sanh.* New York: Ballantine Group, 2003.

Vetter, Lawrence C. *Never Without Heroes: Marine Third Reconnaissance Battalion in Vietnam, 1965–70.* New York: Ivy, 1996.

Staff Sergeant James Lee VanBendegom

Moore, Harold G., and Joseph L. Galloway. *We Were Soldiers Once... and Young: Ia Drang, the Battle that Changed the War in Vietnam.* New York: Random House, 1992.

Colonel Robert Frederick Wilke

Crosby, Francis. "The History of Fighter Aircraft." *A Handbook of Fighter Aircraft.* New York: Hermes House, 2002.

McIlmoyle, Gerald E. "The Chosen Few." *Remembering the Dragon Lady: Memoirs of the Men Who Experienced the Legend of the U-2 Spy Plane.* Solihull: Casemate, 2013.

Polmar, Norman. "Spyplanes Over Cuba." *Spyplane: The U-2 History Declassified.* Osceola: MBI, 2001.

Sheehan, Neil. *A Fiery Peace in a Cold War: Bernard Schriever and the Ultimate Weapon.* New York: Random House, 2009.

Tilford, Earl H., Jr. *Search and Rescue in Southeast Asia.* Washington, D.C.: Office of Air Force History, 1980. *Air Force Historical Studies Division.* AFHSO.

University of Wisconsin–Madison. *1947 Badger.*

Online Resources

The following online articles and resources were used in the research.

Lieutenant Michael John Allard

"A-4 Skyhawk in Vietnam." *A-4 Skyhawk Association.* Skyhawk Association, Inc.

Commander William Tamm Arnold

Drake, Major Ricky J. *The Rules of Defeat: The Impact of Aerial Rules of Engagement on USAF Operations in North Vietnam, 1965–1968.* Thesis. Air University, 1992. Maxwell AFB: Air University Press, 1992. *Stanford University Libraries.*

Greer, W. L. "The 1972 Mining of Haiphong Harbor: A Case Study in Naval Mining and Diplomacy." Institute for Defense Analyses (1997). *Defense Technical Information Center.*

"Summer Cruise." *Georgia Tech Naval ROTC.* NROTCUGIT, 2012.

"USS Coral Sea (CVA 43)." *America's Navy.* United States Department of the Navy.

Major Norman Karl Billipp

"Gordon K. (Bill) Billipp." *LancasterOnline.* LancasterOnline, 2 July 2009.

Kennedy, Tyler, and David Null. "Protests & Social Action at UW–Madison During the 20th Century: 1960–1969." *UW Archives and Records Management.* University of Wisconsin.

Private First Class Thomas Joseph Blackman

Defense POW/MIA Accounting Agency. Department of Defense. *Twelve MIAs From Vietnam War Are Identified (King, Cook, Heyne, Mitchell, Fritsch, Blackman, Czerwonka, Hempel, Lopez, McGonigle, Sargent, Miller). Defense POW/MIA Accounting Agency.* DPAA, 9 Aug. 2005.

Kennan, George. "An Island in the Sea of History: The Highlands of Daghestan." *National Geographic* magazine July 1913: 1087–140.

Captain Robert Ira Bush

"Douglas A-1 Skyraider and the Stanley YANKEE System." *Ejection History.* Ejection-History. UK.

Jacoby, Charles H. "A Brief History of NORAD." *NORAD.* North American Aerospace Defense Command.

Captain Paul David Derby

"Fragments: Wisconsin Vietnam Veterans Tribute." *The High Ground.* Wisconsin Vietnam Veterans Memorial Project, Inc.

Swanson, Jerry Dean. "Paul David Derby Memorial." *The Dockstader–Wegert Family Tree.* CompAssist. 24 Sept. 2016.

Lieutenant Colonel Donald William Downing

"Downing, Donald William." *The Coffelt Database of Vietnam Casualties.* The Coffelt Group.

Captain Walter Frank Draeger, Jr.

Anderson, Erich. "Walter F. Draeger, Jr." *Veteran Tributes.*

Johnson, Lyndon B. "Peace Without Conquest." Johns Hopkins University, Baltimore. 7 Aug. 1965. *LBJ Presidential Library.*

Johnson, Lyndon B. "Remarks at Syracuse University on the Communist Challenge in Southeast Asia." Syracuse University, Syracuse. 5 Aug. 1964. *The American Presidency Project.*

Johnson, Lyndon B. "Remarks in Memorial Hall, Akron University." The University of Akron, Akron. 21 Oct. 1964. *The American Presidency Project.*

Sergeant William Anthony Evans

"Introduction/Note on the MACV Command Historical Program." Introduction. *Records of the Military Assistance Command Vietnam Part 1. The War in Vietnam, 1954–1973 MACV Historical Office Documentary Collection.* Ed. Robert E. Lester. Bethesda: University Publications of America, 1988. xiii–vii. *LexisNexis Academic [LexisNexis].*

Chief Master Sergeant Charles Richard Fellenz

Friedman, Herbert A. "Ho Chi Minh Trail Campaign." *PSYOPS.*

Chief Petty Officer Donald Louis Gallagher

"Aviation Ordnanceman." *Navy Personnel Command.* U.S. Navy.

"History of Patrol Squadron Two Six." *Commander, Naval Air Forces, San Diego, CA.* Ed. LTJG Hepfinger and LTJG Billhardt. United States Navy, June 2010.

"P-3 Orion: The All-Terrain Hunter." *Lockheed Martin.* Lockheed Martin Corporation, 2016.

Tulich, Eugene N. "The United States Coast Guard in South East Asia During the Vietnam Conflict." *United States Coast Guard.* Department of Homeland Security.

Captain Paul Stuart Gee

"Carroll University History." *Carroll University.* Carroll University.

McBride, James. "Electronic Warfare in Vietnam." *Marine Corps Gazette* Jan. 2015: 39–42. *Marine Corps Association and Foundation.* Marine Corps Association.

"Our History." *Forest Park Presbyterian.* Forest Park Presbyterian Church.

Whitten, Col. H. Wayne. "Marine Composite Reconnaissance Squadron One (VMCJ-1) History." *MCARA.* Marine Corps Aviation Reconnaissance Association, June 2008.

Petty Officer Second Class John Francis Hartzheim

"VO-67 Shipmate Awards: Navy Presidential Unit Citation." *VO-67 Association.* VO-67 Association.

Specialist Fifth Class Richard Jay Hentz

"Appendix 2i: Smith 324 Compelling Cases." Included in: U.S. Senate. Committee on POW-MIA Affairs. *Report of the Senate Select Committee on POW-MIA Affairs.*
Buley, Dennis, and Mark Scott. "Origins of the Army Security Agency." *National Security Agency.* Ed. James L. Gilbert. NSA/CSS, 15 Jan. 2009.
Fuller, Warren E. "The Glorious History of the 138th." *138th Avn Company (RR), 224th Avn Battalion.*

Lance Corporal Raymond Thomas Heyne

Defense POW/MIA Accounting Agency. Department of Defense. *Twelve MIAs From Vietnam War Are Identified (King, Cook, Heyne, Mitchell, Fritsch, Blackman, Czerwonka, Hempel, Lopez, McGonigle, Sargent, Miller). Defense POW/MIA Accounting Agency.* DPAA, 9 Aug. 2005.
"The History of the USS Shadwell (LSD-15)." *U.S. Naval Research Laboratory.* US Navy.

Lieutenant (Junior Grade) Roy Arthur Huss

"Abbotsford, Clark Co., Wisconsin History." *Clark County, Wisconsin.* Web. 27 Dec. 2016.
"Huss, Roy Arthur." *The Coffelt Database of Vietnam Casualties.* The Coffelt Group.
"Weideman, Judy Lynn (26 JUN 1965)." *Tribune-Phonograph* [Abbotsford]. 8 July 1965. *Usgennet.org.* USGenNet.

Major James Alan Ketterer

"Historical Snapshot: F-4 Phantom II Fighter." *Boeing.* The Boeing Company.
Joiner, Stephen. "What Couldn't the F-4 Phantom Do?" *Air & Space* magazine. Smithsonian Institution, Mar. 2015.

Captain Roy Robert Kubley

Abbott, Bill F. "Names on the Wall: A Closer Look at Those Who Died in Vietnam." *Vietnam* magazine, June 1993. *HistoryNet.* World History Group.
Buckingham, William A., Jr. *Operation Ranch Hand: The Air Force and Herbicides in Southeast Asia 1961–1971.* Washington, D.C.: Office of Air Force History, 1982. *AFHSO.* Air Force Historical Support Division.
"Captain Kubley Profile." *Frank Kresen Post 24.* The American Legion.
Gelman, Andrew. "How Many Vietnam Veterans Are Still Alive?" *The New York Times.* The New York Times Company, 25 Mar. 2013.

Commander James David La Haye

"History of the USS Bonhomme Richard." *America's Navy.* United States Department of the Navy.
"F-8 Crusader." *National Naval Aviation Museum.* Naval Aviation Museum Foundation.
"Limited Time Aboard Midway?" *USS Midway Museum.* USS Midway Aircraft Carrier Museum San Diego.

Captain David Leverett Leet

"Marine Tactical Electronic Warfare Squadron 1 (VMAQ-1) History)." *MCARA.* Marine Corps Aviation Reconnaissance Association, June 2008.
"Somers American Legion." *Town of Somers.* Village and Town of Somers.

Staff Sergeant Todd Michael Melton

"Baron 52." *6994th Security Squadron.* 6994th Security Squadron.
"SSgt. Todd M. Melton." *6994th Security Squadron.* 6994th Security Squadron.
"U.S. Military Fatal Casualties of the Vietnam War for Home-State-of-Record: Wisconsin." *National Archives.* The U.S. National Archives and Records Administration.

Chief Warrant Officer William Cooper Pierson III

"Pierson, William Cooper, III." *The Coffelt Database of Vietnam Casualties.* The Coffelt Group.

Major Dale Wayne Richardson

"Dale W. Richardson Obituary." *Roller-Crouch Funeral Home.* Roller Funeral Homes.

Specialist Fourth Class Peter Alden Schmidt

"Regimental History." *16th Infantry Regiment Association.* 16th Infantry Regiment Association.

Private First Class Duwayne Marshall Soulier

Allnutt, Bruce C. *Marine Combined Action Capabilities: The Vietnam Experience.* Office of Naval Research Group Psychology Programs, 1969. *Defense Technical Information Center.*

Castle, Michael. "June 20, 2001." *Congressional Record, V. 147, Pt. 8, June 12, 2001 to June 25 2001.* Washington, D.C.: Government Printing Office, 2005. 11176.

"Command Chronology, 1 May–67." *US Marine Corps History Division Vietnam War Documents Collection—The Vietnam Center and Archive.* Texas Tech University. Web. 20 Aug. 2016.

Holm, Tom. "Forgotten Warriors: American Indian Service Men in Vietnam." *Vietnam Generation.* Vol. 1, Article 6 (1989): 56–68. *La Salle University Digital Commons.*

Telfer, Gary L., Lane Rogers, and V. Keith Flemming, Jr. "Spring Fighting in Southern I Corps." *U.S. Marines in Vietnam: Fighting the North Vietnamese, 1967.* Washington, D.C.: History and Museums Division, Headquarters, U.S. Marine Corps, 1984. 51–104. *Marines.mil.* U.S. Marine Corps.

Warrant Officer Albert Raymond Trudeau

"Class 70–33 Photograph." *VHPA.* Vietnam Helicopter Pilots Association.

Staff Sergeant James Lee VanBendegom

Defense Prisoner of War/Missing Personnel Office. "Soldier Missing from Vietnam Accounted For." *Defense POW/MIA Accounting Agency.* Department of Defense, 31 Oct. 2014.

Hill, Roger. *POW's Red Warriors.* Battle Report. 17 June 2015.

Colonel Robert Frederick Wilke

Anderson, Erich. "Colonel Robert Wilke Tribute." *Veteran Tributes.* Web. 06 Jan. 2016.

Andrews, Hal. "OE/O-1 Bird Dog." *Naval Aviation News.* Mar.–Apr. 2000: 26–27. *Naval History and Heritage Command.* U.S. Navy.

"B-47 Stratojet." *Boeing.* The Boeing Company. Web. 07 Jan. 2016.

Bolkcom, Christopher. *Congressional Research Service Reports.* Air Force Aerial Refueling Methods: Flying Boom versus Hose-and-Drogue. Federation of American Sciences, 5 June 2006.

Carroll, John T. "The Air Force in the Vietnam War." *The Air Force Association.* Aerospace Education Foundation, Dec. 2004.

"Combat Search and Rescue in Southeast Asia." *National Museum of the Air Force.* U.S. Air Force, 18 May 2015.

Joiner, Stephen. "Airman Down." *Air & Space* magazine. Smithsonian, Sept. 2012.

Lohman, Major E. A. "Army Air Service Observation School." *U.S. Air Service* 7.1 (1922): 24–27. Google Books. Web.

Moe, Thomas. "Colonel Thomas Moe: American POW in North Vietnam." Interview by Ed McKaul. *HistoryNet.* History Net, 12 June 2006.

Pocock, Chris. "The Early U2 Overflights of the Soviet Union." Allied Museum Conference, Berlin. 24 Apr. 2006. *The Cold War Museum.*

Portz, Matt. "Aviation Training and Expansion: Part 1." *Naval Aviation News* (July–Aug. 1990): 22–27. *Naval History and Heritage Command.* U.S. Navy.

"The U-2 Dragon Lady." *Lockheed Martin.* Lockheed Martin Corporation.

The following websites were used throughout to crosscheck facts and to locate individuals:

Coffeltdatabase.org
Thewall-usa.com
Togetherweserved.com
Vvmf.org
Virtualwall.org

Index

Numbers in **bold italics** indicate pages with illustrations